The Logic of ''Maoism''

edited by
James Chieh Hsiung

The Praeger Special Studies program—
utilizing the most modern and efficient book
production techniques and a selective
worldwide distribution network-—makes
available to the academic, government, and
business communities significant, timely
research in U.S. and international economic, social, and political development.

The Logic of "Maoism"
Critiques and Explication

PRAEGER SPECIAL STUDIES IN INTERNATIONAL POLITICS AND GOVERNMENT

Praeger Publishers   New York   Washington   London

Library of Congress Cataloging in Publication Data

Hsiung, James Chieh, 1935-
    The logic of "Maoism."

    (Praeger special studies in international politics
and government)
    Bibliography: p.
    1. Communism—China—Addresses, essays, lectures.
2. China—Foreign relations—Addresses, essays,
lectures.   I. Title.
HX387.H77   335.43'4'0951   74-3515
ISBN 0-275-09070-1

PRAEGER PUBLISHERS
111 Fourth Avenue, New York, N.Y. 10003, U.S.A.
5, Cromwell Place, London SW7 2JL, England

Published in the United States of America in 1974
by Praeger Publishers, Inc.

Printed in the United States of America

To a Redeemable World and Those
Whose Faith Never Fades

The idea of this book germinated at the time I was organizing a panel for the 1973 annual conference of the Association for Asian Studies (AAS), bearing the title: "'Maoism': Domestic and International Applications." The four papers presented at the panel (by Chen, Dorrill, Ginsburgs, and Yu) have since been revised for inclusion in the present volume, and four papers (by Hsiung, Urken, Whyte, and Womack) have been added. The change in the title and subtitle indicates the addition of a more serious epistemological concern to the original substantive interests in interpreting the ways in which Chairman Mao's ideas and programs have been applied, as will be explained in the Introduction below.

In the preparation of the book, the editor, no less than the four fellow-panelists, has gained immensely from the profuse comments made during the enthusiastic audience participation at the packed 1973 panel session and from suggestions offered in private by others. The dialogue thus generated continued to flow beyond the panel, whereby the present eight contributors were able to exchange views or otherwise communicate with or through the editor. Some of the common themes and theoretical threads came into sharper focus through this running informal dialogue, occasionally joined by other colleagues with a common interest in the subject matter. In different capacities and at different stages, Professors James T. C. Liu (Princeton), Shao-chuan Leng (Virginia), Benjamin I. Schwartz (Harvard), T. K. Tong (City College of New York), Ilpyong Kim (Connecticut), and Tang Tsou (Chicago), among others, were either parties to the dialogue or offered aid and comfort. Inquiries from some among the audience at the AAS panel regarding the volume's subsequent delayed appearance amounted to a ground swell of moral support no less reinvigorating than a Mao-sent mango to a Red Guard tyro.

Through this informal dialogue a consensus seemed to appear, reflecting a number of dissatisfactions with the current state of the trade, which may be outlined as follows:

1. In the existing scholarship too much attention has been directed to exegetical wrangles over whether Mao is "orthodox" or "original" in his Marxist belief and not enough has been directed to how he shaped Marxist tenets to fit Chinese reality, with the result that many of the debates are not only unwarranted but also irrelevant to a realistic grasp and "feel" of modern Chinese politics.

2. There is a "static" bias in the views held by many students of Mao's thought, as though it had remained the same ever since 1920, regardless of changing times and circumstances.

3. Studies of the domestic application and of the international application of Mao's ideas and scenarios have often been compartmentalized, either because the two are considered to be unrelated or because it is thought that one can be approached without the other.

4. The subject of Mao's thought and praxis has been studied in ways that can be described as "ideographic," or looked at without being related to a larger frame of reference capable of yielding inferences applicable or useful for other situations or political systems.

This broad critique therefore called for a different orientation, one that would emphasize (1) Mao's synthesis of theory and practice and of various intellectual precursors of Mao (both Marxist and non-Marxist), (2) a diachronic or cross-temporal analysis of the growth of Mao's thought in response to the challenges posed by the changing times, (3) a binary approach to the domestic and external applications so that meaningful comparisons can be made inter se, and (4) where possible, a judicious blending of the "area studies" approach and social-science methodology. The resultant volume may not have all the answers, but it is hoped that it will serve to point out new directions and chart new paths for further excursions by a new breed of scholars whose inquisitive minds are matched by sophisticated analytic skills.

Many other persons have helped in the making of this volume. Ms. Jeanne Lawrence and Mrs. Barbara Wasser typed parts of the edited manuscript and rendered other clerical assistance. My daughter Susette, aged 10, helped in the grown-up job of collating and typing the bibliography and other sundry chores; her brother Eric, 9, and sister Cynthia, 8, chipped in, leaving a bewildered mother, Susie, in a state of utter disbelief.

It would have been impossible to put together a volume of this large scope of intellectual concerns that is intellectually coherent and schematically threaded together without the indulgent cooperation of its contributors, which is in itself an epitome of what the Maoist spirit is purportedly capable of generating in an edifying social milieu. This example of scholastic camaraderie is sufficient to reinforce one's faith in a redeemable world, to which this book is dedicated.

New York City   J. C. H.

CONTENTS

059737

LIST OF ABBREVIATIONS

CCP   Chinese Communist Party

CFCP   <u>Chieh-fang chün-pao</u> (The Liberation Army Daily)

CPSU   Communist Party of the Soviet Union

GPCR   Great Proletarian Cultural Revolution

HC   <u>Hsuan-chi</u> (The Selected Works of Mao Tse-tung)

HCh   <u>Hung-ch'i</u> (The Red Flag)

JMJP   <u>Jen-min Jih-pao</u> (The People's Daily)

KMT   Kuomintang

PRC   People's Republic of China

The term "Maoism," though discouraged in official Chinese usage, is purposely chosen in this volume to encompass the broad spectrum of topics covered by the eight essays, from ideology, to strategy, to political scenarios associated with the name of the venerated Chairman of the Chinese Communist Party, Mao Tse-tung.[1] The eight contributors not only address themselves to the domestic and international application of Mao's thought and program but also attempt to offer substantive critiques and, furthermore, methodological suggestions on how to make our studies more "scientific," the last two even making use of formal modeling to demonstrate the point. To accentuate its "unofficial" status and the convenient umbrella it provides for the diverse topics under study, the term "Maoism" is used in the title with quotation marks around it.

Despite the salience and topicality of the subject matter, no one volume has yet appeared in print that ventures into questions of interpretation, critique, and explication as systematically as this book attempts to do. The word "logic" in the main title and the words "critiques" and "explication" in the subtitle must be read together in two senses: First, in those essays in the volume that have a more "substantive" interest, there is an implicit but recurrent effort to examine whether there is any logical consistency in the application of Mao's thought by its adherents, both over time and between the domestic and international arenas. The authors spare no critiques where their search for consistency runs into serious problems concerning theory and practice or other problems of an even more severe intellectual nature. Second, those essays concerned with "explication" (that is, systematic explanation) aim at developing some prototypes of "scientific" theory. By definition, "theory" denotes an explanatory relationship in which observed or observable phenomena, loosely defined, are brought together and related systematically in accordance with a logic of the postulated axioms. These explicative essays, therefore, attempt to discover and establish this logic within Mao's system of thought and, moreover, to examine what constitutes "rational behavior" when the Maoist ethic is pushed to its "logical" end in real life, as contrasted with other political systems premised on a totally different ethic or ethos. Preferably, theory does more than explicate, offering testable inferences as well. This question of inferential fertility, or predictive power, is very much the concern of the authors of the explicative essays.

To varying degrees, the eight essays that follow are all concerned with the "logic" of what is identified by the shorthand label "Maoism." Some of the essays are more "substantive-minded," while others are more concerned with the epistemological and theoretical dimensions. Among those essays that are more directed toward the substantive study of the application of Maoism, certain common themes occupy the authors' attention or are implicit in their views. The first theme is the extent to which Mao synthesizes from Marxist and Chinese thinkers before him, in response to practical conditions. It may be noted that just as originality is a Western value, the ability to synthesize has been held dear by almost all Chinese thinkers, including Confucius.[2] Application of the Marxist theory to practice requires not only resourcefulness, even originality, but also the ability to synthesize, to unify diverse conceptual and empirical components in a given spatial-temporal frame. More important, synthesis postulates a frame of reference—a continuum—that is different from the dichotomy inherent in the search for originality.

The second theme is whether Mao's situational flexibility, both over time and between issues, poses any question for doctrinal consistency. A corollary, the third theme, is whether Mao's creative application of the Marxist-Leninist tenets has produced any "intrinsic" or qualitative changes in doctrine. The fourth proposed theme concerns only those studies that offer comparisons of domestic and external applications of Mao's thought: whether any noticeable degree of consistency is maintained in the two discrete arenas of application. Because of the preoccupations and priorities of their authors, some of the essays are more or less governed by the suggested themes than others; but the variations in no way diminish the importance of the four themes to any serious and meaningful study of Mao's thought and scenarios.

Brantly Womack links theory and practice in Mao's thought and finds unique theoretical unity and significant innovations, despite what Mao's detractors in the West have to say. An examination of the Marxist and Chinese "contexts" (the latter refers to the demands posed by reality for modifications of theory) leads him to discount any allegation that Mao merely did what any prudent Communist would do under the circumstances. To understand Mao properly, Womack suggests, it is necessary to study the whole ensemble of the Marxist strand in Mao and the innovative policies and decisions (or applications of Marxism-Leninism) that were not necessarily orthodox Marxism but were crucial to the success of Mao's revolution.

Womack weighs Mao's place as a thinker in a broad consideration that probes into Confucianism, the modern non-Marxist intellectual climate in China, and comparisons of Marx and Hegel. While Mao's theory absorbs the "core" tenets of Marx and Lenin, Womack finds, his style and emphasis differ greatly from the Communist classics. But situational flexibility, which is Mao's hallmark, is the product of the unity of theory and practice. To Mao, a good Marxist is known by his "manner of thinking"—not by his literal adherence to the dead letter of Marxist writings—which holds the key to success-fully unifying theory and practice both in the practical and the epistemological senses.

In an attempt to illustrate Mao's ontology, Womack looks at some basic assumptions of Mao's theory. Assumptions are important be-cause they limit the value of theory, the validity of which is no greater than the a priori validity of its assumptions. According to Womack, one such assumption is Mao's developmental view of theory: that existing tenets have temporally-bound (transient) empirical referents and old formulas may have to be discarded under new conditions. A second set of assumptions is related to Mao's goals and values, such as his faith in the people as a source of energy and power, his na-tionalistic bent, a "Rousseauist" idea of progress, and his empathy with the lower classes. The third assumption is Mao's faith in the "universal truth of Marxism-Leninism" (Mao's own words), which is, Womack points out, no bookworm's blind faith, since truth is found only through unifying theory and practice.

To offer a balanced analysis, Womack also discusses certain limitations of Mao's unity of theory and practice, the first being the very finite character of human experience. No matter how elastic a view one adopts about theory, changing reality poses significant ques-tions for the relevance of Marxism, regardless of its validity vis-à-vis the old reality that has informed it. Creative interpretation may offer a temporary or intermediate solution, but to what extent can this doctrinal stretching go without resulting in a qualitative erosion of ideology? Mao's own demurrer to the contrary does not seem to offer a satisfactory answer to this nagging question. Another diffi-culty, Womack states, arises from Mao's deliberate shifting from borrowed foreign formulas (including the earlier anachronistic Com-intern policies in China and the Soviet heavy-industrialization ap-proach to development) to Chinese history and practical reality. The same spatial-temporal limitations that condemned the former, how-ever, seem to infest the latter if it is to be projected as an exemplary model to other parts of the world. What makes the Maoist model more universal than the bookish Marxist doctrine? In the same breath, Womack discusses the implications of bridging from the individual to the collective individual (through the Party and propaganda avenues, in the socialist milieu) and the problems of transferring Mao's per-sonal genius and experience to a successor, on which the future of China depends—unless the Maoist ethos is totally internalized and sufficiently institutionalized.

Martin King Whyte is concerned with the kinds of societal dynamics that Western theorists such as Weber and Michels consider as leading to bureaucratization and monopoly of decision-making power by a few (oligarchy). At the same time Whyte questions whether Maoist mass-participation practices are able to check these tendencies in China. In Weber's analysis, the forces producing bureaucratization were closely intertwined with those giving rise to capitalism. A prima facie conclusion would seem to be that the bureaucratization trend would not develop in noncapitalist or socialist systems. Quite to the contrary, both Weber and Michels, in separate studies, found that socialism in power resulted not in a reversal, but in an enhancement, of bureaucratization. Weber then found that bureaucratization did not arise from the pursuit of private profit but from the crushing pressures of the momentum of the organizational form itself, features that socialism shared with capitalism. Weber's disregard of the possible corrective or mitigating effects of education or inculcation of antibureaucratic attitudes seems to part company with Mao, who falls back on the corrigibility of human nature as a hope for amelioration.

If Weber still remotely anticipated Mao in his view that forceful and imaginative elites could turn the tables and mold the bureaucracy to their will, Michels believed in the "iron law of oligarchy," arguing that modern large-scale organizations called bureaucracies simply directed human nature toward oligarchical directions. Whyte believes that despite Mao's antibureaucratic bent, Michels' "iron law" is not irrelevant to the Chinese experience. With all Mao's exhortations against bureaucratization, Whyte argues, China under Communism since 1949 has become more, not less, "bureaucratic." Here, admittedly, Whyte's measure is the size of large-scale organizations, which include the agricultural cooperatives and communes, and the number of salaried personnel in a complex hierarchical division of labor. Bureaucracy in this view is considered synonymous with organization or division of labor, the common criterion being "hierarchical," with no regard to the question of proportionality, or the proportional relation of the size of bureaucratic organization to the magnitude of the modern tasks it is called on to perform.

But Whyte also notes Mao's differences with Weber in regard to the "ideal" bureaucracy. Whereas Weber's ideal type hews to routinization and consists of a class of civil servants possessing specialized knowledge, the Maoist model epitomizes the mobilized zeal and ingenuity of organizational subordinates. At the same time, other aspects of the Weberian bureaucratic model, such as the hierarchical structure and the rule-abiding nature of its officers, are shared by the Maoist model. Mao, however, has repeatedly resorted to devices such as hsia fang and other ideological purification campaigns to arrest and correct the trend toward what he considers to be excessive bureaucratization. (Hsia fang, literally "sending down," denotes periodic downward transfers of "elites" to share the experience of and to learn from the masses.) Sociologists normally look for answers more in social structure than in personality or human nature. Nevertheless, one is tempted in this connection to ask whether Mao's strong (and at times romantic) meliorist view regarding bureaucracy is not due to his Marxist-anthropologist credentials. For Marx, Communism promised a society in which the form and structure of its organization conformed to the naturalistic or anthropological nature of man; and there is a perfect coincidence between Being and social organization, in which the former predicates the latter. The Promethean concept of man in the edifice of Marx's thought prescribes man's role as a force humanizing nature, and history is man's autogenesis.[3] Mao's view regarding man and his organization (including bureaucracy) strikes one as being a very real part of this Marxist anthropological legacy.

In any event, all of Mao's devices to counter excessive bureaucratization, Whyte cogently points out, are meant to make bureaucracy more responsive and efficient, not to obliterate it. While agreeing that not all organizations are equally hierarchical, Whyte reminds us that the Maoists have not seen fit to tamper with their Leninist legacy, whose antidemocratic tendencies, together with the requirements of all large-scale organizations, militate against the Maoist attempts to maintain a mass (antibureaucratic) orientation. The true answer to excessive bureaucratization, thus far, lies in the "charismatic intrusions" from Mao himself; but the future, Whyte notes, seems to depend on a similar commitment by Mao's successor.

William F. Dorrill's study analyzes the elusive topic of authority and legitimacy in the Maoist efforts to establish a legend of Mao's ideological prescience through reinterpreting the Party history. He offers a concrete example, the Ningtu Conference of August 1932, to illustrate his point. According to the official Party history laid down in 1945 (and still accepted) by the Maoists, the Party had suffered from the ideological "errors" and deviations of the earlier Comintern-supported leaders, especially the dogmatic "third 'Left' line" that allegedly dominated the Party after 1931 and resulted in the 1934 loss of the Central Soviet base in Kiangsi.

Since Mao was the founder of the Kiangsi base and remained its administrative head, the specific role he played during 1931-34 and the extent of his responsibility for the Communist defeat during the Kuomintang Fifth Encirclement campaign seemed to be a missing link in the crucial but muddled phase of the Party's history directly before the Long March. A search for the missing link led Dorrill to a careful reexamination of the jigsaw puzzle surrounding the Ningtu meeting, interpretations of which are varied for lack of primary documentation. One common view is that the conference effected a sweeping change in both Party and army leadership at the expense of Mao, as evidenced in his loss to Chou En-lai of the post of General Political Commissar. It is maintained that the anticipated Kuomintang campaign had triggered a strategic debate among Party leaders over whether to follow the old (Mao's) scenario of "luring the enemy deep" or, alternatively, to "halt the enemy beyond the gate" (some attribute the latter to Chou).

Dorrill put together the bits and pieces of information available: Mao himself recounted that he did not relinquish his military command functions until October, two months after the Ningtu meeting. On the other hand, Chou did not take up the post until the following May; he endorsed neither of the two alternatives but a third strategy, of anticipatory attacks. Documents made available during the Cultural Revolution served to put to rest any speculation about a Mao-Chou dispute over strategy at Ningtu. More recently, Otto Braun (Li Teh), Comintern's military advisor in Kiangsi, contended that despite criticism, Mao continued to play a very influential role in military affairs. Mao was reelevated to the Politburo in early 1933. And so on.

From this mosaic picture, Dorrill draws a different interpretation: that if Mao relinquished his involvement in military decisions late in 1932, he probably did so voluntarily, perhaps to concentrate fully on the equally pressing problems of political and economic mobilization in preparation for the Kuomintang onslaught. Whatever happened, there was good reason why the Maoist historians would want to continue to blur the question of Mao's military authority and extent of responsibility. Now that the Party had reestablished itself in Yenan, under the full control of Mao, there was a strategic need to rebuild confidence in the Party and, more especially, in Mao's leadership. The continued "mystery" surrounding the Ningtu conference would serve to absolve Mao of any responsibilities for the devastating military defeat in late 1934, since his "correct" guidance had been thrust aside, beginning at Ningtu.

The remarkable political and military recovery in Yenan gave weighty support to the Mao-centered interpretation of Party history, which began to be articulated in the 1942-44 Cheng Feng rectification, aimed at consolidating Mao's authority and legitimacy as the invariably correct strategist of the revolution. The legend of Mao's thought, extolled in the 1940s with the downfall of the "returned students" group, was canonized in the Party's Constitution of 1945. Its subsequent expunction from the 1956 Party document and its reinstitution in the Constitution adopted in 1969, as we have learned, coincided with Mao's waning and waxing leadership. The political use of historiography, Dorrill concludes, is in accord not only with Chinese political culture but also with the Maoist tenet of leadership through "correct" thought. This is not surprising for a society traditionally governed by an internalized body of norms (ideology) with the combined force of law and morality. Reinterpretation of history in this light, Dorrill argues, is an application of an aspect of Maoism in which its Marxist and Chinese strands intertwine.

In his study of the appeal, relevance, and applicability of Maoism, George T. Yu addresses a number of issues, including the Maoist scenario of capturing political power (war of national liberation), the strategy of wholesale sociopolitical change, and the approach to China's diplomacy in a new age of international relations beyond the Cold War. He assesses the symbolic value of the Maoist example to the Third World, those nations in Africa, Asia, and Latin America that are open to or are consciously seeking an alternative to the ideology and social system represented by either of the two superpowers. Rather than a static paradigm, Yu's model of the Maoist experience is an incremental one, evolving and developing in response to changing requirements and circumstances over time, through the pre-1949 liberation-war phase to the developmental experiments of the 1950s, upheavals in the 1960s, and the crystallization of a more definitive genre beyond 1971.

No model operates in a void, Yu stresses, and each model has meaning only within a given situational context; its transferability to other spatial and temporal contexts is relative not only to the objective conditions but also to the other competitive models. Yu's "model" thus refers to the exemplary value of a particular body of human or societal experience. From a relativist perspective, Yu finds that, all other means failing, the Maoist formula of armed struggle or national liberation war holds out an alternative answer to the needs of many desperate and frustrated anticolonial revolutionaries (in Algeria and Mozambique, for instance), and the Chinese national experience provides a reservoir of inspiration. But if the Maoist experience in this respect offers an appeal, the same experience is not to be duplicated. Here enters the question of relevance, which means that translation of the inspirational value of the Maoist example into concrete action has to pass the test of the local conditions (such as in southern Africa). The limiting conditions in each locale pose challenges to the applicability of the Maoist model, no less than to any other borrowed model.

As though aware of this problem, the Maoists themselves have assumed a relatively low posture in the actual supply of aid and comfort (including small arms) to national-liberation movements in the Third World. On the other hand, Yu adds, the Maoists have consciously endeavored to maintain a high visibility of the armed-struggle approach. The constant references in Peking's policy statements to the success of the Chinese revolutionary experience, often peppered with militant language, are designed to provide that visibility or, in Yu's words, "revolutionary credibility" to the formula.

Looking at the question from the "symbolic value" standpoint, Yu discovers reasons why China's support of national liberations does not necessarily stand in the way of her normal conduct of foreign relations. Quite to the contrary, the desire to maximize the symbolic value of the Maoist model generates a counterpressure for China to demonstrate an example of "good behavior," in contradistinction to the alleged bullyish and domineering behavior of the two superpowers. This ulterior motive, according to Yu, may explain why China supports the principles of equality, mutual respect, and noninterference, and vehemently condemns Soviet acts in Czechoslovakia and the U.S. role in Vietnam. Presumably, the same is true of China's persistent disclaimer about any aspirations to become another superpower.

A similar motivation to offer an antithesis to the alleged negative examples presented by the two superpowers, Yu states, characterizes China's posture regarding domestic developmental strategy in the developing countries. To those Third World nations that aspire to rapid industrial and socioeconomic development, the Chinese offer their own experience as a living example, emphasizing that they shared some common historical problems (such as backwardness and Western exploitation). Among concrete programs attractive to other Third World nations, Yu mentions the structural changes in public health care and resource-allocation control in industrial development, such as emphasis on labor-intensive projects and balanced rural-urban development. Here too, the Maoist example is important not because of its direct relevance and ready applicability, Yu reiterates, but because it offers a hope to Third World leaders (as in Tanzania) who are willing to listen. The value of Maoism, Yu concludes, exists in the beholder's eye.

Another study concerned with the external dimensions of the application of Maoism is Vincent Chen's analysis of the Maoist "united front" strategy used in China's diplomacy. In political-science parlance, "united front" is a process involving the use of coalitions to achieve certain common goals for the constituent members. In Communist practice, the forming of united front coalitions reflects a conscious startification of social classes in the Marxist notion of class struggle. The idea of a united front of diverse classes, Chen points out, originated with Lenin and Stalin, who first used it to offset the strategic weakness of the Communist Party in the initial years of the Bolshevik Revolution, but Mao has enriched the idea through adroit application. The operational code of the strategy requires that the Communist Party maintain its independence within the coalition and that both variant forms, the "united front from above" (teaming up with the leaders of the other classes in the coalition) and the "united front from below" (exploiting the divisive forces among the rank and file of the other classes), be used, either alternately or in concert, to help the Communists ultimately gain monopoly of power.

The existence of the various social classes both necessitates and makes possible the united front strategy in effecting the Marxist armed struggle. The specific class composition in a coalition depends on the situation. Mao's united front during the crucial phases (roughly from 1937 on) of the Chinese Communist revolution included the proletariat, the peasantry, the (urban) petite bourgeoisie, and the national(ist) bourgeoisie. The rationale for the four-class coalition was not only the "small number" of the proletariat but also its low "cultural level." Yet, Chen notes, the class coalition as such is supposed to retain the contradictions in the larger society; and hence class struggle (qua Marxist redemptive process for humanity) continues within the coalition as well as outside it. For this reason, Mao stresses that the Communist Party's independence within the coalition is as important as its unity with the other constituent groups. Mao owes his success, Chen adds, to an ability to limit the target of the class struggle at any given time or place to the smallest possible number, treating all others as allies for the moment. In its practical aspect, Mao's united front resembles political coalitions in the electoral systems; but in its ideological (redemptive) aspect, where the class struggle continues, the united front is a quite different phenomenon.

In a speculative but interesting projection, Chen tries to establish a link in the use of the united front in China's diplomacy, juxtaposing the domestic proletariat-peasantry and bourgeoisie stratification with the external alignment of the Communist and Third World countries, on the one hand, and Western capitalist and imperialist states, on the other. He also notes that Mao's initial acceptance of Soviet leadership in the Communist bloc did not negate China's independence. The domestic-external analogy therefore seems to break down. Within the Chinese domestic scene, the Communist Party's independence within the united front could be maintained without upsetting the coalition per se. But externally China's independent stance eventually led to the breakup of the Sino-Soviet alliance. The crucial difference that distinguishes international politics (consisting of latitudinal relations between legally coequal sovereigns but politically disparate units of power) from domestic politics (consisting of superordinate-subordinate relations) calls into question the possibility of applying the united front internationally in a manner consistent with its domestic application. Nationalism or interstate conflicts of interests and the disparate distribution of power between states present complications for the analyst, who can hardly speak about an "international Communist movement" with the same certitude as about a domestic Communist movement.

However, Chen is quick to point out that an appreciation of Mao's domestic united front offers a guide to a better understanding of China's international behavior: she is trying to isolate the Soviet Union within the Communist camp by cultivating a pro-Chinese coalition and, in a parallel move, to rally a broad coalition of countries with diverse social systems to oppose the condominium of the two superpowers. As in the domestic application, the united front in China's diplomacy consists in shifting alliances and tactics, while the goals set by the Party purportedly remain consistent. Nevertheless, goals and tactics are dialectically interrelated. It can hardly be definitively stated whether the substitution of the United States for the Soviet Union as China's main adversary in the early 1970s is a mere change in tactics and not in policy. Certain intermediate goals become means or tactics for attaining other goals of longer range; and since longer or shorter is only relative, the dialectical relationship is not totally unreal. In this light, the experience from the application of the united front strategy in China's diplomacy, as on the domestic scene, seems to confirm Mao's view that contradictions continue to exist in all stages of the development of the human world, though their specific nature changes over time as the composition and relations of the social forces change.

It is in this dialectic fashion that one can appreciate the meaning of the doctrine of "peaceful coexistence" that China champions, Chen suggests. Because "unity" and "struggle" coexist in the Maoist united front thinking, peaceful coexistence and liberation struggle likewise exist side by side without any inconsistency. In all fairness, Chen adds, the united front strategy is not totally unknown in the diplomacy of other nations, though not necessarily identified by the same nomenclature, such as West Germany's Ostpolitik and the United States' bridge-building and détente politics. But the difference is in the ideological master that the strategy is employed to serve.

There is a further difference, however. Because of the inherent "redemptive" value mentioned earlier, the united front strategy in its ideological aspect assumes dimensions unknown to political coalitions in Western electoral systems. In the latter, Chen points out, self-interest causes coalition leaders to keep their coalition strength to the "minimal winning" size (known as the "size" principle in William Riker's theory deduced from coalition behavior). The reason is to avoid undue burden of the side payments that leaders are obligated to make to maintain the coalition (the "side-payment" principle). For like reason, some dispensable partners in a coalition are dropped toward the later stages so that the leaders can maximize their shares of the spoils (the "strategic" principle).[4] In contrast, by its additional "redemptive" goals there is in Mao's united front a counterpremise about the value of maintaining a grand coalition (as opposed to minimal-winning coalition). In other words, Chen suggests, the axiom of maximizing the ranks of the ideologically "redeemed" impinges on the axiom of maximizing the practical gains or spoils.

George Ginsburgs offers what is perhaps the first systematic account of the Soviet critique of Mao and what he stands for on a broad range of issues. Western analysts have focused primarily on the ideological and economic dimensions of the running Sino-Soviet polemic dialogue. But, drawing from Soviet primary sources, Ginsburgs quite appropriately turns his attention to the charges the Soviets have hurled at Mao for innovations in political organization and operation, including the constitutional-administrative structure of the Chinese state, administration of justice, the nationality question, the commune as a social and political organization, and Mao's approach to class struggle and the peasantry. Ginsburgs also tries to find the possible reasons why Moscow has picked the particular items for denunciation. The occasional personal comments Ginsburgs interjects into his discussion throw additional light on the questions touched by Soviet critics.

Partly because the Chinese initially were consciously following the example of the Soviet state and partly because of an unwillingness to criticize the young Chinese people's republic, the Soviets withheld their harsh words in the early years, at least until the Sino-Soviet split. In a streak of charges since then, according to Ginsburgs, the Soviets have attacked Mao for his anti-institutional bias, his "pseudo-Marxist" democracy because of his tolerance of the residual continuance of traditional Chinese localism, and his dubious theory about the persistence of class struggle for an indefinite duration even after the overthrow of the bourgeoisie and the assumption of power by a people's democratic regime. To all these shortcomings, which are laid to Mao himself, the Soviets attribute the problems that have confronted the Chinese nation since the 1950s. The extensive use of the military, especially during the Red Guard phase of the Cultural Revolution, was condemned by the Soviet critics as having brought about a full-fledged "military-bureaucratic state" in China.

Mao's four-class "united front," Ginsburgs adds, was taken to task by Moscow as subversive to socialism and the precept of the dictatorship of the proletariat. Mao's emphasis on the peasantry and his choice of the rural sector for priority in China's developmental program, the Soviets alleged, merely reflected a preference for the peasant's universe of semifeudal traditions, and traditional predilection for deifying the country's leaders was said to serve Mao's personal purpose. Persistent criticisms have been heaped on the Maoist penchant for the minimal use of legal codes and the avoidance of the formal procedures of adjudication, which Moscow reviles as Chinese "legal nihilism." As Ginsburgs cogently argues, these charges demonstrate how legalistic and, for that matter, "Western" Soviet thinking is on social and political organization.

From the various cases he examines, Ginsburgs finds that the Soviet critics have let it be known that Mao's sins are not temporary failings but endemic to the "Maoist phenomenon." Soviet attempts to portray Mao as the source of the poison infecting the entire Chinese nation are schematically designed to discredit Mao and to incite domestic denunciations of him. The broadside of Soviet fire is often reserved for areas where potential dissident groups may be incited to act against Mao. In this light, the motive of Soviet vilification of Mao's handling of the relations between the Han majority and the ethnic nationalities in China's outlying regions, many of them adjacent to Soviet frontiers, has more content than meets the eye.

In another insightful comment, Ginsburgs speaks of the Soviet commentators as possibly indulging in vicarious castigation of the various disturbing tendencies closer to home. One example he gives is the possible domestic allusion in the Soviet criticism of Chinese rejection of the concept of presumption of innocence in criminal justice. Representations of the alleged Chinese excesses or failings, in this and other instances, may offer domestic liberals an opportunity to warn against possible duplication of the same in the Soviet Union, Ginsburgs continues. Viewed in this total context, much of Moscow's critique is politically motivated, and not just concerned with ideological purity or even the universality of the Soviet experience, as the official polemicists convey.

A study of the Soviet critique of Maoism is important to the interests of this volume, since the critique offers not only a mirror of Soviet fears of the competition from the Maoist model but also a counterpoint against which the relevance of Maoism can be better evaluated in view of the different conditions prevailing in China. For example, when the Soviets accused Mao of standing at the apex of a "hierarchical autocracy," their definition of autocracy reminds one of either Tsarist or Stalinist rule: "A form of administration in which the plenitude of power in a given territory rests in the hands of an individual who to all intents and purposes is answerable only to the person standing on the next higher rung of the bureaucratic ladder" (Ginsburgs' paraphrase). The Maoist "committee type" approach to organization, which stands in contrast with the Soviet "branch type,"[5] renders the critique totally anachronistic, unless the Soviet critics were indeed, as Ginsburgs suggests, engaged in vicarious castigation. Moscow, in another instance, invoked Lenin to denigrate Mao's mass-line policy, which it described as pandering to "arbitrary behavior of faceless crows" and as allowing "grass-roots activities of the masses" to be a counterweight to the "job performed by the representative institutions of the proletarian state" (again, Ginsburgs' paraphrase). The vast differences betwen Mao's and the Soviet approaches to the question of the "masses" become at once crystal clear, regardless of what Moscow says about proletarian democracy.

The last two essays, by Arnold B. Urken and myself, respectively
use "rational choice models" to explain behavior of the actors as if they
acted in accordance with the goals and constraints of the prevailing
norms in the model. "Model," used in this connection, refers to a
telescoped structure of symbols, or an analog or isomorph of the
reality. Analogy is a useful tool for human understanding. When
confronted with a new set of circumstances, we consciously or un-
consciously seek to find similarities to familiar circumstances. The
latter are used as a model and serve to organize perceptions and
focus attention. Strictly speaking, models are abstract structures of
symbols, devoid of empirical reference. But through "retroduction"
(that is, tinkering with and refining the models through testing against
reality), models can help lead to the discovery of theory (in which,
as already defined, observable phenomena are related together in a
systematic relationship explainable by some basic postulates). There
are no set rules for choosing one competitive model over another.
The "flash of insight" by which a particular model is chosen is a creative process, but the use of models in the cognitive process is a
rigorous exercise. The superiority of one model over another is
demonstrated through test, and the dialogue between model and empirical data ultimately converges on explanation (theory).

Models may be classified in accordance with their varying theoretical value, ranging from "representational" to "explicative" to
"theoretical," as Urken points out. The last category, which usually
subsumes the first two, attempts to rigorously deduce predictions
about political behavior from systematically related sets of assumptions. By examining the logical (or "formal") relationship between
postulated goals or norms and derived behavior, theoretical models
enable the analyst to make "positive" causal inferences about the
assumptions of a model. "Positive" is so used as to suggest that the
outcomes are only logical inferences within the model, apart from
the real world. The validity of the "positive" inferences is yet to be
verified through testing against empirical facts. Both Urken and I
employ theoretical models in an attempt not only to explicate the logic
of certain types of behavior in the Maoist system but also to make
inferences and suggest a prevision of what behavior is expected
or likely if the actors behave according to the postulated rules of the
game.

Urken was troubled by the conflicting interpretations among
Western analysts of what Mao actually did during the Cultural Revolution and by the conflicting predictions about the effects of the upheaval
on the viability of Maoist leadership of China's modernization. He
was prompted to analyze the bases for these claims. The result is a
persuasive case for reorienting the study of the Maoist system toward
the development of theoretical explanations of political behavior, as

opposed to ad hoc, intuitive, or propaganda-colored statements unequal to the demands of scientific scrutiny.

Urken distinguishes those predictive statements about Maoist political communication and modernization based on tested scientific theory (as defined above) from those predictions whose basis is speculative, or motivated by ideological concerns, or both. As an epistemological problem, the science-propaganda dichotomy is not found exclusively between the private analyst and the official propagandist, but between scientific and unscientific analysts as well. In either case the dichotomy inheres in the lack of congruence between "scientific explanations" and "official explanations." After comparing the behavior of the Maoist propagandists with their Western and Kuomintang counterparts, Urken finds much greater compatibility than is generally acknowledged in much of the published literature in the West. The goal of giving "official explanations" is to mobilize facts in order to support a particular political outlook. By contrast, "scientific explanations" depend on empirically verified consequences derived as part of the trial-and-error process of improving knowledge. Yet Western analysts of Maoist policies do not always provide scientific explanations; on the contrary, their statements are often based on intuitive observation or personal values, and their explanatory power is limited. Despite their claim to be "scientific," these explanations maximize simplicity and minimize information, very much like statements made by official propagandists.

To bring greater scientific rigor to their theorizing about Maoist political communication, Urken urges fellow analysts to adopt theoretical concepts and analytical techniques. He sets an example by proposing a spatial model. Acknowledging that the goals and constraints imposed on actors in the Maoist political system are quite different from those found in electoral systems, Urken proceeds from the assumption that the leader in the system is concerned with maintaining a position on an imagined spectrum of possible policy alternatives—which Urken calls "policy space"—that will maximize his popular support and avoid a losing coalition. Urken assumes further that unlike the situation in an electoral system, where support may be measured in terms of votes, the support of geopolitical factions or protocoalitions is required in China to maintain power. Though the identity and composition of the protocoalitions may change, he postulates that the leader seeks their support as if the protocoalitions possessed unequal shares of a finite amount of voting power. Here again, Urken assumes that the decision rules are simple majority in nonelectoral, as in electoral, systems.

On the basis of these postulates, Urken defines the leader's problem as adopting a policy orientation that will attract 51 percent of the units of power, given a particular distribution of actor preferences.

Further assuming that units of power are unimodal (clustering of phenomena under one mode) and somehow evenly distributed, the probability of encountering a unit of power increases as one moves toward the center of policy space. The optimal strategy for the leader, under the postulated circumstances, would be to locate himself next to the median position. The occupancy of the median position would also demonstrate to a potential competitor that the chances of forming a winning countercoalition are slim. Deviations too far to the left or the right would constitute "adventurism" or "tailism," respectively.

The validity of substituting geopolitical groupings (involving size of population, among other things) for the number of votes as measures of support and power, needless to say, has yet to be verified by test. Nevertheless, inferences from Urken's set of axioms anticipate Mao's own admission about his "left of center" position or, in Urken's language, occupying the policy space next to the median, steering clear of both "left" adventurism and right "tailism."[6] Furthermore, Urken's example suggests how several points about Mao's conception of the distribution of preferences in China may be interpreted. First, Mao acts as if he believes that the distribution of preferences is unimodal and gradually moving to the left. Second, Mao seems to assume that opponents on the left and right possess an insignificant amount of power to threaten him. Third, since information on the actual distribution of preferences is imperfect, the "mass line" serves as a feedback mechanism for indicating the distribution of preferences. Fourth, if Party bureaucrats deviate significantly from a dominant position in policy space, Mao can either (1) adopt various degrees of mass mobilization to bring pressure on them to conform to the Maoist policy, or (2) change the distribution of preferences by introducing new elements into the competition for power.

These interpretations, flowing from Urken's postulates, seem to stand up squarely against the data available during the Cultural Revolution. By his suggestions on how the logical connections between factors and outcomes can be postulated as part of a theory, Urken has demonstrated the kind of analyses that allow one to make systematic, theoretical inferences about similar cases; they are no doubt more scientific than analyses based on implicit or explicit ad hoc assumptions. Even more valuable for the purpose of this volume is his exemplification of how these theoretical analyses can actually be brought to bear on studies of aspects of Maoism.

In a similar vein, Chapter 8, on internal logic in the Maoist society, offers a set of interpretations deduced from a basic postulate: that the willful imposition of social rationality over private interests in the nonmarket ambience of the Maoist polity has significantly modified the game of politics. In constructing a model of the Maoist political system on this basic postulate, I make close comparisons with the market-economy model of electoral democracy developed by Anthony Downs. Close comparisons of two models are potentially most productive, methodologically, in discovering which properties are common and which are unique. The Downs model is used as a point of departure and as a counterpoint for theorizing because it represents a seminal work in linking economics and politics in a unified theory of social action. Besides, the Downs model is explicitly constructed on the basic assumption that the same "self-interest" axiom operates in both the economic and the political sectors of the Western capitalist democracy.

In the Maoist polity one can note a belief in the corrigibility of man, which, with the Communist Party's political predominance, has produced an enforced primacy of collective over individual ends. The introduction of the enforced sociability norm changes the set of axioms and derived behavior in the model. Self-interests are not completely absent in the motivations of the actors but exist in different forms. For example, more acute competition growing from private motives continues to exist among the top circles of the Party, because society's capability of enforcing the collective norm diminishes at that level.

Where the collective norm is enforced, at lower levels and especially among the masses, behavior in violation of the primacy of public ends will be destructive of self-interests. Coercion may be used to enforce the primacy of collective interests, since human nature is subject to molding by the edifying social environment. But once the collective norm is internalized, individuals acting rationally are expected to voluntarily uphold public interests at the expense of their own selfish ends. By contrast, whereas no coercion is used specifically against the self-interest axiom in the Downs model, government coercion is necessary in the collection of costs (such as taxes) for the "collective goods" (police protection, highways, and other services). The latter are enjoyed by all, no matter who pays for them; and unless government coercion is applied, nobody will pay the costs. With the shift in the role of the self-interest norm, the point at which government coercion is applied likewise changes. Where self-interests are allowed to play a residual role in the Maoist polity, I suggest, rules of behavior deduced by such Western theorists as Riker, Downs, and Mancur Olson, Jr. are relatively applicable, but not in areas where the collective norm is more effectively enforced. For example, Riker's coalition theory can explain the intramural power-struggle alignment patterns among the top Party leaders during the Cultural Revolution, but not the grand coalition pattern in the Party's "mass line" relations with the masses.

In direct inversion of the Western model, the symbiosis in the Maoist model of relative economic egalitarianism and an unequal distribution of political power has distinct outcomes. The most significant one is an interdependent relationship between the Party and the masses, perhaps to a larger degree than is usually realized, in that both have a common stake in the elimination of the erstwhile pouvoir intermédiaires (economic blocs intervening between the Party and the masses) and the prevention of their new counterparts from arising, so as to control resource allocation. Economic egalitarianism is essential to the Party for blocking the ascendancy of any recurrent intermediate power blocs and for rallying the support of the masses on its side, including the latter's acceptance of the Party's uncontested power. The masses, on their part, support the Party's political dominance for its guarantee of the benefits they receive from the egalitarian economy. To the extent that the Party remains the only system in which significant social mobility is still open to those more enterprising and qualified individuals hailing from the larger society (the Party is not a closed hereditary aristocracy, though recruitment follows very stringent standards), the prospect of self-elevation through the Party's channels is an additional cause of the masses' support for the Party's political dominance. In this sense, private motivation does not completely run against the grain of the collective dictum, but by and large with it. The duality in motives complicates analysis.

In contrast with the vote-maximizing (as opposed to welfare-maximizing) preoccupation of the electoral party-government in the Downs model, in my model the Maoist government is freed of the many obstacles to achieving optimal social states. Downs argues forcefully (1) that when citizen preferences are diverse and under uncertain circumstances, the government's choice is foreclosed—this happens where there is a conflict between different optimal states or between an optimal position (reflecting social rationality) and a dominant preoccupation of a majority of the voters (following individual self-interests)—and (2) that every optimum is dominated by a suboptimal position. (Downs develops this point quite extensively, as is shown in my discussion. A ready illustration of the problem Downs is alluding to is the predominance of the gun lobby's interests over those of the American public in a ban on arms sales.) The government in the Maoist nonelectoral system, however, has the power—because of its accepted dominance—to equalize the costs and benefits of collective goods for every citizen and to determine, or arbitrate, what optimal position is to be pursued in the event of competing alternative optimal positions. This government potential to move society is a central theme in my study. Among other things, I define optimality as essentially the achievement of such goals as the equitable distribution of the costs and benefits of "collective goods."

Certainty, however, is relative in the real world, even in a socialist system such as China. Given the fact that the Party stakes its legitimacy on its optimality-pursuing capacity, the government cannot completely ignore the possible conflicting preferences of the citizen groups. Mao's "mass line" is therefore a form of consultation or channel of communication with the masses, designed to generate the information necessary to help the state planners in decisions regarding optimal choices and to mobilize citizen acceptance of the policies once they are adopted. The deliberate interjection of the "mass line" approach makes it possible for the Maoist leadership to avoid duplicating the Stalinist errors of overly centralized planning and ubiquitous external surveillance. The postulated differences in Mao's assumption about human nature in an edifying social environment anticipate the difference of his approach from Stalin's to such questions as the Party's relationships with the masses.

In my inchoate model, I have attempted to draw "positive" causal inferences about the systematic relationship between assumptions and outcomes. In a limited way some of the inferences are individually related to the empirical data, but I believe that those not yet so related are also testable. Since it is logically possible to deduce confirmed predictions from false assumptions, just as it is possible to deduce false inferences (with faulty logical reasoning) from correct assumptions, the validity of the "positive" inferences must be held as tentative, subject to systematic testing. Neither Urken nor I claim to have offered anything more than tentative, but other scholars may offer alternative models, or sets of assumptions, that will prove to have more explanatory and predictive power than ours.

I also suggest an element of self-fulfilling prophecy in regard to Mao's premise about the perfectibility of man within the "correct" social environment. Just as this assumption provides the raison d'être for the enforcement of the sociability norm, to generate a social environment believed to be "redemptive" to man, so once the norm has its paramountcy established, the individuals in the morally pressurized society are then conditioned to defer to public well-being over and above their own selfish ends. In a circular way, the end result then corroborates and reinforces the corrigibility premise. Methodologically, this point suggests that scientific positivism should be complemented by considerations of normative dimensions (such as the effects of meliorist action) that normally fall outside scientific inquiry. A substantive inference from this point is that, by the workings of self-fulfilling prophecy, the future of China perhaps depends critically on both (1) the internalization in the individual of the (enforced) Maoist social rationality and (2) the "momentum" of the edifying social environment created in pursuance of the collective dictum, more than on Mao's longevity or even his "reincarnation" through a successor, though the latter is also important.

It goes without saying that overemphasis on methodology is as false as its total neglect. For example, what limits the usefulness of modeling (or formal theorizing in general) is not usually an inadequacy in our knowledge of logic (or mathematics), though sometimes it could be that, but an inadequacy in our knowledge of the subject matter. The requirements of a model sometimes prematurely close out our ideas and limit our awareness of unexplored possibilities of conceptualization. Incorporating folk wisdom in a model does not automatically give such knowledge scientific status.[7] Likewise, cross-cultural borrowing of concepts developed in Western social science could be productive and useful only if the background assumptions are closely examined and compared. This general cautious attitude runs through all the chapters in the present volume, though each has its own methodological mix and slant.

Together the eight contributors display a balanced concern with both practical knowledge of the subject matter and the methodological dimensions. Each in his way directs attention to one or more areas where one's understanding of "Maoism" can be enriched substantively, or methodologically, or both. Even where they fail, the contributors will have demonstrated by their "negative examples" what pitfalls others should avoid and what better paths they could take. Besides demonstrating the importance of mutual dependency of substantive knowledge and methodological sophistication, the contributors have amply demonstrated the "mirror effects" that comparative studies of the kind undertaken in the present volume can offer for a richer understanding of comparable social phenomena, values, and problems in the Western world.

NOTES

1. For a discussion of the etymology of "Maoism" and possible reasons why the term (in Chinese and translations) is officially discouraged in China, see James C. Hsiung, Ideology and Practice: The Evolution of Chinese Communism (New York: Praeger, 1970), pp. 128 ff.

2. Ibid., pp. 143-47.

3. See Karl Marx, "Private Property and Communism," in Early Writings, T. B. Tottomore, trans. (New York: McGraw-Hill, 1963), p. 155.

4. William H. Riker, The Theory of Political Coalitions (New Haven: Yale University Press, 1962).

5. Franz Schurmann, Ideology and Organization in Communist China (enl. ed.; Berkeley: University of California Press, 1968), pp. 178 ff., 313-15.

6. Edgar Snow, "A Conversation with Mao Tse-tung," Life, Apr. 30, 1971, pp. 46-48. Mao's left-of-center position is also

enshrined in the 1956 and 1969 Party Constitutions, in the drafting of which Mao was known to have had an active part.

7. Abram Kaplan, Conduct of Inquiry (Scranton, Pa.: Chandler, 1964), p. 279.

The Logic of ''Maoism''

1

**THEORY AND PRACTICE
IN THE THOUGHT OF
MAO TSE-TUNG**
Brantly Womack

Although Mao's dominant position in the shaping of China's politics and society is undeniable, the role of the "thought of Mao Tse-tung" in his success seems difficult to specify. It does not seem likely that Mao merely did what any prudent Communist would do under the circumstances; a number of timely policies and practical innovations that were not within normal Marxist patterns of action and institutions contributed significantly to the success of the revolution and influenced the kind of Communism established in China. The "thought of Mao Tse-tung" as the ensemble of these innovative policies and decisions is thus of essential importance in comprehending the successes of Chinese Communism and perhaps the key to grasping the peculiar character of the ongoing Chinese revolution.

Two aspects of this ensemble have hampered the understanding of Mao as a creative revolutionary. One is the concreteness of formulation. Mao always addresses himself to a pressing problem of the movement. Although some formulations are more or less generally applicable, he rarely ventures into a discussion of abstractions. He commonly recommends ways for cadres to behave, but he doesn't often proceed to discuss human nature. The other aspect is a seeming lack of a unifying theory behind these practical innovations other than a general acceptance of the Marxist-Leninist world view. Mao thus appears to be merely a good engineer of Communism, successfully applying its theory to Chinese reality.

The writer is deeply grateful to Professor Tang Tsou for his constant help and would also like to thank Professors Philip Kuhn, William Parrish, Leonard Binder, James C. Hsiung, and Lloyd Rudolph for their comments.

The Chinese Communist evaluation of Mao's endeavors seems by and large to correspond to this view. He has creatively applied Marxist-Leninist theory to Chinese conditions. In the West this might be seen as a certain devaluation: S. M. Lipset speaks for his culture when he says, "The height of intellectual achievement is to be original. This is as true of the social sciences as it is in the arts or the natural sciences."[1] Regardless of its defensibility within the context of a specialized society oriented toward progress, this judgment should not be accepted uncritically as a transcultural value. A predilection for synthesis that derives from a basically intuitive-aesthetic attitude has been typical for Chinese philosophy;[2] this has led to a theoretical style that often finds security in unelaborated analogies and syncretism and avoids bald claims of derivation, distinction, or novelty. Whether this style is superior or inferior to the "modern scientific" style, which often accentuates trivial novelties in the dark corners and frayed edges of accepted systems, is obviously not a question to be decided generically. In any case, given the variety and novelty of Chinese conditions and the infinite number of possible inapt derivations from Marxist theory, Mao's frequent success is no mean intellectual achievement, even though it is not primarily intellectual.

The fact that Mao's role is that of an applier rather than that of a theoretician does not rule out the possibility that his thought possesses its own unique theoretical unity and makes significant theoretical innovations. If Mao's thought did not have its own unity, his actions would be erratic; coherence would not have emerged spontaneously from Chinese conditions or descended from Communist theory. The fact that Mao's policies vary greatly over time and yet are successful implies a very sophisticated unity. Mao's conviction that the cadre's capacity for objective (and hence effective) rationality is determined in constant practical struggle differs fundamentally from the assumptions of what he calls dogmatism, but it does not despair of the accessibility of objective reality or of the individual's ability to make a notable contribution to history.[3] My thesis is that the theoretical thread unifying Mao's thought is his notion of the relationship between theory and practice, and that this unity was a significant theoretical triumph within the context of Chinese and Marxist thought. The proposition that theory depends on practice is neither startling nor original with Mao; the reader is asked to consider this principle as central to Mao's thought and to judge the novelty of this orientation within the context of Chinese intellectual history and Marxist theory.

Since Mao's stress is on the importance of practice rather than on theory, the most appropriate way to discuss their relationship would be to analyze series of his solutions to concrete problems. Although this has always been an important aspect of scholarship on

Mao, attention to his ideological flexibility and the development of his thought has become particularly marked recently.[4] The study of the historical interrelationship of Mao's own theory and practice and the consequent development in the content of his thought is the ultimate test of the meaningfulness of the model of Mao's thought to be presented here, but it is a task too vast and reticulated to be included in this paper. By pursuing the notion of the unity of theory and practice and examining its ramifications, we not only take the less cumbersome and more comprehensive alternative but also are able to present more clearly the general assumptions and problems of Mao's method. The explicit content and importance of Mao's notion of theory and practice can be most easily documented from the pre-1949 period, but the strong continuity of his political style and theoretical orientation into the postliberation period is also evident. We would hope to be charting the course for a detailed and systematic study of the interaction of Mao's thought and the Chinese political context.

I begin with a sketch of the Chinese and the Marxist intellectual background. The next section deals with Mao's unity of theory and practice and its policy ramifications. The third section discusses assumptions necessary to Mao's notion, and the last treats its inherent difficulties.

THE CHINESE AND MARXIST CONTEXTS OF MAO'S THOUGHT

"On Practice" (1937) was a more general effort in a long series of attempts to dislodge the dogmatic habit of learning and applying theoretical knowledge without regard to practical conditions and needs. In his "Hunan Report" (1927), Mao had criticized those who sat in the towns and were misled by bourgeois rumors about the peasant movement instead of investigating it themselves.[5] In the pamphlet Oppose Book Worship (1930), he proposed the slogan "No investigation, no right to speak" and criticized "blindly carrying out directives without discussing and examining them in the light of actual conditions."[6] Mao's continual criticism of dogmatic complacency and its fruits was not based merely on a different understanding of the foundation of authority and the necessity of participation; theoretical rigidity was endangering the movement by formulating policies without reference to actual conditions and by allowing established policies and attitudes to continue despite drastic changes of situation. The general theoretical justification provided by "On Practice" for Mao's exhortation to pay attention to objective conditions had its own practical roots in the vastly different conditions of establishing the Yenan base and the United Front against Japan. In such a fundamental change of situation, the

3

blunting of political perception and the artifical limitation of alternatives produced by an overdose of books was a considerable hazard; and to be practical only within the guidelines of the Comintern was perhaps an even greater danger.

Both types of dogmatism had borne bitter fruit in the past: deference to mistaken Russian strategy and loyalty to old policies in new situations had essentially contributed to the catastrophes of 1927 and 1934. Mao himself had always been associated with the real power of the movement, the peasants and the army. But association with the practical aspects of the Party, despite the failures of its theoreticians, did not lead to the type of pragmatism that would have allowed a permanent accommodation with the Kuomintang or the traditional peasant societies. The solution he found was within the Communist framework, but it stressed a dependence of theory on practice and consequently gave theoretical freedom to alertness and creativity in decision-making.

Despite its naturalness to Mao's experience and circumstances, his concern with the unity of theory and practice had a peculiar novelty in China. The concern of the Confucian classics with the relation of knowledge and action, or "principle and affairs," was not an analytic one and hence did not emphasize the differentiation of their relationship. The Sung Neo-Confucianist Chu Hsi first posed the more general philosophic problem of the relationship between "what is above shapes" and "what is within shapes," deriving from this Plato-like distinction between principle and its embodiment in things a special emphasis on studying principle.[7] Three centuries later the Ming philosopher Wang Shou-jen (Wang Yang-ming) countered this dualistic tendency with an idealistic monism and a corresponding emphasis on the unity of knowledge and conduct; and despite opposition to his idealism, the monist frame of mind persisted down to the mid-19th century.[8] At that time the emergence of Western imperialism as a real threat to China presented China's intellectuals with a dilemma that rendered monism difficult. The military inferiority that awakened China to the existence of an alien and more powerful civilization had forced some of its officials to find a specific remedy in the study of Western science and technology, but these subjects were alien to the values and structure of traditional Chinese culture. The antagonism produced by the temptation of these new, non-Confucian disciplines is well described by Chang Chih-tung in his essay An Exhortation to Learning: "Not knowing how to accommodate to special circumstances, the conservatives have no way to confront the enemy and deal with the crisis; not knowing the fundamental, the innovators look with contempt upon the teachings of the sages." An admirer of Chu Hsi, Chang proposed as a unifying formula his famous dichotomy: "Chinese learning for substance (ti), Western learning for function (yung)." As Joseph

Levenson points out in his brilliant analysis of this slogan, Chang attempted to justify a radical dualism of social means and ends on the basis of a forced interpretation of Chu Hsi's dualistic philosophical tendency.9 But this artificial combination of the yung of Western technology and the ti of Confucianism was not viable: the rapidly growing Western-style modernization necessarily implied a restructuring of values, and the appeal of Confucian scholarship dwindled as its own yung of being "the necessary passport to the best of all careers"10 was challenged by the increasing prestige of Western learning. The philosophical separation and practical amalgamation of ti and yung, of the fundamental beliefs of the society and the rules governing its practical activity, was the last traditional Confucian formula attempting to encompass the whole of Chinese development. A nationalistic sacrificing of the traditional Chinese ideology to the perceived needs of a modern nation was already covertly under way in the works of reformers like K'ang Yu-wei. Their sacrifice of orthodox Confucianism, which so quickly followed Chang's sacrifice of a total Confucianism, met its own debacle in the collapse of the "100 days reforms" (1898), leaving the Chinese intellectual to make what sense he could out of a new and turbulent world.

The role of ideology as a cultural system filling the vacuum of a discredited traditional order11 is apparent in the proliferation of "isms" in the early 20th century in China. Since a more successful belief system was sought, the ideas seemingly responsible for the power and success of the West—"Mr. Democracy" and "Mr. Science" in various forms—were most popular and were energetically and devoutly propounded. Even the materialists felt a millenarian fervor, as shown by this passage from Wu Chih-hui, a famous popularizer of industrialization and a Kuomintang member:

> When the world of great harmony is reached, all forms
> of labor shall have been replaced by machinery . . .
> every human being will have an exalted, pure, and ex-
> emplary character . . . man will have a head—because
> of the overuse of his brain—as big as a five-pound melon,
> while his body will be small and delicate. . . . This is
> not a utopian idealization. There is already some evi-
> dence of its realization in countries which possess better
> and more skillful machines.12

The aftermath of World War I contributed greatly to an alienation of Chinese intellectuals from the West. The assignment of the German possessions in Shantung to Japan by the peace negotiations at Versailles both antagonized Chinese nationalists and disenchanted admirers of Western democracy. New, anti-Western sources of ideological inspiration were soon found. Many, following Liang Ch'i-ch'ao and Liang Sou-ming, rediscovered in Chinese culture a spiritualism superior to the materialism of the West. This trend culminated in a polemic against studying science by Carsun Chang, which precipitated the famous debate over "science" vs. "metaphysics."[13] Another trend encouraged by disenchantment and the threat of foreign domination was toward revolutionary Western ideologies, particularly anarchism and Communism.

Sun Yat-sen, whose doctrine precipitately absorbed many of these currents, was very much in the spirit of the ideologists. To encourage political activism he raised the slogan "Action is easy and knowledge is difficult," thus reversing a classical saying. This reflects the overriding concern both with correct general orientation and with the urgent need for action characteristic of this period. It does not imply that Chinese reality was satisfactory; on the contrary, the thesis is that action is impossible without knowledge, although it is easy enough once the truth is attained and firmly believed in.[14] For Sun, the relationship between knowledge and action was never problematic; it was a simple matter of application. The resulting emphasis in Kuomintang ideology on knowledgeable leaders who acted resolutely with conviction and sincerity grew apace with the trend toward conservative culturalism fostered by Chiang Kai-shek. Its inchoate and eclectic nature gave rise to an impression of political activism that lacked ultimate and integrated ideological guidance.

The polar opponent to the welter of abstract, nationalistic ideologies was Hu Shih. An American education had considerably reinforced his pragmatic bent, and had given him an idea of the duties of a man of letters far closer to an American academic than to a Confucian scholar. Brilliantly successful in his own academic research, Hu Shih castigated those who would rather preach abstract solutions than solve specific problems ("Study more problems, talk less of isms"):

> We don't study the standard of living of the ricksha coolie
> but rant instead about socialism; we don't study the ways
> in which women can be emancipated, or the family system
> set right, but instead we rave about wife-sharing and free
> love; we don't examine the ways in which the Anfu Clique
> might be broken up . . . but instead we rave about anar-
> chism. . . .
> The great danger of "isms" is that they render
> men satisfied and complacent, believing that they are
> seeking the panacea of a "fundamental solution," and
> that it is therefore unnecessary for them to waste their
> energies by studying the way to solve this or that con-
> crete problem.[15]

Behind this criticism was the view that theories are mere generalizations of specific situations, and lose their validity if they are torn from their practical roots and applied in different circumstances. Hence, in his essay "Knowledge Is Difficult, But Action Is Not Easy Either," Hu Shih attacked Sun Yat-sen's emphasis on the theorist because "knowledge is the result of action and the function of knowledge is to assist action."[16] As an alternative to imported theories, Hu Shih suggested experimentalism: "Experimentalism is of course also a kind of ism, but it is only a method for the study of problems. Experimentalism emphasizes concrete facts and problems, and consequently does not acknowledge [that there can be] any fundamental solutions."[17] The correct approach was not political, but specific: Specific investigations should be made and concrete solutions to limited problems enacted. The only real possibility of progress was the accumulation of these concrete solutions. This type of science demands independent thinkers who discipline themselves to pursuing particular problems. Despite this picture of the concerned scholar involved in research and politically active only in criticism, Hu Shih felt that an overall plan for government activity was essential. In 1917 he resolved not to talk politics for 20 years, but by 1922 he was recommending "a militant and decisive public opinion" as the first labor of political reform.[18] The "ideals, plans and absolute faith" of the Soviet Union impressed him more than the "negligent government" of England.[19] He preferred "real revolution" against "poverty, disease, ignorance, greed and disorder" rather than unconscious evolution or violent political revolution.

Any plan of political action has value presuppositions that help define its perception of social reality and judge the importance and urgency of alternatives for action. The implicit values of experimentalism's insistence on factual investigation were the imported ones of political meliorism and social equality. In a less volatile situation, Hu Shih's Americanized political ideas would have been more popular. In China, however, experimentalism, like most of the foreign isms he criticized, proved not to be viable. Hu Shih should not be judged by the success of his political ideas; they were merely one aspect of his rich and productive career. But a judgment informed by hindsight must find his political ideas too idealistic: the complacent pursuit of individual investigations and the voicing of reasoned criticism implies a political framework and an ideological consensus in which reforms will be effected and criticisms heeded— one obviously not existent in China at that time. However, pragmatism and empirical method did not allow the formulation or adoption of a general framework necessary to specific improvements, and Hu Shih's exclusive concentration on practice met the same fate as the ideologist's exclusive concentration on theory.

Mao Tse-tung's emphasis on practice has some similarities to Hu Shih's experimentalism. But Mao's criticism of dogmatism and emphasis on investigation interact with a general commitment to Communism; thus, it is an emphasis on practice within a unity of theory and practice and not a substitute for theory. The ideologists' emphasis on theory necessitated a lack of realism and flexibility, whereas Hu Shih's exclusive concentration on practice made him skeptical of any general solutions; Mao, as a "pragmatic ideologist,"[20] used his ideology to specify real political tasks and allowed the political experience thus gained to modify his theory. This reunification of theory and practice was a powerful alternative to the intellectual directions taken since the fall of the Empire. It could combine the confident commitment and direction of an ideology with the prudence and perceptual acuity of empiricism. Since the individual is neither a blind executor of correct dogma nor a specialized researcher, Mao developed a hortative, communally oriented cadre morality that is remotely reminiscent of the classical emphasis on morality. According to Mencius, any well-intentional ruler can become a sage, and according to Mao, any well-intentioned worker can become a Communist hero; both cases involve exemplary devotion to the public good.

The unity of theory and practice and the primacy of practice in this relationship is a doctrine of high and explicit importance in Marxist theory. In his early writings, Karl Marx distinguished his philosophy from those of the merely speculative Young Hegelians by his conviction that fundamentally economic social relationships were the real basis of theory; therefore revolutionary theory must be concrete and must issue in revolutionary praxis. With the additional thesis that the proletariat was the material basis for revolution in capitalist society, the general framework of Marxism was set. But the Hegelian heritage of Marxism did not emphasize that the relation of theory and practice is problematic; so rather than develop a methodology of the constant control of theory by practice, Marxism tended to consider it more a question of philosophic priorities.[21] This is not to say that unrealistic dogmatism is the position of the Marxist classics[22]—without a high degree of practical shrewdness, a revolutionary organization could not survive, let alone be successful. This political realism in practice, however, was considered a technical problem of executing the revolutionary plan, not a vitally important feedback for the content of those plans.

It is not difficult to imagine G. W. F. Hegel as the origin of dialectical materialism's confidence in possessing the truth. Though his pretensions to definitive personal status in matters of philosophy are no more than most great philosophers',[23] his system acquires a special sort of omniscient aura from its thesis of the rational unity of subject and object. Hegel's philosophy is not an investigation of reality in the sense of using some method to pry out its secrets for the observer. His Wissenschaft is the self-unfolding of the rational, because the object in itself (an sich) is no different from the object as it exists for us (für uns). If reality were fundamentally alien to us, then investigation of it would be impossible. If it is not alien, then the assumption of its alienation (the systematic doubt of most modern philosophy), is arbitrary and unscientific.

Science may start from either the subjective or the objective world: their fundamental equivalence guarantees that the result will be the same truth. Hegel therefore has as great a respect for experience as he does for logic, and regards it as "at least an external test of the truth of a philosophy."[24] However, his method of determining what is included in this rule of thumb is hardly rigorous: "A thoughtful consideration of the world distinguishes what in the wide range of inner and outer being is only appearance, transitory and meaningless, and what truly earns the name of reality."[25]

This attitude provides a framework for Hegel's explicit view of the theory-practice relation.[26] The theoretical mind tries to make the data of the objective world its own through knowledge; its weakness is its assumption that the facts with which it works are beyond its influence. This problem is negated by the practical will, which in action demonstrates its ability to impose itself on reality. Gradually, however, it finds that the unity of its designs with nature's laws— "insight into necessity"—brings concrete freedom.

The almost quietist reconciliation of theory and practice that Hegel sees as their natural end is of course contradicted by Marx's call that philosophy change the world. Marx does not simply reject Hegel, but "stands him on his feet"[27]: rather than proceed from theory through practice to an intellectual contemplation, Marx emphasizes that man's theory concerns how to change his existing situation. Man's social situation is his reality. The proper function of theory, according to Marx, is not to mystify this situation and thus impede its improvement, but to be the active element of its revolution. But both revolutionary and reactionary philosophies have only a transitory existence. The latter loses its medium of existence when reality is depicted,[28] the former extinguishes itself in achieving "socialized mankind."

Marx thus introduced a fundamental doctrine into Communist ideology: the primacy of practice as both root and goal of theory. The social consciousness of men arises from the actual production relationships in which they find themselves, and the task of true theory is to change these relationships. But it is far more characteristic of Marx's own development to proceed from the critique of existing theory to his theory and then to empirical research and revolutionary activity. The original determination of theory by economic and social conditions is not a problematic relationship to be perfected, but a fact to be exposed: "The reform of consciousness exists merely in the fact that one makes the world aware of its consciousness, that one awakens the world out of its own dream, that one explains to the world its own acts.29 The fact that Marx was engaged in delineating a Hegelian-materialist standpoint from idealist and vulgar materialist ones makes emphasis on the practical fruit of true revolutionary philosophy and the profane roots of supposedly independent bourgeois philosophy his first tasks. The possibility of difficulties with the mechanism of the dependence of theory and practice, with the suitability of data to theory and theory to reality, is rarely hinted at. Despite his reversal of Hegel, Marx continued to consider the separation of the wheat from the chaff in practice not to be basically problematic.

Marx's attitude toward political economy best portrays this attitude toward practice. Because the forces and relations of production are the real foundation of society, this is the most practical social science. The contents of Capital evidence a tremendous thoroughness in Marx's study of English economic conditions. The method of political economy, however, is not to proceed from concrete reality to abstract concepts, but to start with the abstract and build toward the more complex concrete realities.30 Society is always in the back of the economist's mind as the object of his endeavors, but his scientific task is to construct a rational model of society, "to reproduce it as a mental concretum."31 This is not an abstract speculative effort: the theoretician is limited by the level of development of his epoch and of course must be cognizant of the facts in the area that his theory tries to rationalize. But a problem that history allows to be posed can be understood and solved.32

Marx's contribution to socialism was, according to Engels, making it "scientific": applying the dialectic to the facts of political economy.33 He thereby discovered the materialistic conception of history and surplus value as the secret of capitalist production.34 In his own theoretical struggles with a much less worthy opponent than the Young Hegelians, Engels was obliged to develop the views of dialectical materialism well beyond the general theory of Marx's early works and the economic and political analysis of his later works. In Engels' hands Marxism grew into a comprehensive Weltanschauung that viewed itself as a materialistic inversion of Hegel's system. Dialectical materialism replaced philosophy by providing a theoretical unification of the sciences. Its self-confidence stemmed not from the Hegelian confidence in the unity of subject and object, which is fresh in Marx's early writings, but from a faith in science engendered by the accomplishments of the 19th century.

The unquestioned confidence in the science of socialism was fundamentally shaken in 1898 by Eduard Bernstein, a close friend of

Engels and author of the practical section of the Marxist Erfurt Program (1892). It was precisely the Hegelian framework of Marxism that Bernstein objected to: "The great things which Marx and Engels have accomplished have not been achieved because of the Hegelian dialectic, but in spite of it."[35] Too much faith in theory had led socialism away from the facts and away from its practical tasks. Bernstein's own orientation was eminently practical:

> The historical right and goal of the working class's great war of liberation does not depend on any ready-made formula, but is determined by the historical conditions of existence and the resulting economic, political, and ethical needs of this class. The working class must strive to realize ideals, but not doctrines. If one wants to call this "revisionism," then so be it."[36]

Bernstein demonstrated that the predicted polarization of capitalist society and its impending doom were belied by empirical study. He wanted "to overcome the split between the theory and the practice of the Party" by eliminating outmoded phraseology and promoting theoretical eclecticism.[37] Though Bernstein believed that he was faithful to Marx and Engels, the continuity was far more in his dedication to concretely furthering working-class interests than in theoretical matters.

Bernstein's critique of the dialectic was the theoretical side of his demand that socialist politics be directed exclusively toward promoting the practical welfare of the masses. In both respects V. I. Lenin was the polar opposite of the founder of revisionism. Politically, "What Is to Be Done?" condemns Bernstein's Russian followers for worshipping workers' spontaneity and ignoring the revolutionary tasks of the movement. Philosophically, Lenin in his Philosophic Notebooks shows an even greater respect for Hegel's philosophy than do Marx and Engels. He never criticizes the Hegelian notion of practice and is particularly impressed with his "absolute Idea."[38] With Lenin, materialistic philosophy becomes an independent discipline; practice is still seen as the criterion of theory, but not as its sublation.[39] Lenin's most practical invention, the disciplined party of professional revolutionaries, in particular shows a confidence in Marxism's wisdom and mission. The duties of the Party elite were not systematically worked out by Marx, probably because he assumed that the masses would perceive their class interests and act accordingly. Lenin, however, admits that the masses spontaneously gravitate toward reformism. His conclusion is that the more the masses participate in the political struggle, the more necessary it is to have a stable organization of leaders, because otherwise demogogues—"the worst enemy of the working class"—might sidetrack the more backward sections of the masses.[40] The Party is not characterized by class purity and does not allow such distinctions within its ranks; as for broad democracy, it is "a useless and harmful toy" for a revolutionary party.[41] Its relation to the masses is therefore one-way: it endeavors through agitation and propaganda to raise their class political consciousness. The Leninist party claims to be the legitimate vanguard of the masses, not because of a mandate but because it is an organization of revolutionary specialists that fully devotes itself to their interests. For such a group to admit ignorance or error would be detrimental to both its own espirit de corps and to its claims to legitimacy. The tutelage of the masses implies possession of a theory that permits a sure formulation of correct policy. The party line has no necessary connection with the current thought of the masses; it proceeds from that which is in possession of the leadership: a correct, scientific theory and total, professional devotion to the best interests of the workers. As correct theory becomes more univocally defined in the course of the movement's factional struggles, subjective deviation from the responsibilities of leadership becomes the sole admissible ground for error.

Although the Chinese Communist Party was founded with the guidance of a Comintern agent, the Leninist posture of infallibility was untenable for its first 15 years. Not only was it responsible for obvious and costly mistakes, but as subordinate to the Comintern it lacked final authority in policy matters. This position of intermediate leadership encouraged irresponsibility and contentiousness among the Chinese leaders, while ignorance of Chinese conditions and the pressure of conflicting interests led the Comintern to abuse its authority. As Mao later said: "Without adequate experience it would have been impossible to sufficiently recognize the laws governing the Chinese revolution . . . This objective world of China, generally speaking, was recognized by China [sic], not by those comrades in the Comintern in charge of the Chinese problem. These comrades in the Comintern did not, or one may say, did not at all understand Chinese society, Chinese nationality, or the Chinese revolution."[42]

Meanwhile, Mao himself gained firsthand knowledge of these conditions as an organizer of peasant movements and of the Red Army. After the Shanghai massacre and the crushing of the early Soviets, the Party was ripe for Mao's stress on studying the actual conditions of China and avoiding dogmatism. The ability demanded by the diverse and chaotic conditions that permitted the continued existence of Communist base areas in China was that of correctly differentiating policy in order to exploit the variety and development of political and military situations. The origin of the theoretical views characteristic of Mao is in this type of practical guerrilla experience. To a great extent his theory assumed a framework of the more unifying and centralizing theories of Marx and Lenin, but his style and emphasis differ greatly from the Communist classics.

While Mao's stress on practice in the relationship "between knowing and doing" was understandable for a Chinese Communist with his experience, it stressed an area in the cognitive process that was passed over as not problematic in previous orthodox theory. The state of European social philosophy and epistemology made the Marxist formulation of the relation of theory and practice relevant and innovative, but it did not force a prolonged consideration of the practical problem of how to arrive at correct theory and policy from practice, or how to amend incorrect or superseded theories and policies. Although Hegel, Marx, Engels, and Lenin devoted a tremendous amount of energy to investigation, this research proceeded by and large from a confidence that their theory was correct; and it was done more to convince unbelievers and to concretely articulate theory than to aid in the cautious pursuit of correct and timely policy.[43]

The superficial similarity of Mao's approach to Bernstein's stress on the facts and the workers' immediate needs is misleading: Bernstein rejects revolutionary theory and practice as outmoded and substitutes a class empiricism for ideology; Mao stresses the investigation of the concrete possibilities of revolutionary action within the constant flux of the situation.[44] The question of the orthodoxy of Mao's Marxism is as problematic as it is meaningless in itself—how much deviation constitutes heresy is a matter of taste. But he is undoubtedly a revolutionary dedicated to the success of Communism in China. That the Chinese conditions made an untried path seem more propitious and, one might say, led to a redefinition of success is the source of the problem of Mao's orthodoxy.

The relation of Mao's notion of theory and practice to both Chinese and Marxist intellectual traditions is that of a novelty but not a foreign body. In neither case did he shatter a primeval quiet: the range of controversy in both traditions and the state of things at the time of his formulation render this novelty intelligible. But in it was a "radical" innovation, in Marx's sense of being at the root of the matter; the relationship of theory and practice maintained by Mao gives a distinctive character to every aspect of Maoist China.

DEPENDENCE OF THEORY ON PRACTICE AND THE RESULTING PROCEDURAL RULES

The most important source for Mao's idea of practice and its relationship to theory is the essay "On Practice: On the Relationship Between Knowledge and Practice, Between Knowing and Doing," which was originally delivered as a lecture at the Anti-Japanese Military and Political College in July 1937.[45] Because this work is short and generally available, only the most important references will be given. Although the problem is not treated as systematically in Mao's other writings, they do occasionally provide relevant insights and corroborate the importance of the thesis of "On Practice," so they will be cited. I will avoid references to statements not attributed to Mao—for instance, editorials in Jen-min jih-pao, because his degree of personal responsibility for even the authoritative views expressed therein is problematic.

The essential interrelation of theory and practice makes any discussion of the priority of any particular somewhat simplistic, but there are three basic ways in which theory is dependent on practice.

1. Practice is prior to theory because the scope and character of one's thought are defined by one's interactions with the world. The primary sphere of practical activity is production; but social practice also includes class struggle, political life, and scientific and artistic pursuits. Class cleavages exist in all these forms of practice: each class develops its own politics and culture from its own practical base. In a class society, theory must be the theory of a particular class.

2. The individual theory is also determined by its relationship to practice. Knowledge of a thing is gained by the experience of trying to change it. First impressions cannot identify the essence of a thing: practical firsthand experience is needed as a basis for meaningful thinking. After the proposition or system is formed on the basis of experience, it must be tested against objective reality. The truth of a theory does not lie in its logical relationship to other theories, but in its ability to correctly describe and predict the objective world. "Generally speaking, those [theories, policies, plans, or measures] that succeed are correct and those that fail are incorrect, and this is especially true of men's struggle with nature."[46]

3. Besides this dependence of theory on practice in its formation and testing and the definition of its scope by objective conditions, theory derives its values for man from its ability to improve his life. Theory originates in practice and attempts to grasp the essence of things through practice, in order to improve practice by applying new knowledge. The significance of theory is its effectiveness in actively changing the world. By changing the world, theory also changes its own practical cognitive basis; and old formulas must then be reexamined in the light of new circumstances. Thus execution of theory is the final step of the old cognitive process (verification) and forms the practical basis of the new one, and man's understanding and improvement proceed in this dialectic indefinitely.

14

As was indicated earlier, there is little propositional novelty in the principles of Mao's theory-practice relation. Marx says in the "Preface to the Critique of Political Economy": "It is not the consciousness of men that determines their being, but, on the contrary, their social being that determines their consciousness."[47] Moreover, the "Theses on Feuerbach" observe that "the educator himself needs educating" and that the important task is not to interpret the world but to change it.[48] The difference is that what Marx states as a premise for theoretical criticism, Mao takes as a fundamental problem area for action. Hence Marx uses his emphasis on practice as a weapon of criticism against Feuerbachian "contemplative materialism" and the antitheology of the Young Hegelians; Mao uses it to criticize Marxist dogmatists who are unrealistic in practice, and positively as a basis for a flexible and pragmatic policy-making.

Mao is not attempting to subordinate theory to practice in the sense of allowing it only unimportant functions of abstraction. Mechanical materialism is criticized because in it "mind was given a passive function only and was regarded as a mirror which reflects nature."[49] Mao delineates the essential relations of theory to practice in order to show that theory cannot be pursued or applied for its own sake, that to pursue correct theory alone is to have an incorrect grasp of the nature of one's object. After one has gathered sufficient data on a problem, rationality performs two functions essential to human endeavor. The first is conversion of perceptual phenomena into cenceptual knowledge. That is, by reflecting on the varied information one has on a thing, one can arrive at concepts that "grasp the essence, the totality, and the internal relations of things."[50] This process changes random perceptual data into knowledge of the thing's internal contradictions and the necessary relations between one process and another. It cannot be separated from extensive investigation and testing: Subjectivist mistakes are often made "not because of failure to make careful plans, but because of failure to study the specific social situation carefully before making the plans."[51]

The second function, the more important one, of rationality is the leap from rational knowledge to revolutionary practice. "The knowledge which grasps the laws of the world, must be directed to the practice of changing the world, must be applied anew in the struggle and in the practice of scientific experiment."[52] The application of concepts and theories to practice has its main value in the improvement of practice, but even discrepancies between expectation and result can be useful because they can locate mistakes in theory.

The conscious disciplining of oneself to this practical learning would be unnecessary if a correct understanding of a situation were obvious and unmistakable, and would be to no avail if the truth were completely unattainable. Mao's view is that first ideas of things are seldom completely correct, but after a period of trial and error a basically complete view of "a certain objective process at a certain stage of its development"[53] can be attained. This truth is relative, since one mind cannot grasp the object as a whole;[54] and because this stage will, as the process develops, lose its importance, one must always be ready to change one's subjective convictions in accordance with the changed reality. At present, men cling to old experiences that have lost their truth, and established classes fight the emergence of a new world order. "The epoch of world communism will be reached when all mankind voluntarily and consciously changes itself and the world."[55]

The practical effect of such a view of the unity of theory and practice is not one of univocal determination of policy, because the theoretical importance of experience and changing conditions precludes any simple derivation from theory of the best concrete policy. Thus there can be no immediate sign of its actual effect on the contents of Mao's policies. But this does not deny it the possibility of an essential role in Mao's success, for self-preservation and victory in the incredible variety of conditions in which the Chinese Communist Party survived and prospered required a practical appreciation of the movement's possibilities and an alertness in perceiving changes in the objective situation and their possible policy ramifications. This interdependence of policy and situation amid the changing fortunes of the Party makes its success very difficult to correlate with particular sociological variables. One of the most recent and comprehensive attempts at a social science answer to the question of what factor accounts for Communism's success in China—Roy Hoffheinz's article "The Ecology of Chinese Communist Success: Rural Influence Patterns, 1923-1945"—concludes that "there was no single pattern of Communist success or influence in China."[56]

Although various sociological factors, such as peasant nationalism, are characteristic for a particular phase of CCP activity, it seems untenable to claim that in a different situation or without utilizing this factor they would have failed. Mao claimed in 1930 that "the proletariat has to depend for its victory entirely on the correct and firm tactics of its own party, the Communist Party."[57] Conservatives have long agreed that civil disorder is due mainly to organized agitators, but in this case even a political scientist agrees that "the behavior of the Chinese Communists themselves" is "the most important and least examined of all the possible explanations of Chinese Communist successes."[58]

Mao's idea of the unity of theory and practice promotes the success of this behavior in two fundamental ways. The first is the emphasis on experience and objective conditions as opposed to dogmatic or subjective dictation of policy. Organizationally, this favors local responsibility and initiative and discourages bureaucratic centralization.59 Second, and perhaps more important, is the encouragement of two types of policy change: from erroneous policy to correct policy, and change in accordance with situational development.

The dependence of correct theory upon experience renders mistakes at the initial stage of a situation almost inevitable. This is of course no justification for timidity.[60] As Francis Bacon put it, "Truth emerges more readily from error than from confusion."[61] The goal is of course to commit fewer errors;[62] but knowledge about a situation is gained through mistakes, and these point to needs for policy modification. When the failure of the Great Leap Forward became apparent in 1959, Mao gave a particularly strong formulation of the importance of mistakes:

> What is dialectics? Dialectics means analyzing every-
> thing and accepting that a person cannot avoid making mis-
> takes and must not be denied because of his mistakes . . .
> I have made many errors and have derived great benefit
> from them since they taught me many lessons.[63]

The difficulty of correctly interpreting changing situations leads also to greater tolerance of differing views:

> So long as they [the cadres] do not violate discipline and
> do not engage in secret clique activities, we will always
> allow them to speak. Furthermore, there will not be any
> punishment for saying anything wrong. When what is said
> is wrong, it can be criticized. We must, however, apply
> reasoning to convince others. What then should we do if
> they remain unconvinced after we explain the truth? They
> may keep their opinions . . . so long as they obey resolu-
> tions and decisions adopted by the majority. . . . At first
> the truth is not in the hands of the majority, but in those
> of the minority.[64]

Even more fundamental errors, such as dogmatism and empiricism, which provide the subjectivist foundation for avoidable mistakes, are considered curable, in the belief that once the culprit is educated to the correct view, a repetition is unlikely to occur. Errors are not tolerated, "because poisons are uneatable."[65] In most cases, is considered a mistake capable of rectification and not the sign of a traitor: "We should never create an atmosphere in which it seems that no one can afford to make a mistake because a mistake inadvertently would condemn a person forever."[66] This view has made the CCP, though perhaps not more ecumenical, at least less violent in its factional struggles than the Soviet Union.

Not only should a policy be corrected when in error, but even well-established policies can become outmoded through a change of situation. It has already been observed that experience allows a firm grasp of a process only at a certain stage of its development; thus "true revolutionary leaders must not only be good at correcting their ideas, theories, plans, or programs when errors are discovered . . . but when a certain objective process has already progressed and changed from one stage of development to another, they must also be good at making themselves and all their fellow revolutionaries progress and change in their subjective knowledge along with it . . . they must ensure that the proposed new revolutionary tasks and new working programs correspond to the new situation."67

The habitual and sentimental attachments to established policy that compose organizational inertia are thus a prime target of Mao's theory; and the Party's major changes in land policy, political alliances, and military strategy involved significant victories of his pragmatic views over various groups of "diehards." On the other hand, it is evident that if the CCP's policy changes were only a matter of narrow Party opportunism, its ideological continuity would have been lost. A party more interested in the survival of its organization than in the programs that it viewed as its only legitimate functions would probably in time become alienated from its popular base and find its own political security in some form of accommodation with the powers that be.68 If Mao's flexibility in policy had not been a matter of conscious theory, the Party of the Kiangsi Soviet would probably have lost its identity in the vastly different conditions of the Anti-Japanese War. It might be argued that a democratic party could, by constantly reflecting the mood of its popular base, change its policies while maintaining its identity; but this type of policy flexibility would involve a degree of organizational inflexibility that probably would not be viable under the stresses of protracted war.

The relativity of theory resulting from its manifold dependence on changing conditions leads to a special stress on the manner of thinking rather than its particular product and, hence, on the rules for correct application and development of policy rather than on the speculative derivation of the policy itself. These principles for the determination and execution of policy have a certain stability, although some types of work and situations may require specific methodologies that become less meaningful if the situation changes. The applicability of guerrilla war or mobile war techniques depends on the current military situation, whereas the art of determining which strategy is applicable is important as long as the war lasts.

The most general methodology is the learning process itself, as outlined in "On Practice": investigate the situation, form a conceptual picture of how to change it, execute this attempt at change, and learn from mistakes. Mao continually emphasizes each of the basic moments of this process; a good example is in "Strategy in China's Revolutionary War," written in December 1936:

> A commander's correct dispositions stem from . . . a thorough and necessary reconnaissance and from pondering on and piecing together the data of various kinds gathered through reconnaissance . . . Then, he takes the conditions of his own side into account, and makes a study of both sides and their interrelations, thereby forming his judgments, making up his mind, and working out his plans. . . .
>
> The process of knowing a situation goes on not only before the formulation of a military plan but after. In carrying out the plan from the moment it is put into effect to the end of the operation, there is another process of knowing the situation, namely, the process of practice. In the course of this process, it is necessary to examine anew whether the plan worked out in the preceding process corresponds with reality. If it does not correspond with reality, or if it does not fully do so, then in the light of our new knowledge, it becomes necessary to form new judgments, make new decisions and change the original plan so as to meet the new situation. The plan is partially changed in almost every operation and sometimes it is even changed completely.[69]

A correlative method to this general military one can easily be found for the Party's political work.[70] Political reconnaissance involves investigation of the condition and opinions of the masses and the general political situation.[71] Policy formulation should be carried out with full discussion on committees, and the masses should be informed of new policies.[72]

Failure to carry through any stage of this process is subjectivism, the foundation of unnecessary mistakes. It is an endemic flaw in human nature, and the path toward its elimination is the way of the good cadre. The major problem is becoming conscious of a subjectivist view, for few people would hold to something they knew was untrue. The pinpointing of mistakes and their subjectivist roots is the task of criticism and self-criticism.[73] The first expresses the communal duty toward the betterment of its members. Complaints should be open, addressed to the responsible person, and conducive to common, not sectional, ends.[74] There should be a careful attitude in handling individuals, and emphasis should be on the analysis of the circumstances in which errors were committed.[75]

19

Self-criticism is the more important stage in the rectification of error, because in it the individual himself recognizes his mistakes and their importance, and resolves to change. Almost everyone is capable of regaining the Party's favor via self-criticism. Even in the Cultural Revolution, the policy was "Cadres who have made mistakes can reestablish themselves, provided that they do not persist with their mistakes, but reform them, and are forgiven by the revolutionary masses."[76] Thus, it was expected that more than 95 percent of the cadres would be reconciled with the Party, although almost 90 percent of the Party's work teams at the beginning of the Cultural Revolution committed general mistakes in their orientation.[77]

The specific methodology for avoiding mistakes in political affairs is the principle of the mass line. "In all the practical work of our Party, all correct leadership is necessarily 'from the masses to the masses.' This means: take the ideas of the masses . . . and concentrate them, . . . then go to the masses and propagate and explain these ideas until the masses embrace them as their own."[78] The Chinese Communist Party has as its legitimacy the claim of scientifically representing the interests of the Chinese masses; and, given the interdependence of theory and practice, the relation of Communist policies to the popular conception of these interests becomes vital. "The relationship between the Party and the masses is comparable to that between fish and water."[79] Hence the Cultural Revolution is seen as the trial by the masses of the Party.[80] And because of the continuing danger even within socialism of capitalist restoration, "all members of the Party and the people of our country must not think that after one, two, three, or four great cultural revolutions there will be peace and quiet."[81] Unity with the masses is not only the constant goal of the Party but also the final test of its success.

The epistemological and methodological interplay of theory and practice is linked to a corresponding world view characterized by the change and essential interdependence of phenomena. The goal of creating a political situation that is "centralist and yet democratic, disciplined and yet free, ideologically united yet individually content, and dynamic and lively"[82] has its justification not only in the belief that human knowledge does not proceed securely from abstract, absolute propositions, but also tends to corroborate this with the view that such a dialectical process is actually the way things work, that the objective processes are at least analogous to the human cognitive process.

The most systematic statement of Mao's Weltanschauung is in "On Contradiction," an essay based on a lecture directed against the dogmatists delivered at the Anti-Japanese Military and Political College one month after "On Practice."[83] The underlying thesis is that internal contradictions are responsible for the development of every phenomenon, but that each thing is particular; and external conditions can be a sine qua non for internal development.[84] For those accustomed to more circumspect philosophical styles, the essay may appear apodictic, but—as may be expected from its antidogmatist intention and Mao's predilection for practice—within the Communist context the emphasis is on the particularity of contradiction and the possibility that external circumstances can sometimes play a dominant role.[85] The practical inference from this is the necessity of experience and investigation in determining in each phase of each aspect of each contradiction how the law of contradiction applies. A grasp of the law of contradiction does not allow one to leap over the moment of practice in understanding something; it merely provides a systematization of practice. Hence Mao's illustrations of his theoretical points are drawn from the history of the CCP.

The function of materialistic dialectics also complements the epistemology of "On Practice": it is the method for correct conceptualization of investigation and experience and reflects nature "more deeply, truly, and completely"[86] in order to revolutionize it— to develop it in accordance with its revolutionary nature. Some general truths with practical meaning emerge—for instance, that each phase of each process has only one primary contradiction, and contradiction has a primary aspect[87]—but they do not determine a priori how to view any concrete situation. Even very Marxist formulas that might prejudice objective examination are criticized. "In the contradiction between the productive forces and the relations of production, the productive forces are the primary aspect; in the contradiction between theory and practice, practice is the primary aspect; in the contradiction between the economic base and the superstructure, the economic base is the primary aspect and there is no change in their relative positions. This is the mechanical materialist conception, not the dialectical materialist conception."[88] In certain conditions, any of these relationships may be reversed.

Nevertheless, the allowable historical and methodological theses limit the possible conceptualizations of practice and experience to certain planes of interpretation. If this is the era of imperialism, then any explanation of a political development must rationalize the latter's subordination to the laws of that era. If the Party represents the masses, then development within the Party must be conceptualized with that in mind. Each level of generality can be considered the universal condition within which more limited developments have their meaning.[89]

ASSUMPTIONS OF MAO'S THEORY

Hitherto I have tried to formulate Mao's idea of the unity of theory and practice and trace its significance: proceeding from his

21

explicit treatment of the relationship, we have considered its implication for the practical methodology of the CCP and finally its relation to Mao's ontology. But even such a general integration of theory and practice is not self-contained, so our next task is to consider its assumptions. Assumptions limit the value of a theory because they indicate dependence on the truth of something that the theory itself cannot defend.

One assumption necessary to the value of any a posteriori theory is the basic identity between the condition in which the theory was derived and the conditions to which it is to be applied. It could justly be said that the necessary lag between the development of a situation and its conceptualization has been a particular bane of Communist theory. Although every theory tends to resist the embarrassment caused by emerging new problems, Communism's claim to have grasped the true laws of historical development renders the recognition and incorporation of novel problems unusually difficult. Major developments tend to be ignored for years before a reformulation takes them into account; examples are imperialism before Lenin's formulation, and the "new class" problem before—and in some places after—Djilas. But Mao is conscious of this problem, and his treatment of it is not naive. He observes that any knowledge is only of a phase of development that could pass, and therefore exhorts revolutionary leaders to be alert to the signs of the times and to be ready to discard old formulas in new conditions. In making predictions, Mao has sometimes been too conservative and sometimes too optimistic.[90] He did, however, make the observation early that "Marxists are not fortune-tellers,"[91] and has always seemed ready to abandon forecasts if they are proved wrong. As observed earlier, Mao's lenient attitude toward mistakes is both a result of and an essential factor in the flexibility of his system.

A deeper level of assumptions necessary to Mao's thought is that of goals and values. The fiction of arbitrariness that the common dichotomy of facts and values suggests is, first of all, significantly limited by the need for a coherent matrix of such principles.[92] In addition, for such values to be promulgated (or for actions derivative from such values to be accepted as legitimate), they must be within the horizons of acceptability of one's associates. Although the cultural location implied by these limitations is a boundary to understanding that must be overcome by "outsiders," Mao's social values were readily understandable to his primary audience.

The aim of Mao's engagement in politics and theory is to institute a social system most conducive to the progress of the Chinese masses. As Jerome Ch'en observes, "Ever since his article, 'The Great Union of the Popular Masses,' published in 1919, Mao does not seem for a moment to have lost his faith in the people as a source

of energy and power."93 Chinese nationalism, a "Rousseauist" idea
of progress, and the identification with the lower classes are the unquestioned "background assumptions" upon which Mao's social goals
depend.94 They also determine the kind of practical investigations
that inform his policy-making.95 These values structure Mao's desire
to lead the people's own efforts to overcome their impediments at
their own rate.96 The form of his ideal society is the thorough integration of selfless individuals, where "all mankind voluntarily and
consciously changes itself and the world"97 and the three great differences—between worker and peasant, city and country, and mental
and manual labor—are abolished. As Maurice Meisner has pointed
out, some of these values have a positive effect on Chinese productive
effort, but it is equally apparent that a certain tension exists between
some of these ideals and the specialization and stratification that
since Adam Smith have been considered necessary to economic pro-
gress.98

The problem of values and goal assumptions is twofold. The
first is that if the values are not universally held, the efforts guided
by them will continually meet various forms of resistance from those
whose convictions run otherwise. The second is that the means used
to express values or attain goals generally are not univocal derivations
from that particular set of values and goals. Dr. Guillotin did not
have his own execution in mind when he proposed the use of what came
to be called the guillotine. Positions of political power are particularly
vulnerable to being used counter to their original purpose; hence the
fear of capitalist restoration is especially terrifying. However, some
of Mao's general procedural rules—for instance, mass-line politics
or guerrilla warfare—would be unimaginable without a significant
degree of mass support.

A third category of assumptions for Mao is the "universal truth
of Marxism-Leninism."99 This is a more problematic category because as a general orientation it is essential, but studying it attracts
bookworms. As Mao complained in a talk with Ch'en Po-ta and K'ang
Sheng in 1965, "The trouble with philosophy is that there is no practical philosophy, only book-learned philosophy. We must come up
with something new. Otherwise what are we here for? What do we
want future generations to do?"100 "Pure ideology," as Franz Schurmann terms it, provides the framework: "Marxism-Leninism can
raise our understanding of the future and the destination we are going
to, can widen our scope, and can free our thought from parochialism."101
It is correct "not because Marx is a 'prophet' but because his theory
has proved correct in our practice and in our struggle."102 As late
as 1958, Mao did not consider his thought to be a substitute for
Marxism-Leninism, as is shown by this comment made in 1958:
"Chang Tsung-hsün said that he has erred because he did not study

Mao Tse tung's works carefully. This is not right; what he should say is that primarily it is his level of Marxism-Leninism which is not high."103

The striking contrast between this deference to Marxism-Leninism and the abuse heaped on dogmatists and academicians who specialize in its study is best explained by referring to James Hsiung's emphasis on the paramount importance of szu-hsiang (thought) in Chinese Communist ideology.104 It is the applicability of theory, and not its universality, that determines its value. The significance of Marxism-Leninism as a practically oriented scientific theory (li-lun) would be perverted if its study caused one's practical leadership responsibilities to be neglected.105 Although Marxism-Leninism has the important function of providing a general framework for Mao's thought, the distinction between "pure ideology" and "practical ideology" is too rigid to describe their relationship. Marx, Lenin, and Mao are all described as having been engaged in practical affairs when they did their "thinking"106; and with the concretization of Marxist revolutions, the writings of each have successively served as the general framework of other revolutionaries. Since this is a historical, incremental process, the preceding "classics" retain most of their theoretical importance, both as original studies and as sources of legitimacy.

Since 1970 there has been a reemphasis on studying Marx, Engels, Lenin, and Stalin,107 although Mao retains much of his Cultural Revolution preeminence. The underlying view seems to be that the Communist "classics" have provided and continue to provide a general conceptual framework within which the Chinese work out their own revolution. Although it is the szu-hsiang of Mao Tse-tung that determines the content of the Chinese revolution, the conceptual range of Marxist li-lun defines the terms of its rationalization.

PROBLEMATIC AREAS

Primarily because of its necessary assumptions, Mao's theory has certain areas of fundamental difficulty whose recognition or resolution would be inconsistent with the theoretical framework presented here. These problematic areas have their roots in the limits placed on any attempt to integrate theory and practice by the finite character of human experience, the Marxist-Leninist framework of Mao's thought, and the historical necessities of the Chinese revolutionary movement.

The interrelationship of theory and practice makes the analysis of conditions other than one's own problematic; hence it questions the basis of the interpretation of the political situation of other countries. The results of the Comintern's dictation of early CCP policy must have confirmed Mao's aversion to relying on foreign experience for advice in deciding policy. By example and in polemics with Moscow-trained dogmatists,[108] Mao insisted on the study of Chinese history and the analysis of Chinese conditions in order to arrive at independent, practical decisions. The converse of this (though statesmen and nations are not always so logical) is that Chinese analysis of world events can never reach the certainty of her domestic experience. As Franz Schurmann has pointed out:

> If the thought of Mao Tse-tung were directly applied to other national liberation movements one would expect to find detailed concrete analyses in official Chinese publications of revolutionary processes in countries other than China, comparable to the voluminous Comintern literature on world revolutionary movements. I have seen few such analyses. In a way, Chinese Communist ideology prevents them from officially presenting such analyses. If practical ideology is the result of the combination of pure ideology with concrete actions, it can only be created and used by someone who is from the country in question. No Chinese could presume to have the requisite knowledge. It is therefore up to the revolutionary forces themselves in each country to produce the kind of analysis that Mao developed for the Chinese Revolution. The Chinese may advise them, but they cannot hand them such an analysis from Peking.[109]

Yet the diplomatic necessity of having definite relations with every country and the ideological problem that "the final victory of a socialist country . . . also involves the victory of the world revolution,"[110] requires policy decisions essentially dependent on the analysis of international affairs, thus forcing theory beyond the limits of practice. Insofar as the relevant conditions are not analogous to Chinese experience (and even this is a problematic judgment), the "universal truth" of Marxism-Leninism must supply the tools and categories of analysis.

Though Chinese foreign policy statements seem to have an equally dogmatic tone, two aspects of priorities in international relations appear to take cognizance of the problem described above; however, both have other sufficient explanations. First, the Chinese direct the thrust of their propaganda toward the underdeveloped countries, and also insist that indigenous revolutionary movements must rely on their own strength. Here the real foreign policy possibilities and Mao's theory coalesce. Second, there is a relative deemphasis of foreign policy and a concentration on internal problems. Though this is no doubt also determined by the great urgency of domestic concerns, this urgency does not work mechanically: many countries with internal problems have engaged in adventurous foreign policies. Still, the theoretical relationship between Maoist prudence and Marxist omniscience is tenuous in this area.

The second area of difficulty is the relationship of the general orientation provided by Marxism-Leninism to the unity of theory and practice as worked out by Mao. The problem of the acceptance of Communism being in some respects a case of "theory first" is evident: "Due to the backwardness of Chinese society, today's philosophical movement of dialectical materialism is not a continuation and reconstruction of China's own heritage. It is, instead, a development from learning Marxism-Leninism."[111] This acceptance is not an act of blind faith: if it were not found useful for Chinese conditions, the movement would either fail or reject it. The service that this imported theory provided for the work of practical revolution in China was much like the use of a scientific paradigm—for instance, Newtonian physics—for scientific experimentation. It provides a general rationalization of the area of endeavor, so that normal research can attack limited, coordinated problems.[112] Accepting such a paradigm enables one to get down to the practical work of creatively applying it rather than having to construct a new world view ab ovo. Moreover, combined with Mao's emphasis of actual success or failure rather than dogmatic faithfulness, the particulars of the orientation are susceptible to infinite modification in practice.

However, the paradigm's service of directing attention to particular problems is offset by the consequent ignoring of the problems that are too obvious to be missed but are not really covered by the ideology. The Hungarian revolt of 1956 and its sympathetic disturbances in China apparently came as a real shock to Mao,[113] because he had believed, with Communist theory, that such things were not possible in a socialist country. The peculiar form of the criticism of the "hidden traitor, renegade, and scab" Liu Shao-ch'i is undoubtedly due to an inability to essentially distinguish elite behavior from class behavior within a Marxist framework. The gradual estrangement of a guiding elite from its mass basis, or, in Mao's and Hegel's terminology,[114] the development of the ruling structure from a faction "in itself" to a faction "for itself" has no necessary connection with private ownership of the means of production; however, calling Liu's faction "capitalist" is the closest rubric in Marxist terminology to the actual problem. The resulting abuse of terminology has two supplementary bad effects: either the terminology is taken seriously and the reality is distorted, or the meaning of the words becomes so devious that discourse becomes impossible. Persistence in an inappropriate framework, which is one manifestation of the erosion of

ideology, can only distort the perception of Chinese reality and lead
to corresponding amounts of either dogmatism or hypocrisy.

The last problematic area is theoretically the most interesting
and practically perhaps the most important: the relation of the inherent demands of political leadership to the unity of theory and practice. Mao's model of the revolutionary movement is the product of
the individual's cognitive process, and this has its individualistic and
collective aspects. On the one hand, everyone is an individual with
his own experience and, hence, with a right to his own ideas: "Cadres
should act like general commanders."[115] On the other hand, the movement has a "soul" that is more important than any formulas or institutions it holds at any particular moment, and it is evident that Mao
is its custodian. Some manner of bridge between the individual and
the collective individual is established by the methodology of the mass
line. This is precarious because of its dependence on the character
of the leader and his correct perception of the needs and abilities of
the masses. But there are two other forms of mediation between the
masses and the leader that further complicate the relation: the Party
and propaganda.

The role of the intermediate leadership is a particularly difficult
one in Mao's China. Emphasis on practice and experience implies
emphasis on leaders as the sole locus of decision, because their own
personal experience is their most important practical basis. Insofar
as cadres are in the position of being "general commanders" in their
own spheres, their responsibility and authority are augmented; but
insofar as they are the arms and legs of a central control, they are
structured toward the effective execution of orders that they played
little part in originating. The policy freedom allowed by Mao's view
of theory and practice also means an indeterminacy of policy that
makes subordinates personally dependent on their leader. The evident contradiction between the role of the subordinate and the behavior
suggested by "On Practice" is mitigated only by the best of conditions:
continuity in policy or universal agreement as to the necessity of the
policy changes made.

This problem does not remain merely a psychological or internal
strain on China's leadership; its ambiguous relationship to final authority structures the leadership's role of mediating information and
decisions. In the Cultural Revolution, when the Party itself was dis-
armed and attacked, this led to the helpless dogmatism of the Little
Red Book and the "latest directives."[116] Even in relatively normal
times, however, the dependence of the Party, on Mao necessitates appeals to his writings and directives as a final authority, and Mao Tse-
tung's thought assumes dogmatic function that belie its own methodological content. Its expressive value in claiming legitimacy was
quickly discovered by both sides in the Cultural Revolution. The

phenomenon of "Waving the Red Flag to oppose the Red Flag" indicates that this type of usage depends neither on content nor on approval. There are also more practical dogmatic uses. The slogans from Mao that intersperse directives and editorials help to insure conformity by legitimizing the line or model being promoted and by providing an ideological weapon against those whose differences of opinion touch the principles involved rather than merely questions of implementation. Finally, the approval of Mao's thought can be awarded to already successful independent initiatives, thus lending prestige to the initiator and further strengthening the legitimacy of Mao Tse-tung thought.

Mao's personal harmony with the masses has the same final dependence on the genius of his leadership that anchors his relationship to the Party, so regardless of his own tolerant attitudes toward mistakes, there must be an image of infallibility. If the program instituted is beyond the abilities of the masses, confidence in the leader is lost, or should be. The principal way of mitigating this loss of confidence is propaganda. One aspect of this is the suppression of bad news: "In the present chaotic situation [1930] we can lead the masses only by positive slogans and a positive attitude."[117] In Mao's self-criticism at the Lushan (Port Arthur) conference the same point is made: "If the newspaper you are publishing will print only bad news, and if you have no heart to work, then it won't take a year [for the nation to collapse], but it will perish in a week's time."[118] The positive side of this distortion is the adulation of Mao in the Chinese media. The problem of the leader's image is alien to the theory-practice relationship, and the artificial maintenance of this image must distort such derivative methodologies as the mass line. This is dangerous, both because of the "credibility gap" that is created and because of the possible distortion of the leader's idea of the abilities and loyalty of the masses.

The most fundamental problem for the continuation of Mao's unity of theory and practice, as established in the leadership of China, is its essential dependence on his own genius and his own experience. Such attributes are too personal to transfer to a successor. Mao's attempt to create a substitute by training a Party elite (the institution of the "first and second lines" in the Central Committee, which was later abandoned) failed because the Party under Liu Shao-ch'i was developing a bureaucratic-elitist spirit. It is almost inevitable that an organization would seek to objectify the locus of decision by binding policy-makers either to an articulated body of theory or to organizational procedures, because this would stabilize policy-making and give greater security to the intermediate leadership.

But succession by a follower could be just as problematic. The personal responsibility for the highest decisions was for Mao both a product of leadership qualities and a condition of his leadership style.

Inherited political power is different: its final legitimacy is appointment, and the founder's flexibility is generally sacrificed to the follower's fidelity to his concrete decisions.[119] The crassest form of sanctification of the dead hero has probably been avoided with the elimination of Lin Piao; but, insofar as the legitimacy of succession is problematic, predecessor-worship is inevitable. Succession by either a faithful follower or an organization would mean that the "thought of Mao Tse-tung" would make the fateful passage from being the legitimizing word to being the sanctified letter. The remaining problem would then perhaps best be formulated as how Maoist the succession will be, and what form the stratification of Mao's legacy will take.

A third possibility is that Mao's notion of the unity of theory and practice and its correlative flexibility in revolutionary politics will maintain its preeminence. It could be used to examine precedents and to resolve the continuing problems generated by the problematic areas for Mao's thought discussed above. If this be the case, new solutions and new experience could lead to new practices and policies that in turn would constitute the basis for fresh understandings and improved theories, just as they did in the most creative acts of Mao's statemanship and his reflections on these acts. In this way, the "thought of Mao Tse-tung" itself would in the hands of his successors continue to evolve to higher levels as Chinese history and human experience continue to develop along their uncharted and unpredictable course.

NOTES

1. S. M. Lipset, Political Man (Garden City, N.Y.: Doubleday Anchor, 1963), p. xix.

2. I owe this observation to James Chieh Hsiung, Ideology and Practice (New York: Praeger, 1970), pp. 143-47.

3. Western reactions to ideological politics often tend toward either affirmation of the given nonrational inertia of social mores or a concentration on the salvation of the enlightened but ineffective few through scientific detachment. For the first, see Michael Oakshott, Rationalism in Politics (New York: Basic Books, 1962). For the second, see Arnhelm Neusüss, Utopisches Bewusstsein und freischwebende Intelligenz (Meisenheim am Glan: Hain, 1968), pp. 11-35. Frederic Wakeman presents a rich pedigree for Mao's dialectic of initiative and circumstance in his brilliant study History and Will (Berkeley: University of California Press, 1973).

4. See James C. Hsiung, Ideology and Practice: Michel Oksenberg, "Policy Making Under Mao" in John M. H. Lindbeck, ed., China:

Management of a Revolutionary Society (Seattle: University of Washington Press, 1971), pp. 79-115; and Chalmers Johnson, ed., Ideology and Politics in Contemporary China (Seattle: University of Washington Press, 1973).

5. Selected Works of Mao Tse-tung, I (Peking: Foreign Language Press, 1967), 27. Hereafter cited as SW.

6. Translation available in Selected Readings from the Works of Mao Tse-tung, in pamphlet form (Peking: Foreign Language Press, 1966), see p. 4 of pamphlet.

7. Cf. Fung Yu-lan, A History of Chinese Philosophy, II (Princeton: Princeton University Press, 1953), 533-71.

8. Cf. David S. Nivison, "'Knowledge' and 'Action' in Chinese Thought Since Wang Yang-ming" in A. F. Wright, ed., Studies in Chinese Thought (Chicago: University of Chicago Press, 1953), pp. 112-45.

9. Joseph Levenson, Modern China and Its Confucian Past: The Problem of Intellectual Continuity (Garden City, N.Y.: Doubleday Anchor, 1964), pp. 81-105.

10. Ibid. p. 84.

11. For a development of this view of ideology, see Clifford Geertz, "Ideology as a Cultural System," in David Apter, ed., Ideology and Discontent (New York: The Free Press, 1964), pp. 47-76.

12. Cf. D. W. Y. Kwok, Scientism in Chinese Thought, 1900-1950 (New Haven: Yale University Press, 1965), pp. 32-58; extract from "Treatise on the Promotion of Universal Harmony by Machines (1918)," p. 39.

13. Cf. Kwok, op. cit., pp. 133-61.

14. Cf. Nivison, op. cit.

15. Quoted in Jerome B. Grieder, Hu Shih and the Chinese Renaissance (Cambridge: Harvard University Press, 1970), p. 124.

16. Ibid., p. 235.

17. Ibid., p. 209.

18. "Our Political Proposals," in ibid., pp. 191-93.

19. Ibid., pp. 193-94.

20. The source of this terminology is Ulf Himmelstrand, "Depoliticization and Political Involvement," in Allard and Rokkan, Mass Politics (New York: Free Press, 1970).

21. Some general studies of the Hegelian heritage of Marxism are Gustav A. Wetter, Die Umkehrung Hegels (Cologne: Verlag Wissenschaft und Politik, 1963); and Karl Ballestrem, Die sowjetische Erkenntnismetaphysik und Hegel (Dordrecht, Holland: D. Riedel, 1968).

22. Though in some cases this is not out of the question. It is claimed that Marx was constantly unrealistic in his evaluation of the German workers' movement. Cf. Helga Grebing, Geschichte der

deutschen Arbeiterbewegung (Munich: Deutscher Taschenbuch Verlag, 1970), pp. 65-66.

23. Kant, for example, claims in the Critique of Pure Reason to have laid the groundwork for the scientific reconstruction of metaphysics, a "revolution" that will bring it to the level of certainty of mathematics and the natural sciences. Cf. Preface to the 2nd ed., passim.

24. Cf. Enzyklopädie der philosophischen Wissenschaften, 1830. (Hamburg: Felix Meiner Verlag, 1959), sec. 6. See also secs. 223-25, 445-82.

25. Ibid., sec. 6, p. 38.

26. Ibid., secs. 445-80.

27. Ballestrem, op. cit., p. 64, points out that Marx's criticisms of Hegel are for the most part either directed at Hegel personally or involve a distortion of Hegel's actual teaching.

28. Karl Marx and Friedrich Engels, The German Ideology (Moscow: Progress Publishers, 1968), p. 38.

29. From a letter in the Deutsch-französische Jahrbücher (1844); in Easton and Guddat, eds., Writings of the Young Marx on Philosophy and Society (Garden City, N.Y.: Doubleday Anchor, 1967), p. 214. Emphasis in the original.

30. This discussion is based on the section "Die Methode der politischen Ökonomie," in "Einleitung zur Kritik der politischen Ökonomie," Marx-Engels Werke, XIII (Berlin: Dietz Verlag, 1968), 631-39.

31. Ibid., p. 632.

32. Cf. "Preface to The Critique of Political Economy," Marx-Engels Selected Works, I (Moscow: Foreign Languages Press, 1962), 363.

33. "Alte Vorrede zum 'Anti-Dühring,'" Marx-Engels Werke, (Berlin: Dietz Verlag, 1968), 334-35.

34. "Socialism, Utopian and Scientific," Marx-Engels Selected Works, II (Moscow: Foreign Languages Press: 1962), 136.

35. E. Bernstein, Die Voraussetzungen des Sozialismus (Reinbeck: Rowohlt, 1969), p. 63.

36. Ibid., p. 26. Emphasis in the original.

37. Quote in Grebing, op. cit., p. 118. See also Bernstein, op. cit., p. 37.

38. A note on this in the Notebooks reads, "In this most idealistic work of Hegel's is the least idealism, the most materialism. Contradictory, but a fact!" Quoted in Ballestrem, op. cit., p. 93.

39. Ballestrem, loc. cit.

40. Cf. "What Is to be Done?" Lenin, Selected Works, 12 vol. (New York: International, n.d.), II, 137-39.

41. Ibid., p. 154.

42. "Democratic Centralism" (1962), in Selections from Chairman Mao (a Red Guard publication), Joint Publications Research Service (JPRS) 50792, p. 48.

43. It is interesting to note that Max Weber calls Marx "by far the most important case of ideal-type constructions." Ideal types are considered necessary for social science research, but dangerous because of the ease of confusing them with reality. About Marxist social laws in particular, Weber says: "The eminent, even unique heuristic significance of these ideal types, when one uses them for comparison with reality, and just as much their danger, as soon as they are imagined to be empirically valid or even real (i.e. metaphysical) "active forces" "tendencies," etc. is evident to anyone who has ever worked with Marxist concepts." From "Die Objektivität sozialwissenschaftlicher Erkenntnis"; emphasis in original. Shlomo Avineri defends Marx against this criticism in his excellent book. The Social and Political Philosophy of Karl Marx (Cambridge: Cambridge University Press, 1970), pp. 157-62, but I doubt that he would extend his defense to Engels and Lenin.

44. Cf. Stuart R. Schram, "Mao Tse-tung and the Theory of Permanent Revolution," China Quarterly 46 (Apr.-June 1971): 221-49.

45. SW, vol. I, pp. 250-310.

46. Where Do Correct Ideas Come from? (May 1963) (Peking: Foreign Languages Press, 1966), p. 2.

47. Marx-Engels Selected Works, vol. I, p. 363.

48. Ibid., vol. II, pp. 403-05.

49. "Outline of Dialectical Materialism," in Selections from Chairman Mao, loc. cit., p. 48.

50. "On Practice," SW, vol. I, p. 298.

51. Oppose Book Worship (May 1930) (Peking: Foreign Languages Press, 1966), p. 6.

52. "On Practice," p. 304.

53. Ibid., p. 306.

54. "Outline of Dialectical Materialism," p. 48.

55. "On Practice," p. 308.

56. Included in A. Doak Barnett, ed., Chinese Communist Politics in Action (Seattle: University of Washington Press, 1969), p. 72.

57. Oppose Book Worship, p. 11.

58. Roy Hoffheinz, "The Ecology of Chinese Communist Success," in A. Doak Barnett, Chinese Communist Politics in Action (University of Washington Press, 1969), p. 77.

59. For an example of Mao's organizational policy, cf. Mark Selden, "The Yenan Legacy: The Mass Line," in Barnett, ed., op. cit., pp. 99-154.

60. Cf. Oppose Book Worship, pp. 2-3.

61. Novum Organum (London, 1620).

62. "Outline of Dialectical Materialism," p. 35.

63. "On Dialectics" (1959), in Selections from Chairman Mao, p. 35.

64. "Democratic Centralism," p. 55.

65. Chinese Law and Government (Winter 1968/69): 62.

66. For the Cultural Revolution see the analysis of cadre quality in Point 8 of the "Sixteen Points" (Aug. 8, 1966). See text in English translation in K. H. Fan, ed., The Chinese Cultural Revolution: Selected Documents (New York: Grove Press, 1968), p. 168. Quotation from "Democratic Centralism," p. 57.

67. "On Practice," p. 306.

68. This is an extrapolation of Robert Michels, Political Parties (1915), trans. by Eden and Cedar Paul (New York: Free Press, 1962).

69. SW, vol. I, pp. 188-89.

70. An excellent description of the policy implementation process at the provincial level is given by Victor Falkenheim, "Provincial Leadership in Fukien: 1949-1966" in Robert A. Scalapino, ed., Elites in the People's Republic of China (Seattle: University of Washington Press, 1972), pp. 220-22.

71. Cf. "Be Concerned with the Well-Being of the Masses, Pay Attention of Methods of Work" (1934), SW, vol. I, p. 148; "Preface to Rural Surveys" (1941), SW, vol. III, Peking: FLP, 1960, p. 12; "Concerning Methods of Leadership" (1943), SW, vol. III, p. 119; "Rectify the Party's Style of Work" (1942), SW, vol. III, pp. 47-49.

72. Cf. "On Strengthening the Party Committee System" (1948), SW, vol. IV, Peking: FLP, 1960, p. 267; "A Talk to the Editorial Staff of the Shansi-Suiyuan Daily" (1948), ibid., pp. 241-43.

73. Lowell Dittmer, in his "Liu Shao-chi and the Chinese Cultural Revolution" (unpub. diss., University of Chicago Dept. of Political Science, 1971), pp. 372-97, presents a detailed account of the structural evolution of criticism and self-criticism.

74. Cf. "On Correcting Mistaken Ideas in the Party" (1929), SW, vol. I, p. 108, no. 3; and "Combat Liberalism" (1937), SW, vol. II, p. 31, second type of "liberalism"; "On Correcting Mistaken Ideas in the Party," p. 110, no 2; Ibid., p. 112, no. 2.

75. Cf. "The Present Situation and Our Tasks" (1947), SW, vol. IV, p. 164.

76. Mao Papers, Jerome Chen, ed. (Oxford: Oxford University Press, 1970), pp. 119ff.

77. "Sixteen Points," point 5, op. cit., p. 166, Mao Papers, p. 128.

78. "Concerning Methods of Leadership," loc. cit. Another general statement of the mass line occurs in "Democratic Centralism," p. 53: "To formulate a comprehensive set of concrete guiding principles, policies, and methods under the guidance of the mass line, it is necessary to have ideas originate from the masses, carry out systematic and thorough investigation and study, and evaluate historically the experience of success and failure in work. Only then can we discover laws inherent in objective things rather than subjective concoctions of people. Only then can we formulate various regulations suitable to the situation. This is very important."

79. Mao Papers, p. 56.

80. Ibid., p. 25.

81. Ibid., p. 139.

82. Ibid., p. 56.

83. For the dispute concerning the dating of this work, see Arthur Cohen, The Communism of Mao Tse-tung (Chicago: University of Chicago Press, 1964), pp. 22-28; and Doolin and Golas, " 'On Contradiction' in the Light of Mao Tse-tung's Essay on 'Dialectical Materialism,' " China Quarterly no. 19 (July-Sept. 1964). Neither "On Practice" nor "On Contradiction" appears in Takeuchi Minoru, ed., Mao Tsetung Chi (Tokyo: Hokubo-sha, 1971) because the earliest texts available to the editors were those of Jen-min Jih-pao, Dec. 29, 1950, and Apr. 1, 1952, respectively. They are reprinted unchanged in SW, vol. I, pp. 295-310, 311-47. Practically-minded passages in other works—for instance, vol. V, pp. 93-98—lend credibility to the alleged dating. Since the historical development of Mao's thought is not a theme of this paper, the question of dating is not particularly relevant.

84. The formal purpose of the essay is to educate his audience to a "fundamental understanding of materialist dialectics" by classifying certain philosophical problems concerning the law of contradiction, "the kernel of dialectics." "On Contradiction," SW, vol. I, p. 311; para. 1.

85. Mao indirectly claims that his analysis of the particularity of contradiction is novel in Marxism by lavishly praising Marx, Engels, Lenin, and Stalin for their contributions to the idea of the universality of contradiction. Ibid., pp. 315-16.

Although external causes are the "condition of change" and internal causes are the "basis of change," both are essential aspects and it would be mechanical to assume that internal causes are dominant in every case. Ibid., pp. 314, 336.

86. "On Practice," p. 299.

87. Mao's philosophy of contradiction is analyzed in detail by Vsevolod Holubnychy, "Mao Tse-tung's Materialist Dialectics," China Quarterly no. 19 (July-Sept. 1964).

88. "On Contradiction," pp. 335-36.

89. Ibid., p. 339.

90. Cf. his predictions of the length of the Civil War, SW, vol. IV, passim. Also "Hunan Report" (1927), SW, vol. I, p, 23; "A Single Spark Can Start a Prairie Fire" (1930), ibid., pp. 121, 125, 126.

91. "A Single Spark . . .," p. 127.

92. Mao's constellation of social values is described in Tang Tsou, "The Values of the Chinese Revolution," in "China's Developmental Experience", Michel Oksenberg, ed., Proceedings of the Academy of Political Science 31 (Mar. 1973): 27-41.

93. Jerome Ch'en, "Development and Logic of Mao Tse-tung's Thought," in Chalmers Johnson, ed., Ideology and Politics in Contemporary China (Seattle: University of Washington Press, 1973), p. 105.

94. Cf. Benjamin Schwartz, "China and the West in the 'Thought of Mao Tse-tung,'" China in Crisis, Ho and Tsou, eds. (Chicago: University of Chicago Press, 1968).

The term "background assumptions" is borrowed from Alvin Gouldner, The Coming Crisis of Western Sociology (New York: Avon, 1970), p. 29. He finds this type of assumption essential to any empirical social research.

95. Cf., for example, Nung-min Yün-tung yü Nung-ts'un Tiao-ch'a (Hong Kong: Hsin Min-chu Ch'u-pan She, 1949); and "Hunan Report," in SW, vol. I, pp. 13-59.

96. "A Talk to the Editorial Staff of the Shansi-Suiyuan Daily," p. 243.

97. "On Practice," p. 308.

98. Maurice Meisner, "Utopian Goals and Ascetic Values in Chinese Communist Ideology," Journal of Asian Studies 28, no. 1 (Nov. 1968): 101-10.

99. "Reform Our Study" (1941), SW, vol. III, pp. 16-17.

100. Selections from Chairman Mao, p. 28.

101. See Franz Schurman's discussion of ideology in Ideology and Organization in Communist China (Berkeley: University of California Press, 1968), pp. 17-104. Quotation from a 1963 instruction, Mao Papers, p. 91.

102. Oppose Book Worship, p. 5.

103. Chinese Law and Government 1 (Winter 1968/69): 15.

104. Hsiung, Ideology and Practice, pp. 126-47.

105. Ibid., p. 131. See "Reform Our Study," SW, vol. III, p. 19.

106. "Rectify the Party's Style of Work," ibid., p. 37.

107. "Chin liang-nien lai tsai wo-men kuo ta-liang pien-yi ch'u-pan Ma-ke-szu En-ke-szu Le-ning Szu-ta-ling chu-tso" (In the last two years many works of Marx, Engels, Lenin, and Stalin have been translated and published in our country), Jen-min Jih-pao, Nov. 6, 1972, p. 1.

108. The best example is "Reform Our Study," SW, vol. III, pp. 17-26.

109. Ideology and Organization in Communist China, p. 123, note.

110. Introductory quotation (Oct. 1968) to Important Documents of the Cultural Revolution (Peking: Foreign Languages Press, 1970), also cited on pp. 62-63.

111. "Outline of Dialectical Materialism," p. 8.

112. These concepts are developed by Thomas Kuhn, The Structure of Scientific Revolutions (Chicago: University of Chicago Press, 1962).

113. Cf. On the Correct Handling of Contradictions Among the People (1957) (Peking: Foreign Languages Press, 1966).

114. This estrangement is described in the European socialist parties by Robert Michels, Political Parties (see note 68). For Mao's terminology, see "On Practice," p. 308.

115. "On the Mass Line" (Sept. 1959), Selections from Chairman Mao.

116. Cultural Revolution policy-making is described by Harry Harding, "Maoist Theories of Policy-making and Organization," in Thomas Robinson, ed., The Cultural Revolution in China (Berkeley: University of California Press, 1971). Since the Cultural Revolution was a time of acute crisis for Party organization and activities, and involved questions of loyalty to the center and general reorientation, directives of that time should not be assumed to be typical for Mao or for a Maoist party.

117. "A Single Spark Can Start a Prairie Fire," p. 122.

118. Chinese Law and Government 1 (Winter 1968/69): 35.

119. This possibility of development is exemplified by a speech of Lin Piao's at the 11th plenary session of the 8th Central Committee: "My heart has been quite heavy recently. I am not equal to my task. . . . We must do everything according to Mao Tse-tung's thought and not by any other method. We must not oppose but firmly follow the Chairman. He gives overall consideration to problems; he is far-sighted. What is more, he has his ideas, many of which we don't understand. We must resolutely carry out Chairman Mao's instructions, whether we understand them or not. I have no talent, I rely on the wisdom of the masses and do everything according to the Chairman's directives . . . The Chairman is the genius of the world revolution." From Selections from Chairman Mao, JPRS 49826, p. 17.

2

IRON LAW VERSUS
MASS DEMOCRACY:
WEBER, MICHELS,
AND THE MAOIST VISION
Martin King Whyte

Does the Chinese revolution have to become routinized and institutionalized, or can policies and structures be found to produce a meaningful form of "continuing revolution?" Does economic modernization in China have to entail bureaucratization, or can a formula be found for some sort of nonbureaucratic development? Is it inevitable that cadres and intellectuals in China develop elitist tendencies and the masses sink into submissiveness and apathy, or can ways be found to propagate and maintain "humble" leaders and creative and aggressive followers? Large and amorphous questions such as these have generated considerable debate in Western China studies in recent years, and in these debates the arguments of the skeptics or pessimists are often grounded in the analyses carried out by two turn-of-the-century German sociologists, Max Weber and Robert Michels. In this paper we return to the original arguments of Weber and Michels in an effort to figure out what they did (and did not) say that may be relevant to an understanding of China's efforts to deal with the problems of our age.[1] One of the major themes of the Cultural Revolution (1966-69) and subsequent institutional reforms in China has been the assault on bureaucratic tendencies and the effort to find new ways to get subordinates actively involved in presenting ideas and criticisms to their superiors. Our purpose in summarizing the Western theories here is to see whether recent events in China

An earlier version of some of the ideas presented here was given at the conference "China in Theoretical Perspective," organized by Gordon Bennett in the spring of 1973 at the University of Texas. I am grateful to the participants in that conference and to James C. Hsiung and Ying-mao Kao for their comments and criticisms.

should lead us to question the inevitability of the modern bureaucratic and oligarchical tendencies analyzed by Weber and Robert Michels more than half a century ago. Have the Chinese found answers or checks on these tendencies that we in the West have somehow missed?

WEBER ON BUREAUCRACY

According to Weber, bureaucracy is a form of organization approaching the following ideal typical characteristics:[2]

1. The organizational structure is divided into specialized offices with relatively fixed duties and authority.

2. These offices are arranged in a hierarchy of super- and subordination.

3. The office is separate from the officeholder, who can be replaced, and the facilities of the organization are divorced from the private property of the officeholders. Management of the office is carried out through written documents and files.

4. Selection for office depends upon specialized training.

5. Official activity demands the full working capacity of the officeholder.

6. The management of the office follows general rules that are more or less stable, and that can be learned.

These traits provide just the bare bones of Weber's ideal typical conception; but they should be sufficient to convey the familiar picture of bureaucracy ideally as a complex organizational form with a high division of labor, detailed rules, and an emphasis on specialized knowledge rather than emotions or personal ties.

Weber made clear that bureaucracies were nothing novel on the world scene in his detailed discussions of the Egyptian and Chinese state bureaucracies, the Catholic Church, and other historical examples. However, only with the advent of capitalism did bureaucratization (the process of replacement of other forms of organization by bureaucratic forms) become the dominant trend in society at large, and did bureaucracies become fully developed (relatively close to the ideal type). The forces producing this trend toward bureaucratization were thus closely intertwined with those giving rise to capitalism. Weber enumerated the following long list of forces and preconditions: the emergence of money economies, the increasing complexity of the administrative tasks faced by societies and elites, the growth of the state form of political rule, the development of extensive systems of modern transportation (canals, railways, and so on), the emergence of formal legal systems, the growth of science, the rise of mass democracies, and the formation of capitalist industrial and commercial institutions. Weber, of course, also emphasized the importance of ideological factors, particularly the trends away from mysticism and superstition and toward rationality in Western religions.[3] The relationship between all of these trends and bureaucratization was, of course, reciprocal, since, once in existence, bureaucratic forms of organization facilitated the growth of railroads, factories, large territorial states, and rational-skeptical ideas.

For Weber the bureaucratic trend was not simply the result of the confluence of unrelated historical trends. Rather, all of these forces were linked with bureaucratization in the common implications they held for increasing rationality. The term "rationality" has caused more debate and confusion than any other in Weber's conceptual inventory, in part because Weber was not always consistent in his usage. Generally he used rationality not as the opposite of irrationality, in the common sense of the terms, but as a part of larger and more subtle sets of categories: rational authority as distinct from traditional or charismatic authority; rational action as distinct from habitual or affectual action. Weber's primary meaning when he spoke of rationality was the emphasis on logical consideration of means-ends relationships, unencumbered by emotions, habits, personal loyalties, and so forth.*

Bureaucracy was seen as an organizational form that led to the maximization of rationality. Weber at various points used the analogy of bureaucracy with a machine, with all the positive and negative connotations this brings to mind:

> The decisive reason for the advance of bureaucratic organization has always been its purely technical superiority over any other form of organization. The fully developed bureaucratic apparatus compares with other organizations as does the machine with nonmechanical modes of production. Precision, speed, unambiguity, discretion, unity, strict subordination, reduction of friction and of material and personal costs—these are raised to the optimum point in the strictly bureaucratic administration.[4]

_____

*There is at least one additional complication here, the distinction Weber made between instrumentally rational and value-rational action. The former is concerned with finding the best means to reach any given goal in given circumstances, while the latter is concerned with the best means to realize ultimate values. He also used a somewhat overlapping dichotomy (formal vs. substantive rationality) to categorize economic action. It is clear that the rationality of bureaucratic organizations is, for Weber, primarily of the formal and instrumental type.

In the great majority of cases [the professional bureaucrat] is only a small cog in a ceaselessly moving mechanism which prescribes to him an essentially fixed route of march. The official is entrusted with specialized tasks, and normally the mechanism cannot be put into motion or arrested by him, but only at the very top. The individual bureaucrat is, above all, forged to the common interest of all the functionaries in the perpetuation of the apparatus and the persistence of its rationally organized domination.[5]

Weber saw the bureaucratic trend advancing, then, not just as a historical accident but also as a result of the superiority of the organizational form itself. He did not claim that actual bureaucracies were perfectly efficient or were not subject to inefficiencies and irrationalities of their own. He did make the lesser claim, as seen above, that bureaucracies could perform all kinds of complex tasks better (in the technical senses referred to) than previous forms of organization (those based on kinship, faith, or personal loyalties). Weber even allowed for limited exceptions: for instance, he noted the efficiency (but limited applicability) of the model of economic activities carried out by monastic organizations.[6] Nor was Weber so naive as to suppose that bureaucratization progressed simply because of its technical efficiency—for instance, with elites rationally comparing competing forms of organization and giving the nod to bureaucracy. He stressed in his writings that bureaucracies created systems of dependencies affecting rules, officeholders, and subordinates alike, in large part because of the very complexity and importance of the tasks these organizations performed and the system of interpersonal ties they spawned. The concentration of powers that bureaucratization entailed, combined with the monopolization of expertise and maintenance of administrative secrecy in relation to other groups, made these organizations active and potent competitors for power.

Weber's views on the consequences of bureaucratization were, of course, decidely mixed. On the one hand, the technical superiority of the bureaucratic form allowed dynamic capitalist economic institutions and nation-states to prosper; and as an ardent nationalist (though a liberal), Weber saw the benefits of these trends for Germany. On the other hand, Weber was clearly aware of, and critical of, the negative aspects of bureaucracy that have surrounded this term: the tendency of officials to ignore questions of substantive justice in adhering to formal rules, the impersonality of organizational relationships, the "amorality" of bureaucracies willing to serve whatever elements gain control over them, and the antidemocratic implications of bureaucratic hierarchy.[7]

How did Weber see the future development of this good and evil bureaucratic trend? First we should consider his well-known comments on socialism. Weber died in 1924, before the development of the "Soviet experiment" could be adequately evaluated; and the main exposition of his views on bureaucracy in Economy and Society was written in 1911-13, before the Bolshevik Revolution. His comments on socialism, then, are based mainly on comparing the aims and claims of socialist parties in Europe with the trends he discerned in historical and capitalist societies. His conclusion was that socialism in power would result not in a reversal of bureaucratization but, if anything, in its enhancement. "Only by reversion in every field—political, religious, economic, etc. to small-scale organization would it be possible to any considerable extent to escape [bureaucracy's] influence. . . . Socialism would, in fact, require a still higher degree of formal bureaucratization than capitalism."[8] Public or state ownership of the means of production and the institution of centralized economic planning and price-setting would provide fertile grounds indeed for the growth of bureaucracies. Bureaucratization, in Weber's analysis, did not significantly depend upon such things as the pursuit of private profit or the elevation of efficiency above other social values. Rather, the trend was fostered for the most part by features that socialism and capitalism would share. And Weber was quite clear that the antidemocratic implications of bureaucracy should hold under socialism as well, since they were largely the product of the organizational form itself, rather than of a particular type of property relations or attitude toward, or education of, the masses.

The discussion thus far reveals some of Weber's ideas on the origins and significance of the modern bureaucratic trend, but it should also be noted that Weber's views on this trend were not as deterministic as many of his subsequent vulgarizers have thought. His writings do not predict a future of total bureaucratization of society, or of a technocratic utopia à la Saint-Simon or B. F. Skinner, with experts making rational and wise decisions and guaranteeing human harmony. Rather, Weber saw the trend toward bureaucratization as very long and complex, with other forces often retarding or reversing it. In this respect we might say that Weber operated with more of a Chinese time perspective than do most contemporary Western academics, some of whom have used Weber to support the judgment that Maoist attacks on bureaucratic trends in China two decades after victory in the revolution are irrational and utopian.

In spite of Weber's many comments on the force of the trend toward bureaucracy ("Once fully established, bureaucracy is among those social structures which are the hardest to destroy. . . . Where administration has been completely bureaucratized, the resulting system of domination is practically indestructible."),[9] he did not see a unilinear trend toward domination by bureaucratic officials. In part his more complex views stemmed from the very nature of the bureaucratic form of organization. In most cases the leaders of bureaucracies were "outsiders," chosen by various means (election, revolution, inheritance), who did not fit the bureaucratic pattern. Although there was a tendency for officials to strive for autonomy from, or even domination over, their "dilettantish" political masters, forceful and imaginative elites could turn the tables and mold the bureaucracy to their will. Weber argued that the functional indispensability of bureaucracies did not guarantee predominant power for officials any more than it did for earlier indispensable slaves or proletarians;[10] and the "amorality" of bureaucracies consisted precisely in their willingness to serve all kinds of masters.

Weber strikes the same note in his comments on charismatic authority. Although some scholars have cited Weber to support the view that charismatic authority is outmoded in the modern age, Weber said quite explicitly, "Charismatic domination is by no means limited to primitive stages of development, and the three basic types of domination [traditional, charismatic, and legal-rational] cannot be placed into a simple evolutionary line: they in fact appear together in the most diverse combinations."[11] He did see charismatic authority as relatively unstable and short-lived, tending to recede in the face of everyday life and economic concerns. Yet again and again throughout history charismatic leaders and movements kept arising, most often at the time of some "extraordinary event," such as a war or depression. Charismatic authority eventually became routinized and institutionalized, but this did not mean that bureaucratic authority replaced it easily or automatically (or permanently), or that charismatic origins left no trace.

Instead of an ever-growing and irreversible bureaucratization, then, Weber saw the continual alternation of competing claims for loyalty and authority. In his political writings, as opposed to his scholarly works, it becomes quite clear that he placed great importance on this continued tension between charismatic and bureaucratic tendencies. He despaired of the sources of imaginative political leaders in Germany who could restrict bureaucrats to administration and prevent them from taking over policy-making, a development he felt would reduce any nation to unimportance in world affairs.[12] He felt that the continuing tension between charismatic and bureaucratic tendencies in Germany could also play an important role in the end of autocracy and the creation of a legal-rational democratic order. At the same time, he would not have agreed with the optimistic tone some later interpreters have read into his emphasis on rationality; and his analysis did not rule out the possibility that a new charismatic leader might use the bureaucratic structure to pervert, rather than to foster, democratic trends, as in fact happened in Germany scarcely a decade after Weber's death.

BUREAUCRACY IN MAOIST CHINA

From some of Mao's earliest writings we can see his great antagonism toward bureaucracy and bureaucratic styles of work, for instance, in his call in 1933, "This great evil, bureaucracy, must be thrown into the cesspool."[13] For Mao and many other Chinese Communist leaders, bureaucracy bore the connotation of the venal and oppressive officialdom that had ruled China for centuries. The experience of ruling China in no way seems to have diminished Mao's animus toward bureaucracy, which emerges clearly in his most explicit treatment of the subject, his 1967 "Twenty Manifestations of Bureaucracy." A few excerpts from this document convey the tone:[14]

> 2. They [bureaucrats] are conceited, complacent, and they aimlessly discuss politics. They do not grasp their work; they are subjective and one-sided; they are careless; they do not listen to people; they are truculent and arbitrary; they force orders; they do not care about reality; they maintain blind control. This is authoritarian bureaucracy. . . .
> 5. They are ignorant; they are ashamed to ask anything; they exaggerate and they lie; they are very false; they attribute errors to people; they attribute merit to themselves; they swindle the central government; they deceive those above them and fool those below them; they conceal faults and gloss over wrongs. This is dishonest bureaucracy. . . .
> 16. They fight among themselves for power and money; they extend their hands into the Party; they want fame and fortune; they want positions, and if they do not get it they are not satisfied; they choose to be fat and to be lean; they pay a great deal of attention to wages; they are cosy when it comes to cadres but they care nothing about the masses. This is the bureaucracy that is fighting for power and money. . . .

Mao's criticisms cover the range from the aspects of red tape and rigidity familiar to students of Western bureaucracy to the corruption and disdain for the common man that has roots equally in China's own bureaucratic tradition.

When viewed in the context of Mao's criticisms of bureaucracy, the actual development of organizations in post-1949 China has been quite complex. In consolidating their victory in the revolution the Chinese Communists did not, of course, "revert to small-scale organization in every field." Quite the contrary, the consolidation of power led to the creation of new and larger organizational forms: youth and women's associations, trade unions, economic planning agencies. At least in the sense of large-scale organizations with salaried personnel arranged in a complex hierarchical division of labor, post-1949 China has been, and still is, considerably more bureaucratic than its traditional and republican predecessors. A comparison can be made of the number of government officials and functionaries in Nationalist China just prior to the Communists' victory, and the increase in the number of "state cadres" (white collar and administrative personnel in government organs and enterprises) since 1949. (These figures leave out administrative personnel serving outside of formal governmental organs.)[15]

1948	1949	1952	1955	1958
2,000,000	720,000	3,310,000	5,270,000	7,920,000

This comparison admittedly is highly inexact, but it does give evidence of the rapid growth of one type of administrative personnel in China since 1949.[16]

It might be argued that part of the expansion of bureaucracy after 1949 was due not to the organizational requirements of socialism, as described by Weber, but to the Chinese decision to follow the particular socialist path to industrialization established by the Soviet Union. This path, which clearly emphasizes the virtues of large-scale organization, was increasingly rejected by Chinese elites after 1957. If this is the case, it still is not clear in what sense the Chinese have rejected bureaucratization since setting off on their own path to development. The early culmination of this search for an independent path, the Great Leap Forward of 1958-60, contained, in at least a partial sense, a huge push toward bureaucratization. From a pre-1949 agriculture of predominantly individual cultivators, the Chinese Communists had progressed by stages to the creation (in 1955-56) of collective farms (agricultural producers' cooperatives) roughly similar in size and organization to Soviet kolkhozy. Then with the Great Leap Forward communes were formed, resulting in the centralized administration of farming and other activities of often 20,000 or more people, units considerably larger than Soviet collective or state farms. The original communes were subsequently split into units roughly one-third their original size (still larger than their Soviet counterparts), with many administrative matters handled at the brigade and team subdivisions rather than in the commune headquarters itself. To staff the brigade and team levels (the two lower levels of the three-tiered commune hierarchy) required more than 20 million cadres as of 1963,[17] although these admittedly were not full-time officials in the Weberian mode.

Furthermore, the arguments made for each stage of agricultural collectivization, including the communes, are in many cases precisely those made by the advocates of the virtures of bureaucracy: the realization of economies of scale, the ability to handle larger and more complex undertakings, and the reduction of duplication of effort. Mao Tse-tung's succinct praise of the communes as "big and public" reflects the realization that there are virtues, and not merely evils, in large-scale organizations.

In many ways, then, events and policies since 1949 have tended to encourage bureaucratization while Mao and others around him have continued to criticize bureaucratic tendencies and behavior. Thus the "antibureaucratic spirit" in China is something much more subtle and complex than a simple rejection of bureaucracy as an organizing principle of society. This can be seen in the sorts of ideals the Chinese Communists proclaim for their large scale organizations. As I have argued elsewhere, on a number of points the "Maoist ideal" for such organizations is quite different from the Weberian ideal type of rational bureaucracy.[18] For instance, organizational autonomy to allow officials and experts to apply their specialized knowledge is supposed to give way before outside political mobilization and evaluation of organizational performance, while interpersonal relations characterized by formalistic impersonality and unemotionality are supposed to be replaced by a spirit of comradeship and mobilized collective political zeal. On balance, the most important difference between the Weberian and Maoist conceptions of the ideal large-scale organization is that the Weberian model sees the source of organizational strength primarily in the application of specialized knowledge of the officials, while the Maoist model looks more to the mobilized zeal and ingenuity of organizational subordinates. At the same time other aspects of the Weberian model are shared by the Maoist ideal: offices are arranged in a hierarchy bound by rules, with rewards greater for higher levels, and the influence of personal ties and likes and dislikes in hiring and in job performance are supposed to be minimized.

What happens in practice is that the growth of large-scale organizations in China encourages tendencies that make it harder to approach the Maoist organizational ideal. For instance, the growth of bureaucratic staffs and the devolution of decision-making upward make it more difficult to generate the zeal among subordinates upon which the Maoist model is based. Thus, while changing policies since 1949 have generated bureaucratization, Mao and his supporters have repeatedly launched campaigns and reforms to prevent these trends from having social and political consequences that they are not willing to accept. One of the best-known examples is the repeated launching of hsia fang campaigns, especially since 1957. These campaigns have a number of objectives, one of them the reduction in the size of administrative staffs of large organizations. In some cases cuts of 50 percent or more are made in such staffs, with those cut sent to lower posts, either in the same organization or elsewhere. In the process, the organizational structure is often consolidated and simplified in line with the spirit of "crack troops and simple administration," a slogan stemming from the Yenan period.[19] The emphasis on hsia fang and "crack troops and simple administration" represents a determination to check the natural tendencies for growth and complexity that develop in bureaucratic staffs.

Another aspect of the effort to avoid excessive bureaucratization is the policy of "walking on two legs." This means emphasizing small, rural, locally financed enterprises as well as large, modern, centrally financed urban ones. For instance, in the wake of the Cultural Revolution a new push was given to the organization of rural local industries, particularly cement, fertilizer, and agricultural implement factories.[20] These small factories now form an important part of the Chinese industrial base (local factories are said to produce 40 percent of the nation's output of chemical fertilizers) and, while they are not as efficient as larger, more technically advanced factories producing similar items, some other advantages are claimed for them. They can make use of surplus rural manpower, particularly during slack agricultural seasons; they can adapt their production to local needs; and they can help retain skilled manpower in the countryside. By "walking on two legs" the Chinese are saying that, just because larger and more complex enterprises are more efficient in an economic sense, their development should not be stressed to the detriment of other, less bureaucratic, organizational forms.

Another aspect of the Chinese assault on bureaucratic tendencies has been the launching of periodic decentralization campaigns. At various times, efforts have been made to transfer some powers from the central government to the provinces and within individual enterprises to give more powers to subunits. The downward transfer of power from communes to their subordinate brigades and teams after 1960 has already been mentioned. In the wake of the Cultural Revolution a number of central government ministries were disbanded, with their powers consolidated or transferred down to the provinces, while on a local level the running of schools was placed more under the authority of local productive and residential units and less under the direct control of the local offices of the Ministry of Education. The rationale for such moves is that decision-making that is too centralized will lead to apathetic responses from subordinates and to rigidities that will make it difficult to adapt programs to local needs and peculiarities.

In a number of significant ways, then, the Chinese Communists, and particularly Mao personally, have emphasized the curbing of some aspects of the bureaucratic trend rather than simply accepting it as inevitable and desirable. To a large extent it is a semantic question (depending upon one's definition of criteria of bureaucracy) whether and to what degree Mao and his followers are antibureaucratic. They are certainly against the abuses and irrationalities of bureaucracies in both the Chinese and Western traditions, but most of the measures taken by the Maoists constitute not so much a rejection of bureaucracy in toto as an effort to make bureaucratic Chinese organizations more responsive and more efficient. In this sense these efforts have much in common with similar ideas of Western theorists of "participative management."[21] The aim is not to destroy the large complex divisions of labor that have emerged in the modern age, but to make them work better.

If this conclusion is correct, the Maoists cannot be said to have found a refutation of Weber or a replacement for bureaucracy as a principle for organizing modern societies. Most of what Weber said about the factors favoring the growth of bureaucracy and the tenacity of this trend seems to be borne out in post-1949 China, as have his feelings about the good and evil aspects of this development. While the Chinese Communists emphasize somewhat different sources of the evil side of bureaucracy than Weber (bad ideology left over from before 1949 or propagated by modern revisionists and bourgeois-liners, rather than the requirements of the organizational form itself), on balance bureaucracy comes across as something both powerful and in some sense good, but at the same time dangerous.

We should not infer that complex organizations in China function just like those in any other society. Both traditional styles of behavior and the post-1949 revolutionary ethos affect the way large organizations function in China. Weber would not have been at all surprised at this, for he recognized that bureaucracies born in traditional and charismatic settings would continue to bear the stamp of their origin. It also is not clear that Weber would have felt that the periodic mass campaigns waged in China against the bureaucratic trend are anachronistic or irrational. He saw charisma as an important source of innovation and social dynamism, as a potent instrument for breaking through established behavior patterns and institutions and checking the power of established elites and officials. Weber did not deal with the sort of situation we find in post-1949 China—charismatic mobilization of the masses against bureaucratic evils every few years—so his works contain no predictions about how long or how well China's leaders can maintain this sort of dialectical alternation between bureaucratic and antibureaucratic phases. But clearly Weber felt that periodic "charismatic intrusion" into bureaucratic realms was both possible and important, even though charisma could never serve as the primary basis for the day-to-day running of a society over the long run. In terms of the problem of guaranteeing official responsiveness to the needs of the people, as long as it is impossible for autonomous mass movements to arise from below from the existing political institutions in China, bureaucratic evils can be checked only by charismatic movements initiated from above. At the same time we should keep in mind the lesson of events in post-Weber Germany. When there are no effective checks on the power of those charismatic leaders who succeed in dominating the bureaucratic structure, there are no guarantees that they will use their power to guarantee sensitivity to popular sentiments and to preserve the dignity of their people.

MICHELS ON OLIGARCHY

In dealing with the problems created by large-scale, complex organizations, the Chinese Communists devote a great deal of attention to assuring responsiveness to the "masses"—that is, to subordinates within, and to the public being served outside, the organization. The most specific treatment of the obstacles to such responsiveness is contained in Michels's Political Parties, in which he enunciated the "iron law of oligarchy": "It is organization which gives birth to the domination of the elected over the electors, of the mandataries over the mandators, of the delegates over the delegators. Who says organization says oligarchy."[22] This pessimistic conclusion was based on Michels' analysis of European socialist parties and trade unions, particularly the German Social Democratic Party. To amplify the "iron law" somewhat, Michels found that no matter how strong the commitment of socialist leaders to internal democracy and the wisdom of the masses, and no matter what devices were adopted to make those leaders responsive to their followers, the very act of organizing to pursue their goals inevitably produced an oligarchic elite that monopolized decision-making and manipulated their followers to accept the outcome. Parties avowing anti-elitist and democratic ideologies came to look very similar to aristocratic and autocratic parties, at least in terms of their internal workings. Michels's work overlaps with Weber's to the extent that both were concerned with the antidemocratic implications of large-scale organizations, but Michels was concerned primarily with the internal processes of organizations, while Weber was more oriented to the role such organizations played in the power structure of the larger society.

For Michels the iron law got its "iron" quality from the fact that oligarchy was unalterably predetermined. A large number of psychological, structural, and environmental forces were seen as contributing, and even the elimination of several would still leave oligarchic tendencies dominant. Some of his analysis focused on psychological factors—for instance, the desire of Party leaders to preserve their power and status, and the apathy of their followers that allowed them to do so. It is important to note, however, that Michels was not for the most part making an argument about the inherent selfishness of human nature or blaming oligarchic subversion of democratic parties on the influence of patterns of child-rearing or the general or class-specific values and norms prevalent in modern societies.[23] This is the implication of his focus on the absence of real internal democracy in the parties and unions in which it was a fervently held value and deep personal commitment of most members. Take away any assumptions of inherent human selfishness and simply assume, in the Maoist fashion, that individual human nature is "blank" and can be influenced by the surrounding social milieu in a variety of directions, and Michels's argument is that the activities and division of roles required in large-scale organizations will mold such "blank" personalities in an oligarchic direction. For Michels, as for Weber, the structural features and dynamics of large-scale organizations themselves produce such elitist tendencies, which are not simply the product of the inherent selfishness of participants or of the acquisitiveness of the culture in which they have been raised.

To recapitulate the links in Michels' argument in summary form:[24]

1. Socialists and workers cannot pursue their goals without organization.

2. Direct democracy is impossible (for reasons of efficiency, rapidity of response, unity), and organizations require leaders.

3. Competition with other groups in pursuit of organizational goals requires internal discipline, which in practice means obedience to the leadership.

4. The complex tasks of modern party leadership require special abilities and skills (oratorical, literary, diplomatic, administrative) that are not widely or equally distributed within the membership. Even leaders chosen from among the membership who do not possess relevant training and experience develop special skills through their organizational duties (pretrained and selected leaders, of course, acquire additional valuable skills and experience in office). This experience makes both leaders and followers feel that replacement of the incumbents is a risky undertaking.

5. Leaders have a preponderance of control over organizational resources (means of communication, funds). They will interpret

opposition from below as obstruction of their legitimate pursuit of valued organizational goals, and will be able to use organizational resources to defeat more numerous, but less well endowed, oppositionists.

6. Positions of leadership have higher power and prestige than positions of followership; generally speaking, leaders would rather retain their positions than return to the ranks, and can use the powers of their offices to stay in command.

7. The division of labor within the organization means that leaders have very different daily routines, contacts, and concerns than their followers do; in particular, they must expend much of their time and energy on the maintenance of the organization itself and relations with outside allies and adversaries. Followers are primarily involved with their daily work routine. They cannot expend most of their time in monitoring the minute details of daily organizational administration. When they do concern themselves, it is more with the goals the organization is supposed to be pursuing than with organizational maintenance and discipline.

8. Even where there are institutions for regular election of leaders and representation of subordinates in leadership, these do not significantly affect the oligarchic trends. Incumbents are in an advantageous position in internal elections; and even when a subordinate succeeds in entering the leadership, the day he takes office, he begins to acquire concerns and interests that are not shared by those who remain followers.

All of these organizational or structural features produce the oligarchic tendencies that Michels detected in European socialist parties and unions.

We should clarify here that Michels did not say that the interests and goals of party followers were never furthered by the actions and policies of their oligarchic elites. As mentioned previously, he was concerned primarily with the distribution of internal power rather than with the success of the parties in pursuing professed goals. He did feel that oligarchic tendencies had conservative implications, both because the concern of leaders with organizational maintenance deflected them from pursuit of professed goals, and because these leaders tended to develop vested interests in the stability and calculability of their environment, including their adversaries. But this does not mean that goals were never reached or that members always ended up exploited and deceived, with no benefits to show for it. The oligarchic despot might in fact be benevolent; but if so, it was not due to his insecurity in the face of pressures and demands of his followers.

OLIGARCHY IN MAOIST CHINA

It might be argued that Michels's analysis is not relevant to the Chinese scene, since many of the specific sources of oligarchy (such as the need for discipline and unity in the face of competing parties and state oppression) do not exist with socialism in power. I would argue, however, that Michels's arguments are relevant to China. For instance, the mobilizational nature of the Chinese political system provides "functional equivalents" (distant and demanding goals, unchallengeable ideology, foreign enemies and internal subversion) that produce quite similar demands for unity and discipline. The Chinese Communists in fact recognize the frequent occurrence of oligarchic tendencies in their institutions, to which they have affixed colorful labels over the years: "commandism," "mountaintop strong-hold mentality." And repeatedly they have tried to alter their political institutions to ensure responsiveness to the masses, the post-Cultural Revolution reforms being the latest attempt. Many of these efforts stem from the Chinese commitment to the "mass line" style of leader-ship.[25] Under this principle, leadership is supposed to be exercised not by the giving of commands and demanding of obedience, but through the medium of regular two-way communications and consultations between leaders and followers. Leaders are supposed to exercise persuasion in presenting new programs and demands, while receiving ideas and criticisms from the masses and using these to adapt and improve programs so as to elicit better mass response. Leaders are supposed to admit errors and accept and welcome criticism from below, rather than suppress complaints.[26] They are encouraged to realize that the key to successful leadership is their skill in mobilizing the energies and enthusiasm of their subordinates, rather than their strictness in getting orders obeyed. From the repeated campaigns against elitism and the suppression of the masses in China, we can tell that actual leadership often strays far from these ideals. Here we should remember the thrust of Michels's argument: It is not so much the ideals themselves that are important, but how (or whether) they can be translated into the structure and role requirements of organizations. We turn now to a consideration of some of the specific mechanisms implemented since the Cultural Revolution in the effort to institutionally check oligarchic tendencies.

Richard Pfeffer has discussed the "institutional aftermath" of the Cultural Revolution, the specific devices adopted in recent years in the attempt to revive the Maoist mass orientation.[27] He focuses on four particular institutional changes: open-door rectification, educational reform, May 7 cadre schools, and direct class represen-tation. All are seen as giving the masses more voice and power in relation to their organizational superiors than was formerly the case. How might Michels have viewed these changes?

Open-door rectification refers to the practice of not restricting the criticism of Party organs and members to internal Party councils, but regularly encouraging subordinates and non-Party members to openly join in the voicing of complaints. Pfeffer argues that open-door rectification heightens the sense of mass participation while increasing Party responsiveness and helping to weed out bad Party members. The problem in this analysis is that Party and organizational leaders generally retain powerful mechanisms for directing, manipulating, and even suppressing criticism from below. Party authorities interpret the current political line, direct regular ideological study and indoctrination of subordinates, and can use small study groups and preselected activists to insure that leading critics are tame and that those with strong grievances remain intimidated. Open-door rectification is, of course, not completely new; and in many previous instances (for example, in the New Three-Anti campaign after the Great Leap Forward) the mobilization of criticism from below continued to be directed by those who were supposed to be rectified. The exceptions are circumstances in which work teams were sent into organizations to take over the direction of criticism of local leaders (the rural Four Cleanups campaign of 1964)[28] and campaigns in which higher authorities prevented Party organs from playing their usual directing roles (the "Hundred Flowers" campaign of 1957, the Cultural Revolution). In other words, open-door rectification cannot live up to expectations as long as subordinates are not given free reign to voice all manner of criticism without risking sanctions, and in China this rarely happens. During the Cultural Revolution more radical ideas for facilitating mass control over leaders were proposed: the direct election and recall institutions of the 1871 Paris Commune. However, the Paris Commune model was rejected in short order for reasons that remain obscure, but that may have something to do with the incompatibility of its democratic devices with Leninist principles of Party rule.[29]

Educational reform and the May 7 cadre schools are both seen by Pfeffer as making organizational elites more humble and responsive to subordinates. By placing a heavy emphasis on labor and useful skills in curricula at all levels, by giving local communities and economic institutions administrative control over schools, and by insuring that those who get access to higher education come predominantly from families of worker and poor or lower-middle peasant origins, current educational reforms are supposed to undermine technocratic elitism and the divorce from working realities of those who end up in mental labor occupations. In May 7 schools all over China, cadres above the production unit level regularly go to special farms for periods of agricultural labor and political study lasting six months or so, designed to restore their connection with the masses and prevent the emergence of a separate elite consciousness. Michels would probably have regarded these mechanisms with skepticism. Since he saw organizational structure and requirements as the primary sources of oligarchy, rather than the prior (or intervening) experience and training of the oligarchs, mass-oriented education and cadre labor spells could at best have minor ameliorating effects. Once graduates of these schools entered (or reentered) their offices, their concerns would begin to diverge from those of their subordinates.[30] (Here we ignore the question of how well the reformed regular schools and cadre schools can generate the kinds of attitudinal changes they are supposed to.)

Michels would probably have been similarly skeptical about the impact of what Pfeffer calls direct class representation, the practice of including representatives of the masses in the revolutionary committees and Party organs governing China today. First of all, the workers and peasants who sit on various leading bodies are not there because of the sort of direct election from below that Michels dealt with in the European parties. The actual methods of selection vary and are often unclear, but they generally seem to involve heavy doses of recommendation and selection by higher authorities. Thus the potential for existing leaders to use the representational system to insure that those chosen fit their own requirements, rather than the "true" wishes of subordinates, remains great. With such built-in possibilities for leaders co-opting compliant subordinates, it is not clear in what sense these new representatives are in fact representative of the masses, except in the minimal senses of proper class origins and not having previously served in official posts. Michels clearly felt that even noncompliant subordinates who managed to get themselves chosen for representative posts would, once in office, lose their representative character and begin to acquire the concerns and perspectives of elites.

We might note that prior to the Cultural Revolution, a mass-representative model emerged that differs from Pfeffer's direct class representation. Poor and Lower-Middle Peasant Associations were established in rural communes after 1964, in part to supervise the exercise of authority of commune cadres and to criticize abuses of power. Commune cadres were specifically forbidden from holding posts of Association leadership.[31] Using Michels's ideas, one might expect that this device would have more democratic promise than direct class representation, since it involves masses supervising leaders without becoming involved in the burdens of daily leadership. However, in recent years little has been heard of the Poor and Lower-Middle Peasant Associations, and it is not clear that they are fulfilling the role designated for them.[32] Perhaps the conflict with the Leninist model of unified Party rule is again involved in the watering down of the role of these Associations.

The preceding sections argue that the "institutional aftermath" devices discussed by Pfeffer have not effectively checked the oligarchic tendencies described by Michels, although they may have some ameliorating effects. Leaders of Chinese organizations continue to be subject to pressures to manipulate rather than be responsive to their subordinates; and when they bow to these pressures, they have powerful manipulative devices in their hands. The effectiveness of the kinds of mass-oriented devices discussed by Pfeffer depends at the very least upon the vigilance and vigorous pressure of mass-oriented higher authorities, who can keep these devices from being watered down.

We need to deal here with at least one of the major criticisms later scholars have made of Michels's analysis, the fact that his deterministic emphasis is misleading. Merely focusing on tendencies toward oligarchy is deceptive insofar as it diverts us from considering tendencies toward democracy.[33] One may be led to assume that all organizations are equally oligarchic, which is clearly not the case. Furthermore, one might conclude that no institutional mechanisms can significantly check oligarchic tendencies, which at least may not be the case. Looking at the Israeli kibbutz (which, it is true, is still a fairly small organization), one can see oligarchic tendencies; but such things as fixed terms of office, direct elections, and regular rotation of jobs would seem to place kibbutzim at the relatively low end of the oligarchy scale.[34] Lipset and his associates argue that not all American trade unions are equally oligarchic, and that in the International Typographical Union structural such features as low status differentials, active associational life of members, independent channels of communication for opposition groups, low control of union leaders over employment opportunities, and ample leisure time act to produce such atypical democratic actions as the defeat of incumbent union officials and of proposals to raise the salaries of officials.[35] In another context Arthur Stinchcombe discusses various factors that will act to lower the dependence of subordinates on organizations and organizational superiors, including the capacity of inferiors to organize independently, the availability of alternative sources for the satisfaction of needs now met by superiors, guarantees of the existing rights and status of inferiors, and the degree of institutionalized dependence of superiors on inferiors (for instance, by direct elections).[36] These references suggest that we need to think of oligarchy in variable terms, and to look for the structural bases of democracy as well as oligarchy.

When all of this is said, it is not clear what the implications are for our understanding of Chinese society. It does suggest that we should expect the balance of oligarchic and anti-oligarchic forces to differ in communes, schools, and factories, and even within organizations of one type. But we must also come to grips with the influence of the Leninist legacy, which was referred to briefly in our discussion of Richard Pfeffer's article. Neither Weber nor Michels dealt in detail with the implications for their ideas of Lenin's doctrines on the Party, although Weber did predict in 1906 that the coming to power of left-radical forces in Russia would lead to extreme "centralist-bureaucratic tendencies."[37] Many analysts since have pressed the case that the institutions of Leninist Party rule (democratic centralism, monopolization of the means of communication, prohibition of factionalism, unchallengeable and totalistic ideology, hierarchical and restricted-membership Party, Party control over policy-making and personnel allocation in all areas of social and economic life) have profound antidemocratic consequences. One could cite here not only the arguments of such Western social scientists as Philip Selznick but also critics within the Marxist tradition, such as Rosa Luxemburg, Leon Trotsky, and Milovan Djilas.[38] Some would argue that shortly before his death Lenin, too, began to have misgivings about the organizational weapon (to use Selzinick's term) he had created.[39]

One does not have to accept the accuracy of the model (or ideal type) of totalitarianism for the Soviet or Chinese scene to recognize that Leninist Party rule introduces structural tendencies toward bureaucratization and oligarchy beyond those detailed by Weber and Michels. To put it another way, Maoist attempts to maintain a mass orientation are not undermined simply by the requirements of all large-scale organizations, but also by the specific antidemocratic tendencies of Leninist Party rule (for instance, by the absence of the democratic structural factors discussed in the cited works of Lipset et al., and Stinchcombe). So far in their search for mechanisms to check bureaucratism and oligarchy, the Maoists have not seen fit to tamper, in any significant way, with their Leninist legacy.[40] And so long as this remains true, the effectiveness of the checks the masses have over their leaders will depend to an overwhelming extent upon the pressures maintained on these leaders by Mao and his followers at the top.

CONCLUSIONS

It does not seem necessary here to try to summarize all the heterogeneous issues covered in preceding pages. Instead we will simply reiterate several points that stem from the ideas we have been considering:

1. Simplistic assumptions of inevitable or irreversible bureaucratization, and of the "health" of such a trend, cannot stand up to a close reading of Weber's ideas. Nonbureaucratic claims can have a continued vitality and positive effect even (or perhaps especially) in a complex modernizing society like China.

Organizations and structures in which people spend their daily lives have a vital influence on their perceptions, attitudes, and behavior; in the analyses of Weber and Michels this influence is generally more powerful than that stemming from class background, prior experience, and the generalized values held in the larger society. This suggests that explanations of attitudes and behavior focusing on national character and child-rearing, classes in pre-1949 society, the enemy vs. the people, or competing ideological lines lead to oversimplifications or distortions. A fuller picture must consider the organized system of norms, roles, and interpersonal ties in which individuals are embedded. Mao Tse-tung provides a framework for such a fuller picture in his "On the Correct Handling of Contradictions Among the People," in which he acknowledges the importance of contradictions within socialist society between different strata of intellectuals, between leaders and led, between workers and peasants.[41] This leads to the conclusion that people in different social positions, fulfilling different roles, will have interests that are partially in conflict. But for political reasons, in actual practice, conflicts between different segments of the population or sentiments at variance with official policies are usually ascribed to the influence of harmful ideology rather than to social differentiation. Thus, what might be regarded as a natural expression of diverging interests and perspectives is often branded an ideological deviation.

3. Pressures for oligarchy are variable, as are pressures for democracy, but the Leninist legacy makes the oligarachic side of the equation considerably more powerful than it would otherwise be. It is misleading to attribute oligarchic or bureaucratic tendencies simply to the "survivals" of bourgeois society or even to the general requirements of all large, complex organizations while ignoring the structural tendencies stemming from Leninist party rule.

4. The Chinese Communists have not found any total solutions to the problems of bureaucracy and oligarchy, but they are making earnest efforts. The holding in check of bureaucratic and oligarchic tendencies in China still depends predominantly on pressure from above to keep mass-oriented practices viable, since checks resulting from the independent organization and mobilization of the masses are effectively prohibited. This makes continued "charismatic intrusions" from above important to the masses, but also represents a fundamental instability of the Chinese political system. If elites come to power in Peking who are not committed to the maintenance of mass-oriented policies, then all of our discussion of mass participation and responsiveness of leaders in China may seem irrelevant and naive to future readers.

NOTES

1. Obviously, a full exposition of the views of the two German scholars cannot be presented here. Our focus will be on the trends toward bureaucratization and oligarchy in modern societies, and our method will be the short quotation and capsule summary rather than the lengthy textual exegesis. Most of our attention will be devoted to two works, Weber's Economy and Society and Michels's Political Parties. The work of these two scholars was not, of course, completely independent; and the analysis carried out by Michels followed an outline of research topics laid out by Weber in 1905. Cf. Guenther Roth, postscript to "The Historical Relationship to Marxism," in Reinhard Bendix and Guenther Roth, Scholarship and Partisanship: Essays on Max Weber (Berkeley: University of California Press, 1971), p. 249.

2. These are abbreviated summaries of the main traits listed by Weber in Economy and Society (New York: Bedminister Press, 1968), pp. 956-58. Weber's ideal-typical approach has generated much controversy and confusion. Here we will simply note that it is not profitable to think of organizations in categorical terms, with any organization as either bureaucratic or not, but in variable terms, with any organization more or less bureaucratic, depending upon how closely it approximates the ideal-typical pattern.

3. Weber is best known for his thesis in The Protestant Ethic and the Spirit of Capitalism that ascetic Protestantism, particularly Calvinism, played a key role in the rise of capitalism. What is less often noted is that Weber viewed the Protestant Reformation as only one stage in the long and complex history of the development of rationalism in Western religions. See Max Weber, Ancient Judaism (Glencoe, Ill: The Free Press, 1952).

4. Max Weber, Economy and Society, p. 973.

5. Ibid., p. 988.

6. Ibid., pp. 1168-70.

7. Ibid., pp. 985, 987-94. Weber saw democratic trends in society as fostering bureaucratization by undermining traditional status distinctions. However, bureaucratization did not encourage democratization in the sense of direct rule by the masses but, rather, the leveling of the governed of all strata in the face of the rule of bureaucratic officialdom.

8. Ibid., pp. 224-25.

9. Ibid., p. 987.

10. Ibid., pp. 990-92, 1123.

11. Ibid., p. 1133.

12. Max Weber, Gesammelte politische Schriften (Tübingen: J. C. B. Mohr, 1958), p. 277. Cited and discussed in Alfred Diamant,

"The Bureaucratic Model: Max Weber Rejected, Rediscovered, Reformed," in Ferrel Heady and Sybil L. Stokes, eds., Papers in Comparative Public Administration (Ann Arbor: Institute of Public Administration, University of Michigan, 1962), pp. 80-81. I thank Gordon Bennett for bringing this source to my attention.

13. Quoted in Maurice Meisner, "Leninism and Maoism: Some Populist Perspectives on Marxism-Leninism in China," China Quarterly no. 45 (Jan.-Mar. 1971): 29.

14. Joint Publications Research Service, "Chairman Mao Discusses Twenty Manifestations of Bureaucracy," Translations on Communist China no. 90 (Feb. 12, 1970): 40-43.

15. 1948 figures computed by Ying-mao Kao in "Patterns of Recruitment and Mobility of Urban Cadres," in John W. Lewis, ed., The City in Communist China (Stanford: Stanford University Press, 1971), pp. 98-99. Official figures for 1949-58 cited in Victor C. Funnell, "Bureaucracy and the Chinese Communist Party," Current Scene 9, no. 5 (May 7, 1971): 6.

16. Some of this expansion could be called artificial, representing not the training of new officials but the process by which existing officials became classified as state cadres as a result of the socialization of the enterprises in which they served. But this does not undermine the argument about bureaucratization, since this absorption represents the tying of formerly independent enterprises into larger (in this case national) administrative hierarchies. For a discussion of other bureaucratic trends, such as the formulation of a graded system of cadre ranks with differentiated salaries, see Ezra F. Vogel, "From Revolutionaries to Semi-Bureaucrats: The Regularization of Cadres," China Quarterly no. 29 (Jan.-Mar. 1967).

17. Jen-min Jih-pao, July 4, 1963 p. 1; cited in Funnell, op. cit., p. 7.

18. Martin King Whyte, "Bureaucracy and Modernization in China: The Maoist Critique," American Sociological Review 38, no. 2 (Apr. 1973), pp. 149-65.

19. See the discussion in Mark Selden, The Yenan Way in Revolutionary China (Cambridge: Harvard University Press, 1971), pp. 188-200.

20. Articles 51 and 52 of Mao Tse-tung's 1958 document "Sixty Articles on Work Methods," translated in Chinese Law and Government 5, no. 1 (Spring 1972): 115, deal with the need to establish small local chemical fertilizer and agricultural implement factories.

21. Cf. Rensis Likert, New Patterns of Management (New York: McGraw-Hill, 1961); Douglas McGregor, The Human Side of Enterprise (New York: McGraw-Hill, 1960); Arnold S. Tannenbaum, Control in Organizations (New York: McGraw-Hill, 1968)

22. Robert Michels, Political Parties (New York: Free Press, 1962), p. 15. Originally published in 1911.

23. Part 4 of Michels's work deals with the social origins of party and union leaders, and he concludes that leaders of proletarian origin manifest oligarchic tendencies as much as or more than those from higher stations.

24. Here we briefly summarize points made in parts 1-3 of Political Parties.

25. Cf. Mao Tse-tung et al., Lun ch'ün-chung lu-hsien" (On the mass line) (n. p.: Hsin hua, 1950). See also the discussions in John W. Lewis, Leadership in Communist China (Ithaca: Cornell University Press, 1963); James R. Townsend, Political Participation in Communist China (Berkeley: University of California Press, 1967).

26. "At present, some comrades fear mass discussion very much; they fear that the masses may put forward views different from the leading organs and leaders. When problems are discussed, they suppress the enthusiasm of the masses and forbid them to speak out. This attitude is extremely bad. . . . Only those who adopt the attitude of looking their mistakes in the face, admitting and correcting their mistakes and lending their ears to mass criticism should be welcomed." Mao Tse-tung, "Talk on the Question of Democratic Centralism" (Jan. 30, 1962), translated in Current Background no. 891 (Oct. 8, 1969): 37.

27. Richard M. Pfeffer, "Leaders and Masses," in Michel Oksenberg, ed., China's Developmental Experience (New York: Praeger, 1973).

28. Cf. Richard Baum and Frederick C. Teiwes, Ssu-Ch'ing: The Socialist Education Movement of 1962-1966 (Berkeley: Center for Chinese Studies, University of California, 1968), p. 73.

29. John Bryan Starr, "Revolution in Retrospect: The Paris Commune Through Chinese Eyes," China Quarterly 49 (Jan.-Mar. 1972): pp. 106-25.

30. "The major error in dealing with problems of organizational change, both at the practical and theoretical level, is to disregard the systemic properties of the organization and to confuse individual change with modifications in organizational variables. It is common practice to pull foremen or officials out of their organizational roles and give them training in human relations. Then they return to their customary positions with the same role expectations from their subordinates, the same pressures from superiors, and the same functions to perform as before their special training. Even if the training program has begun to produce a different orientation toward other people on the part of the trainees, they are likely to find little opportunity to express their new orientation in the ongoing structured situation to which they return." Daniel Katz and Robert L. Kahn, The Social Psychology of Organizations (New York: Wiley, 1966), p. 390.

31. Baum and Teiwes, op. cit., pp. 95-101, translates the Association rules.

32. The evidence here is vague. The organization seems still to exist in most communes but to have lost much of its watchdog role, and perhaps its importance. A detailed six-part description of a commune in Kiangsu presented in Peking Review nos. 13-18 (Mar. 30-May 4, 1973), contains no mention of a Poor and Lower-Middle Peasant Association.

33. Alvin W. Gouldner, "The Metaphysical Pathos and the Theory of Bureaucracy," American Political Science Review 49 (1955).

34. Melford E. Spiro, Kibbutz—Venture in Utopia (Cambridge: Harvard University Press, 1956); R. D. Schwartz, "Democracy and Collectivism in the Kibbutz," Social Problems 4 (1957): 137-47.

35. S. M. Lipset, Martin Trow, and James Coleman, Union Democracy (Garden City, N.Y.: Doubleday, 1962).

36. Arthur L. Stinchcombe, "Social Structure and Organizations," in James G. March, ed., Handbook of Organizations (Chicago: Rand-McNally, 1965), pp. 182-83.

37. Max Weber, Gesammelte politische Schriften, pp. 47-48, cited in Diamant, op. cit., p. 81.

38. Philip Selznick, The Organizational Weapon (Glencoe, Ill.: The Free Press, 1960); Rosa Luxemburg, Leninism or Marxism (Glasgow: Anti-Parliamentary Communist Federation, 1935); and The Russian Revolution (New York: Workers Age, 1940), pp. 44-48; Leon Trotsky, The Revolution Betrayed (Garden City, N.Y.: Double-day, 1937); Milovan Djilas, The New Class (New York: Praeger, 1957).

39. Moshe Lewin, Lenin's Last Struggle (New York: Random House, 1968); Adam B. Ulam, The Bolsheviks (New York: Collier, 1968), Ch. 10.

40. During the Cultural Revolution the Party's infallibility was dented as rebels were mobilized to struggle against "high persons in power taking the capitalist road." However, in the wake of the Cultural Revolution the Party has been reconstructed, and the argument is made that the Party in the abstract is still owed obedience and that the struggle was only against revisionists who had usurped power in the Party. At the moment, the Party and its leaders are once again involved in interpreting what the correct policies are, and rebellion is not being encouraged. With the centralism half of the democratic-centralism formula restored, there is, however, a novel feature written into the Party Constitutions adopted at both the 9th and 10th Party Congresses 1969, 1973): Party members who feel that their immediate Party superiors are mistaken can communicate such feelings over the heads of their superiors to higher authorities, even to the Central Committee. Such a provision is missing from

the Party Constitution adopted at the 8th Congress in 1956. It is too early to tell how significant this change will be. For the three constitutions, see T. H. E. Chen, ed., The Chinese Communist Regime (New York: Praeger, 1967), pp. 136-37; Current Background no. 880 (May 9, 1969): 54; and Current Background no. 994 (Sept. 20, 1973): 41-42.

41. Translated in Robert R. Bowie and John K. Fairbank, eds., Communist China 1955-1959 (Cambridge; Harvard University Press, 1962), document 14.

3

**REWRITING HISTORY
TO FURTHER MAOISM:
THE NINGTU CONFERENCE
OF 1932**
William F. Dorrill

The official—and still accepted—version of the Chinese Communist Party's rise to power was laid down in 1945, several years after Mao Tse-tung's achievement of unchallenged supremacy in the leadership.[1] According to this interpretation, the Party had been subjected to recurrent setbacks and defeats throughout its history owing to the "errors" and ideological deviations of previous leaders. Ultimately, the dogmatic "third 'Left' line" of Wang Ming (Ch'en Shao-yü) and Po Ku (Ch'in Pang-hsien), which allegedly dominated the Party after 1931, resulted in the disastrous loss of the Central Soviet base in Kiangsi during the Kuomintang's Fifth Encirclement Campaign in 1934. Total destruction was only narrowly averted by Mao's accession to power at the Tsunyi Conference of the Central Committee in January 1935. Not until then was the CCP set on a "correct" course toward successful completion of the Long March and eventual victory in the Chinese revolution.

The remarkable Communist political and military recovery in the Yenan period gave weighty support to this Mao-centered interpretation of Party history. It began to be articulated in the Cheng Feng campaign for ideological rectification (1942-44), which was to establish Mao's authority as the invariably correct strategist of the revolution. Party members and cadres were urged to study the CCP's historical experience diligently and to arm themselves with Mao's thought so as to avoid the errors of the past and hasten the revolutionary victory.[2] The results were summed up shortly afterward:

Since 1942, under the leadership of Comrade Mao Tse-tung, the Party-wide movement for the rectification of subjectivism, sectarianism, and stereotyped Party writing and also for the study of Party history has corrected, at their very ideological roots, the various "Left" and Right errors that have arisen in the history of the Party.[3]

Besides strengthening the unity and discipline of a new generation of cadres drawn largely from the peasant and intellectual classes, the rectification campaign also marked the beginning within the Party of a new emphasis on "the thought of Mao Tse-tung."[4]

Since Mao claims to have had to struggle against the established Party bureaucracy (and, indirectly, its Comintern sponsors) to win control of the leadership and to put an end to the former "erroneous" lines, it is not surprising that his understanding of fidelity to the Party came less to mean conformity to institutional rules and regulations than "first and foremost an obedience to the author of the Party line (Mao) or the correct ideology (Mao's thought)."[5] The same might also be said about his concept of fidelity to factual details in writing Party history. In April 1945 he secured the Central Committee's formal endorsement of his own interpretation in the lengthy "Resolution on Some Questions in the History of Our Party." It criticized the policies of previous Party leaders, blaming the earlier revolutionary setbacks on them; commended Mao's opposition to the "erroneous" lines; and praised his leadership over the decade since Tsunyi, attributing all successes to it (and even the limited victories achieved earlier).

Immediately after the passage of this resolution the CCP's Seventh Congress was held, during which a new Party constitution was adopted. It was reorganized so the Party structure reflected Mao's dominant power position and, in the preamble, exalted "ideas of Mao Tse-tung," along with other great Communist theoreticians, as necessary to guide the entire work of the CCP.[6] It is probably not an exaggeration to say that a "veritable cult of Mao Tse-tung . . . burst forth into blossom at this Congress.[7]

Mao's achievement of such a dominant position over his rivals depended, of course, to a considerable extent on his ability to relate the Party's successes to his leadership and to absolve himself of any responsibility for its failures—that is, on establishing the legitimacy of his claim to lead. To continue in power and meet the severe challenges to the Party posed by the harsh wartime environment of the early 1940s, there was an urgent necessity for Mao to rebuild confidence in his personal leadership and authority. The rewriting of Party history became an important vehicle to accomplish these tasks. It helped create an aura of infallibility and success around Mao and his allies to offset the CCP's earlier defeats and to inspire faith in the ultimate victory over both Japan and Chiang Kai-shek.

In a broader sense, Mao's attempt to legitimize the authority through the writing of history demonstrated a keen sensitivity to important elements of the Chinese political culture. For centuries in China the legitimacy of rulers was regarded as directly related to their performance, successive dynasties rising or falling as they were seen in practice to possess or lose the "mandate of heaven." In modern times, as Lucien Pye notes, the Chinese people's acceptance of a leadership has depended heavily on its ability to demonstrate success: ". . . the few men who have achieved [national] popularity have quickly lost their appeal as soon as they were confronted with difficulties and setbacks."[8] Leaders operating under the Marxist-Leninist banner have had the additional requirement of justifying their right to lead by demonstrating through the success of their policies that they were carrying out the laws of history in accordance with the dialectical process.

While it may be argued that political leadership in all cultures is based to some considerable degree on a sense of authoritativeness derived from past successes, in China, as Richard Solomon has pointed out, authority has become uniquely identified with "the power of the word." In traditional China, "to exert authority came to mean having the right both to speak and to 'educate' inferiors; while to be compelled to memorize and repeat the words of a teacher became a mark of subordination, a ritual of social control." Even today, he concludes, "when a Chinese political leader has doubts about his authority, the technique he instinctively selects to reaffirm his status is 'education', compelling his subjects to commit to memory his words, his 'thought' (szu-hsiang)."[9]

Thus, in applying his own thought to the writing of Party history in the early 1940s Mao sought to explain the CCP's earlier setbacks and defeats as the result of deviations from the "correct" ideology or line. The disastrous loss of the Kiangsi Soviet base in the Kuomintang's Fifth Encirclement Campaign was attributed to numerous ideological, political, military, and organizational errors of the "Left opportunist" leadership that allegedly dominated the Party hierarchy before Mao's elevation to power at Tsunyi in January 1935. In these dark years Mao's correct guidance was callously thrust aside by the doctrinaire "Leftists" allied with Wang Ming. A critical push in Mao's displacement in the Kiangsi Soviet leadership was said to have occurred at the Ningtu Conference of August 1932.

It will be the aim of the following analysis to reexamine this incident and its impact on the Party in light of the official Maoist interpretation. It is hoped that this detailed case study will contribute to a broader understanding of the application of Mao's thought to Party history.

THE POLITICAL AND MILITARY SETTING

Kuomintang (KMT) military action in the summer and fall of 1932 indicated that, despite the growing external menace of Japanese aggression, the Nanking regime led by Chiang Kai-shek was determined to eradicate the rural Chinese Soviets, the only important base of Communist strength in China. This determination was evident not only from the unprecedented size and elaborate preparation of the government forces committed to the campaign (as well as the willingness of urban financial interests to back the enterprise), but also from Chiang's readiness to accept large and growing casualties without hesitating in the prosectuion of the anti-Communist pacification effort.[10] The KMT effort was characterized by a new political and economic emphasis largely lacking in previous campaigns. Significant improvements were made in governmental administration, civil-military cooperation, police and intelligence work, mass propaganda and education, and various programs that might be categorized today as "civic action." These proved increasingly effective in allowing the KMT to retain control over territory seized from the Communists. This did not, of course, spell an end to ruthless coercion and punitive action against the civilian population, but it helped limit and refine the application of force.

The initial phase of the Fourth Encirclement Campaign against the Central Soviet Area began in June 1932 after the elimination of the O-yü-wan (Hupei-Honan-Anhwei) and Hsiang-o-si (Hunan-West Hupei) bases in central China. The new offensive in Kiangsi raised the specter of a vastly increased KMT military threat to the continued existence of the rural Soviets. In addition to committing overwhelmingly large forces for a coordinated attack, Chiang Kai-shek had begun the construction of a system of interconnected blockhouses around various Communist bases. In time this would permit a basically new tactical approach. Besides forming a tight blockade around the Soviet areas (depriving the Communists of necessary imports and room to maneuver, while securing the KMT rear), the fortified lines could be pushed inward, protecting the penetration of heavily concentrated government units and slowly tightening like a noose around the elusive Red Army. The results of Communist attempts to counter or break through the newly constructed KMT fortifications in the summer of 1932 were not particularly encouraging.[11] This probably caused the Red Army high command much concern as it prepared to meet new and larger KMT attacks.

THE NINGTU CONFERENCE

Political developments within the CCP inevitably reflected the heightened concern and anxiety arising from an increasingly menacing environment. In the face of this threat, tensions within the CCP leadership over questions of military policy, organization, and tactics inevitably sharpened. New decisions had to be made.

According to post-Cheng Feng Maoist sources, an important conference of the CCP Central leadership was held at Ningtu, Kiangsi, in August 1932.[12] This meeting, like the First Party Congress of the Central Soviet Area (October-November 1931), allegedly

> . . . maligned the correct line which had been followed in the base areas of southern Kiangsi and western Fukien, describing it as a "rich peasant line" vitiated by "serious mistakes of persistent Right opportunism," and . . . replaced the former correct Party and military leadership.

Nevertheless,

> Thanks to the profound influence of Comrade Mao Tse-tung's correct strategic principles, the Red Army was still able to win victory in the Fourth Campaign against the enemy's "encirclement and annihilation" in the spring of 1933 before it was permeated with the influence of the provisional Central Committee's erroneous line.[13]

Unfortunately, no contemporary records or primary documents of the Ningtu Conference are presently available for study. However, by fitting together bits and pieces of related information we can attempt to enlarge upon the very sketchy reference to it quoted above—and perhaps even evaluate the latter more critically.

A closer look at the military and political context in which the conference was held might furnish a clue as to its main concerns. In the early summer of 1932 the First Front Red Army had again turned to the offensive, following its successful spring expedition into Fukien. In June and July the Communist forces struck first against comparatively weak Kwangtung units pressing against the Central Soviet Area from the south, then launched a series of attacks against towns on the northern perimeter of the base. While these moves were in tune with current Party slogans urging a "positive, offensive" strategy (but warning against "military adventurism" or recklessness) and calling for an unyielding defense of Soviet territory,[14] urgent requirements of the objective situation in themselves furnished a more than adequate stimulus and rationale. There was an immediate need (1) to help relieve KMT pressure on the beleaguered O-yü-wan and Hsiang-o-si bases, and (2) to disrupt the menacing enemy buildup around the Central Area in Kiangsi in order to delay or even preempt the expected massive attack.

Politically, the Ningtu meeting came during a period of organizational reform within the Party apparatus of the Central Soviet Area and preceded organizational changes in the governmental and military establishments. It should be noted, however, that these organizational changes were primarily concerned with the lower levels of Party, governmental, and military units rather than the top leadership.[15] On June 12, the Central Bureau, Soviet Areas, adopted an ambitious program of expansion and reform of the Party ranks (including CCP units in the Red Army), to be carried out before October 1.[16] Declaring that accomplishments since the First Party Congress of the Soviet Area (October-November 1931) had been inadequate and confined to the top leadership, the Central Bureau called for a thoroughgoing transformation of work and an organizational housecleaning from the lower echelons upward.[17] Four days later the Bureau, in response to an aggressive and critical directive from the Party Center, confessed to past errors of Right opportunism in failure to push more forcefully the "line of offensive" and promised, among other things, to reform the lower levels of Soviet leadership.[18]

On July 21 a letter from the Central Committee again called upon the Central Bureau (and Fukien and Kiangsi Provincial Committees) to undertake certain reforms.[19] While superlative in its praise of the Central Soviet Area's "many glorious achievements" obtained "under the correct leadership of the Central Sub-bureau," the missive dealt mainly with some "politically erroneous viewpoints" that were said to be damaging the execution of the general line of the Comintern and CCP.[20] Finally, several tasks were outlined for the Party in the Central area, including the strengthening and consolidation of the Soviets and Red Army, betterment of mass organization work (especially in labor unions and Poor and Lower-Middle Peasant Associations), heightened self-criticism, and improvement of revolutionary efforts in peripheral KMT areas.

This description of the political and military setting suggests that any conference of Party leaders meeting at Ningtu in August must have been preoccupied with the growing threat posed by the Fourth Encirclement Campaign and how to cope with it. In this context, such a gathering probably would have been concerned with organizational reforms to improve both control and performance at the lower levels of Soviet, CCP, and military establishments. It would likely also have espoused the new shadings of interpretation of the Party line insisted upon in recent letters from the Central Committee (reflecting new Comintern emphases), although it is difficult to see how this could have had any great practical impact on policy.[21] In light of the mounting KMT military pressures, it is also possible that such a meeting might have taken unto itself the concrete planning and tactical decisions normally left to the Red Army high command.

Lacking primary documentation of the conference, attempts to reconstruct its agenda and decisions in any detail tend to be highly conjectural.[22] Nevertheless, since the publication of the Maoist version of Party history in 1945, the Ningtu Conference has been accorded a very important, if brief, place in accounts of the CCP's rise to power and Mao's struggle for leadership within it. There seems to be a general agreement among both Communist and non-Communist historians that the conference produced some highly significant organizational and policy changes that ultimately had an adverse effect on the Chinese Communist movement. However, the actual nature and extent of these results may have been exaggerated or misinterpreted. In the following analysis we shall reeaxmine some of the most prominent conclusions that have been reached about the conference and seek to determine their validity in the light of available evidence.

Professor Hsiao Tso-liang, in his pioneering study of the Kiangsi period, contended that the Ningtu meeting "brought about a sweeping change in the leadership of both the Party and the army at the expense of Mao." He argues that there is "good reason to believe that Mao probably lost his military power as a result of the Ningtu Conference . . . though his personal influence in the Red Army apparently continued." Indeed, for Professor Hsiao, it is "impossible to exaggerate the importance of the Ningtu Conference in Chinese Communist annals."[23] Similarly, John Rue has concluded that at the conference Chou En-lai "took the offensive and forced Mao off the Military Committee of the Central Bureau," with the result that afterward Mao's role was limited to work in the Soviet Government.[24] More recently, Dieter Heinzig has emphasized that the whole process of Mao's loss of power in the Communist movement prior to the Fifth Campaign began at Ningtu, where he "de facto lost his dominant position in the Party leadership of the army to Chou En-lai."[25] Finally, Han Suyin, in her recent biography of Mao, declares that after Ningtu "he had no real voice any longer in political or military decisions."[26]

I believe that these conclusions go much too far, particularly in view of the fact that no records of the conference survive and that its importance—or notoriety—became known only in revised, post-Cheng Feng accounts. Let us examine the collateral evidence adduced by the above and other writers on the subject to support the particular claims of what is supposed to have happened at Ningtu. First, the conclusion that the conference resulted in high-level shifts in the Party and Red Army leadership, changes made at Mao's expense.

IMPACT OF NINGTU ON LEADERSHIP
AND ORGANIZATION

In an interview with Edgar Snow in the summer of 1936, Mao recalled:

> From October, 1932, onward, and until the beginning of the Long March to the Northwest, I myself devoted my time almost exclusively to work with the Soviet Government, leaving the military command to Chu Teh and others.[27]

This leaves the impression that Mao relinquished his post as General Political Commissar of the Red Army about October 1932, retaining only the position of Chairman of the Soviet Government.[28] To be sure, he made no mention of any conference at Ningtu as having a bearing on this change and, indeed, it apparently was not made for nearly two months after the August session. The delay could perhaps be explained as resulting from a period of illness said by some sources to have disabled Mao after the Ningtu meeting.[29] If so, however, one wonders why Mao did not date his relinquishment of military command functions as having occurred in August rather than October. In any event, if he actually was relieved as General Political Commissar in October, why was the post apparently not filled by Chou En-lai until the following May?[30]

Moreover, if Mao was forced out of the military leadership at the Ningtu Conference—evidently the most important Party conclave held in 1932, how does one account for the evidence that he was elevated to the Politburo at about the same time?[31] Or what explanation is there for Mao's purported statement in a Cultural Revolution document, "At the Ningtu Conference, Chang Wen-t'ien [and others] wanted to dismiss me, but Chou En-lai and others disagreed"?[32] Moreover, it is necessary to deal with the recent contention of Otto Braun (Li Teh), the Comintern's military adviser in Kiangsi, that Mao continued, despite all criticisms, to play a very influential role in military affairs through his control over the Revolutionary Military Council of the Central Soviet Government, nominally headed by Chu Teh.[33] This evidence seems curiously at variance with Mao's 1945 charge that the Ningtu Conference "replaced the former correct Party and military leadership" in the Central Soviet Area.[34]

If Mao did indeed relinquish his involvement in military decisions in the late fall of 1932, a more plausible argument could be made that he did so voluntarily, in order to concentrate his full attention and energies on the equally pressing—and no less decisive—problems of political and economic mobilization.[35] Certainly, he gave no hint to

Edgar Snow in 1936 that his relinquishment of military command functions after October 1932 had been anything but voluntary. In view of the extremely grave threat posed by Chiang Kai-shek's Fourth Encirclement Campaign, Mao probably realized that his full time and energy were needed to spur the mobilization of the Central Soviet Area. Always acutely sensitive to the primacy of the political factor in armed struggle, Mao may well have reasoned that whatever the Red Army's skill or success on the battlefield, the defense of the Soviet base would surely flounder without a more effective, all-out mobilization effort.[36] If he had been held personally responsible for any previous shortcomings in the defense of the Soviet Area (and, thus, been punished by demotion at Ningtu), it would seem most unlikely that he would have been rewarded by being left in full charge of the vital war mobilization effort.

Since his old comrade-in-arms Chu Teh remained in command of the Red Army, and other trusted lieutenants continued to hold the major subordinate commands, Mao could have made such a move without undue fears that the effective strategy and tactics worked out over previous years of campaigning would suddenly be discarded in favor of rash or unsound military policies. Moreover, while curtailing his activities in the military field after October, Mao might well have actually retained the title of General Political Commissar until Chou En-lai's appointment in May 1933. Although this interpretation challenges the notion that Mao was forced out of the military leadership as a result of the Ningtu Conference, it would not be inconsistent with the later contention that Mao's "correct" influence remained to guide the army to victory in the second phase of the Fourth Encirclement Campaign in the spring of 1933.

If Mao were not forced out at Ningtu and there is no evidence of any sweeping replacement of his supporters in the principal commands (which is the case),[37] perhaps the objectionable "leadership" changes occurred among the lower echelons of the military establishment. It is also possible that the Maoist indictment should be read as referring to the replacement of institutional forms of leadership rather than to the purge of individual leaders. Certainly, no names were mentioned. This hypothesis seems further strengthened by the fact that in 1932 the Red Army's Party committee and soldiers' committee systems were abolished.[38] Both dated from 1927, having been established by Mao and Chu Teh at Chingkangshan.[39] The abolition of the two types of committees, which had functioned from the company level upward, probably tended to decentralize Party control in the army and to increase the power of the political commissars and General Political Department. Since the latter was headed by the returned student Wang Chia-hsiang, and its functions had already been upgraded at the Central Soviet Area Party Congress (October-November 1931),

it is entirely possible that Mao had some misgivings about the abandonment of the committee system. However, no statement of his views
on the subject is available, although a pre-Cultural Revolution article
by Ho Lung charged that this institutional change had "grave adverse
effects" on the Red Army's "combat activities and on army building."[40]

IMPACT OF NINGTU ON MILITARY POLICY

It has been argued by some historians that the Ningtu Conference, besides making changes in the leadership (whether personal
or institutional), also ordered a new military strategy. According to
Professor Jerome Ch'en, the meeting was convened "in preparation
against the imminent attack of KMT forces against the Central Soviet
Area." Terming it a "conference of the party, army, and government
leaders" (Mao had referred to it as a meeting of the "Party Center"
exclusively), Professor Ch'en continues:

> . . . Mao went straight to the conference from a cam-
> paign in Fukien where at Chang-chow he had cut Chang
> Chen's division to pieces. But again he was severely
> criticized. After that he fell ill, and whatever military
> power he had retained was taken over by Chou En-lai as
> the general political commissar of the Red Army and
> concurrently of the 1st front Army. . . . At the Conference,
> Mao insisted on following the same strategy as the pre-
> vious three campaigns, but Chou En-lai and Liu Po-ch'eng,
> backed by the party centre, prevailed with their plan of
> "halting the enemy beyond the gate."[41]

Unfortunately, this account goes far beyond anything warranted by the
evidence adduced to support it and is in conflict with several established facts. Mao could hardly have gone "straight" to a meeting in
August from a campaign that was concluded in April or early May.
It is doubtful that he had been with the expedition at Changchow, much
less "cut Chang Chen's division to pieces." While it is not clear from
the passage quoted above whether his illness was connected with the
criticism he is said to have received at the conference, we have seen
that he did not relinquish the post of Red Army Political Commissar
to Chou En-lai until the late fall of 1932, at the earliest, or very possibly not until May 1933. I am unable to find clear and persuasive
evidence of any strategic debate or severe criticism of Mao at Ningtu
in the secondary sources cited by Professor Ch'en.[42] Moreover, the
sources referred to provide no evidence that Chou En-lai and Liu
Po-ch'eng (not mentioned), "backed by the party centre," advanced a

plan for "halting the enemy beyond the gate"—much less sold it to the Ningtu Conference (not mentioned).[43]

However, a similar interpretation has been advanced by Warren Kuo, who describes the Ningtu Conference as the scene of a major strategic debate between Mao and Chou En-lai. Relying on the testimony of Ch'en Jan (an ex-Communist, now in Taiwan, who apparently was not present at the meeting), Kuo portrays a debate in which Mao opposed further Red Army preemptive attacks on KMT-held towns north and west of the Soviet base, arguing that the earlier failure to capture Kanchow (followed by the successful March offensive into Fukien) now dictated a defensive strategy of "luring the enemy to penetrate deep." Chou and the other political and military leaders, however, regarded Mao's strategy as outmoded in the new situation and argued for enlarging the Red Army, increasing its effectiveness by emphasizing improvements in military technique, and going ahead with the planned attacks on the weakened KMT defense line north and west of the Soviet base. In the end, "Mao was compelled to give up his ideas in the face of unanimous opposition" and the Red Army adopted a "preventive strategy" of attacks northward to counter the imminent KMT encirclement offensive.[44]

Elements of this analysis can, of course, be corroborated from documentary evidence. However, in certain key points the interpretation seems questionable or doubtful. It is a matter of record, of course, that in late May Chou had argued for launching attacks in White areas to seek out and destroy KMT units, rather than waiting passively for their concentration and invasion or even employing the formerly useful, but now outmoded, tactics of "luring the enemy to penetrate deep." However, he also opposed the slogan "defend the borders," emphasizing instead the necessity for mobility and seizure of the initiative.[45] Besides, if Chou and Liu had overruled Mao and "prevailed with their plan" at the Ningtu Conference, as Jerome Ch'en and Warren Kuo conclude, how could Mao later have claimed that his own "correct strategic principles" were still sufficiently influential to allow victory over the Fourth Encirclement Campaign in the spring of 1933 ?[46] Finally, although the Communist propaganda continued to adopt a "forward and offensive" tone on the rhetorical level, the actual behavior of the Red Army after Ningtu was relatively cautious and restrained. Communist attacks northward against KMT-held towns never reached the scale and intensity of those launched successfully in Fukien the previous spring.[47] Indeed, there is no evidence that the strategy employed after Ningtu either resulted in losses to the Soviet base, through failure to take prudent defensive measures, or led to complete abandonment of the venerated guerrilla tactics through the remainder of the campaign.

THE POLITICAL SIGNIFICANCE OF NINGTU:
A REASSESSMENT

Aside from any military or leadership decisions that may have been made at the Ningtu Conference, it is possible that the topic of agrarian policy figured to some extent in the deliberations. According to Mao, this meeting and the Central Soviet Area Party Congress (October-November 1931) were used as a forum by "Left" deviationists to malign the "correct" line previously followed in the base areas of Kiangsi and Fukien as a "rich peasant line." However, while the earlier meeting was followed by the enactment of important new agrarian measures, the Ningtu session apparently had no such result. This leads me to believe that Mao's indictment was intended to apply primarily to the former rather than the latter meeting. Moreover, CCP reports in the spring of 1932, far from accusing local Soviet leaders of following a "rich peasant line," evinced satisfaction with the way land reform measures were being carried out in the Communist areas of Fukien and Kiangsi.[48] Besides, Mao had not been above using the "rich peasant line" to tar his opponents after the Fut'ien Incident (December 1930) and was to use this issue approvingly again in 1933.

Whatever may have happened at the Ningtu Conference, the fact that a CCP Central leadership meeting convened there in August 1932 was extremely significant as an indication of the growing size and importance of the Party leadership located in the Central Soviet base. It was not a plenary session of the Committee, of course, and the Central Committeemen in attendance may have included few of those not already resident in Kiangsi as members of the Central Bureau, Soviet Areas. The "provisional" central leadership, including the secretariat and "temporary politburo," probably remained in Shanghai until the spring of 1933. Nevertheless, some of its members might have traveled to Kiangsi for this occasion, perhaps to remain permanently.[49]

The fact that a meeting of the Central leadership was held at Ningtu, rather than Shanghai, at this time also probably tended to demonstrate the increased importance of the Soviet Government and Red Army as institutions of power distinct from the Party apparatus. The Party needed them more than they needed it. To an ever-increasing extent, the interests and problems of the Chinese Communist movement were synonymous with the interests and problems of the Soviets and Red Armies.

One revealing indication of the power of the Soviet administration vis-à-vis the Party apparatus, to which it was technically subordinate, may be found in the direct and growing role it played in the non-Soviet or White areas. It sent delegates to Shanghai to organize "a special apparatus" to foster direct connections with anti-imperialist

groups and to participate actively in mass demonstrations.[50] It provided vital financial support for the Shanghai-based Party organization, an increasingly critical factor in the latter's continued operation
as Comintern assistance dwindled and Moscow moved toward a diplomatic rapproachement with Nanking. Communist Party membership
outside the Soviet areas was but a tiny fraction of that in the rural
bases (perhaps 5 or 10 percent of total CCP strength), and even the
direction of the limited Party work still carried on in the KMT regions
was increasingly transferred to leaders and organs in the Soviet districts.[51] Well before the Ningtu Conference the Central Committee
acknowledged the preponderant role and power of the Soviets in the
Chinese Communist movement in a passage of its resolution on the
Fourth Campaign:

> The Soviets not only are the leaders and organizers of
> the worker-peasant revolution in the Soviet areas, but
> also are the leaders and organizers of the revolutionary
> movement in the non-Soviet areas.[52]

In these circumstances it is difficult to believe that the veteran
Soviet leaders Mao and Chu could have suffered a loss of power to the
youthful, urban-oriented returned students in the Party hierarchy.
While the increased size of the Central Soviet Area and the growing
complexity and urgency of its problems in late 1932 clearly suggested
the desirability of a greater division of labor among the Communist
leadership, I can find no persuasive evidence that Mao was forced
aside and the responsibility for critical decisions seized by less capable hands. Certainly, he retained all his prerogatives as Chairman
of the Chinese Soviet Republic and its Central Government. Addi-
tionally, he was elevated to the Politburo of the CCP, hardly an indication of declining power. And, whatever his formal position in the Red
Army after October, his influence through trusted lieutenants and
proven ideas was to remain decisive through the Fourth Encirclement
Campaign, if not longer.

LATER APPLICATIONS

The Maoist historical revisionism begun in the early 1940s and
exhibited in the reinterpretation of significant events in the Party's
past experience, such as the Ningtu Conference, was to have profound
consequences for the CCP's later development in both the Revolutionary
and post-Revolutionary periods. The immediate effect was to legitimize
Mao's leadership and authority in the Party, and that of his supporters,
against all potential rivals and external influences, including the

possibility of Stalinist intervention in CCP affairs after the war against Japan.

By absolving Mao of any responsibility in the earlier defeat of the Kiangsi Soviet (since his "correct" guidance had been thrust aside, beginning at Ningtu), the new historical line helped build a needed confidence in the Yenan leadership and an unshakable faith in ultimate victory. This was especially important for the cadres and rank-and-file membership, the vast majority of whom had been recruited after the Long March. Beyond the Party, the suggestion of Mao's infallibility and invariable success had an important charismatic appeal for the broad, non-Communist masses, giving him in time the stature of a great popular leader and folk hero.

After the defeat of the Kuomintang and establishment of the People's Republic of China in 1949, the claims for applicability of Mao's revolutionary doctrines and leadership were further elaborated and expanded. The "thought of Mao Tse-tung," extolled in the Cheng Feng movement and the CCP Constitution of 1945, was virtually canonized with the publication of his well-edited Selected Works beginning in 1951. Chinese reviews of the latter praised his "heroically creative genius" in integrating the principles of Marxism-Leninism with the practice of the Chinese revolution and compared his theoretical contribution to that of Lenin and Stalin, a point of view not fully appreciated in the Soviet Union.[53] Mao's theory of revolution was soon portrayed as having an applicability far beyond China and Asia to all colonial and semicolonial countries, giving it a universal significance for the world Communist movement.

The authority implied in such ambitious claims of course necessitated full acceptance of the legitimacy of Mao's historical leadership. The official story of his rise to power, depicted as a continuing struggle between his "correct" line and the "Left" or "Right" opportunism of his rivals, became an essential element in the Maoist ideology, a foundation upon which to rest his and the Party's post-Revolutionary policies and pretensions to leadership. It has remained to fill this vital legitimizing function for the regime, despite subsequent divisions in the leadership over the contemporary role of Mao and the applicability of his thought in concrete policies.

In the mid-1950s erosion of support for Mao's policies within the CCP hierarchy was indicated by deletion of the phrase "the thought of Mao Tse-tung" from the Eighth Party Constitution.[54] This conflict deepened in the 1960s as the leadership divided over competing strategies of national development and the relevance of Mao's thought as a concrete guide to action.[55] However, in the Cultural Revolution, Mao was able to reassert his authority and command over the power structure by mobilizing overwhelming popular support on the basis of the enormous prestige and unquestioning faith in the legitimacy of his leadership built up over the years. Thus the Constitutions adopted by the Ninth and Tenth CCP Congresses in 1969 and 1973, while failing to settle many practical issues of policy and succession in the leadership, have firmly reestablished the guiding role of Mao's thought over the Party, very much as the Seventh Congress affirmed it in 1945 following promulgation of the Maoist historical legend.[56]

NOTES

1. See the Central Committee's "Resolution on Some Questions in the History of Our Party" in Mao Tse-tung, Selected Works of Mao Tse-tung, III (Peking: Foreign Languages Press, 1965), pp. 177-225. Hereafter cited as SW. The Chinese text appears in Mao Tse-tung hsüan-chi (Selected works of Mao Tse-tung), III (Peking: Jen-min ch'u-pan she, 1953), pp. 955-1002. Subsequent writings on Party history have conformed to this interpretation while adding details.

2. In a key rectification document Liu Shao-ch'i, then Mao's trusted lieutenant, declared that "twenty-two years of bitter and complex revolutionary struggle" had led the Party to find its leader in Mao and, indeed, that the CCP's history had "developed with Mao Tse-tung as a center." Liu exhorted all cadres and Party members to engage in diligent study of history and try to master Mao's "system of thought" in order to liquidate traces of error. Liu Shao-ch'i, "Liquidation of Menshevik Thought in the Party," in Boyd Compton, trans., Mao's China: Party Reform Documents, 1942-44 (Seattle: University of Washington Press, 1952), pp. 256, 267.

3. Mao Tse-tung, SW, III, p. 193; Mao Tse-tung hsüan-chi, III, pp. 971-72. Emphasis added.

4. See Compton, op. cit., xxix, xlv; also Stuart Schram, Mao Tse-tung (rev. ed.; Baltimore: Penguin, 1967), pp. 220-22, 233.

5. Jerome Ch'en, "The Development and Logic of Mao Tse-tung's Thought, 1928-49," in Chalmers Johnson, ed., Ideology and Politics in Contemporary China (Seattle: University of Washington Press, 1973), p. 93.

6. Conrad Brandt, Benjamin Schwartz, and John K. Fairbank, A Documentary History of Chinese Communism (Cambridge: Harvard University Press, 1952), p. 422.

7. Schram, op. cit., p. 233.

8. Lucien W. Pye, The Spirit of Chinese Politics (Cambridge, Mass.: MIT Press, 1968), p. 192.

9. Richard H. Solomon, Mao's Revolution and the Chinese Political Culture (Berkeley: University of California Press, 1971), p. 87.

10. According to a CCP analysis published in November 1933, the Red Army "annihilated" nearly twice the number of KMT forces

in 1932 than it had in the previous year (which covered the period of the first three Encirclement Campaigns). The Communists claimed to have wiped out over 106,000 White troops in 1932 (including 6 divisions, 12 brigades, and 6 regiments) and to have captured 71,000 officers and enlisted men. Allowing for probable exaggeration, these figures (taken from an internal Party organ rather than a propaganda statement) suggest that the Communists perceived Chiang Kai-shek to be willing to sustain large casualties in pursuit of his anti-Red pacification effort. Hai Lang, "Fen-sui wu-tz'u 'wei-chiao' yü fan-ch'ing-hsiang tou-cheng" (The struggle to smash the Fifth 'Encirclement-Annihilation' and to oppose deviations), Tou-cheng (Struggle) no. 34 (Nov. 12, 1933): 8.

11. In August 1932, elements of the Eighth Red Army operating in the Hunan-Kiangsi border area (under P'eng Teh-huai's Third Corps) attacked a KMT blockhouse situated on a mountain near Fen-i, Kiangsi. Wang Chen, Political Commissar of the Army, led a squad of nine men in the initial assault on the fortress. All nine were killed and Wang was seriously wounded. However, the Communists proceeded to surround the bottom of the mountain and fought a pitched battle with the KMT garrison until it was reinforced by the arrival of four regiments. The battered Red troops then retreated, with approximately 300 killed and wounded. Wang later recalled that despite being so badly defeated, the Communists lost no guns and captured 50 or 60 enemy rifles. See his interview with Nym Wales in Red Dust (Stanford: Stanford University Press, 1952), p. 99. Though conceding that the defending KMT regiment had badly defeated the Red attackers, it should be noted that Wang—as late as mid-1937—apparently found no error in the tactical decision to attack the stronghold.

12. The precise organizational nature of the Conference remains obscure and somewhat confused. The 1945 Central Committee resolution on Party history referred to this as the "Ningtu Conference of the Party Center" (Tang chung-yang ti Ning-tu hui-i). Mao Tse-tung hsüan-chi, III, p. 968. This was later translated "the Ningtu meeting of the Central Committee" in a semiofficial English version of the resolution. See SW, IV (New York: International Publishers, 1956), p. 185. This translation seems to imply an informal and, possibly, enlarged meeting of those Central Committeemen then in the Central Soviet area but something less than a formal convocation of a quorum of the Central Committee. However, in 1965 the Peking Foreign Languages Press translation of the 1945 resolution spoke of the conference as "the Ningtu Meeting of the Central Bureau of the Red Base Areas" (the highest Party organ probably then functioning in the Central Soviet base). SW, III, p. 190. Warren Kuo, relying on the recollection of Chen Jan (an ex-Communist defector now in Taiwan) refers to the Ningtu Conference as an enlarged meeting of the CCP's

Central Bureau of the Soviet Areas (CBSA). He says it was attended by members of the CBSA, the Military Council, the "political department"[?], and representatives from the Kiangsi Military Zone, and the First, Third, and Fifth Armies. Ningtu, scene of the famous revolt of the KMT 26th Route Army in December 1931, was chosen as the site for the conference because it was more convenient to the war front for military commanders. Their participation was needed because the conference would plan strategy to deal with the threatening KMT offensive. Warren Kuo, Analytical History of Chinese Communist Party, II (Taipei: Institute of International Relations, 1968), p. 441.

13. SW, IV, 185-86; Mao Tse-tung hsüan-chi, III, pp. 968-69.

14. The contemporary meaning and implications of these slogans, as well as their later distortion, are examined in detail in an unpublished paper by William F. Dorrill entitled "Mao and the 'Offensive Line': A Reconsideration," which was presented at the 22nd Annual Meeting of the Association for Asian Studies (San Francisco, April 1970).

15. As early as January 9 a Central Committee resolution had called for "rebuilding" (kai-tsao) of lower-level units of the Soviet. Shih-hua [True words] no. 3 (Apr. 20, 1932): 10.

16. "Fa-chan tang ho kai-tsao tang ti kung-tso ta-kang" (Outline for Party development and Party reform), Tang ti Chien-she (Kiangsi) no. 2 (June 15, 1932): 1-30.

17. Noting that at the time of the First Soviet Area Party Congress, CCP membership in Kiangsi was 15,000 and in Western Fukien 5,000—these figures having risen by 8,000 and 1,700-1,800, respectively, by March 1932—the Central Bureau called for the addition by October 1 of 20,000 new Party members in the Kiangsi Soviet Area and 8,000 new members in the Fukien-Kwangtung-Kiangsi Area, as well as for doubling in the Hunan-Kiangsi and Hunan-Hupeh-Kiangsi Areas. At least one-third of the new members were to be women. Improvement of the leadership methods and cadre cultivation were also stressed. The Bureau complained that except for a few Hsién [counties] (such as Hsing-kuo, Kan-hsien, Juichin), CCP branch and local Party headquarters units were weak and inept at mobilizing mass strength, often becoming "the tail of the masses" in such important work as enlarging the Red Army and participation in fighting. The style of leadership was said to be removed from the masses. Tang ti Chien-she (Kiangsi) no. 2 (June 15, 1932): 1-4.

18. The resolution also called for enlarging and strengthening discipline and political leadership in the Red Army. "Chung-yang chih-shih tien yu chung-yang-chu kuan-yu cheng-chu ho wan-ch'eng Chiang-hsi chi ch'i lin-chin sheng-ch'u ko-ming shou-hsien sheng-li ti chueh-i" (Directive telegram of the Central and resolution of the Central Bureau in regard to winning and achieving preliminary

victories of the Revolution in Kiangsi and its neighboring provinces).
The Central Bureau resolution was dated June 16; the Central Committee directive, May 21, 1932. The text has been reproduced (photo-
copy) in Hsiao Tso-liang, Power Relations Within the Chinese Communist Movement 1931-1934, II (Seattle: University of Washington
Press, 1967), pp. 611-20. A brief summary appears in vol. I of the
same work (1961), 209-10.

19. "Chung-yang chi su-ch'u chung-yang-chu chi Min Kan liang
sheng-wei hsin" (Letter of the Central Committee to the Central
Bureau of the Soviet Areas and the two Provincial Committees of
Fukien and Kiangsi), Shih-hua no. 8 (Sept. 20, 1932): 1-9.

20. Among the "glorious achievements" were "the establishment of the Central Soviet Government and its increasingly strong
leadership of the revolutionary movement throughout the nation,"
"the expansion of the Soviet area and occupation of Changchow," and
"enlargement of the Red Army." Ibid., p. 1. Among the politically
erroneous viewpoints criticized were inadequate appreciation of the
imperialist threat to the Soviet Union and failure to understand that
in the Fourth Campaign the imperialists were preparing large military
forces for direct attacks on the Soviet Areas. The reference to the
"correct leadership of the Central Sub-bureau" is somewhat puzzling,
particularly since the letter was addressed to the higher-level Central
Bureau and lower-level Provincial Committees but made no mention
of a Sub-bureau. We know that Sub-bureaus managed CCP affairs in
the O-yü-wan and Hsiang-o-si Soviet Areas, and it is possible that
a sub-bureau functioned also in the Central Area directly below the
Central Bureau, Soviet Areas. If so, it was clearly overshadowed
by the Central Bureau, which played a direct and dominant role in
Kiangsi and Fukien.

21. Beginning in early 1932, Comintern statements reflected
growing apprehension of the threat to the Soviet Union posed by the
Japanese invasion of Manchuria. See Charles McLane, Soviet Policy
and the Chinese Communists 1931-1946 (New York: Columbia University Press, 1958), pp. 48-49. Long before the Mukden Incident,
of course, the Comintern had expressed general fears of a new imperialist attack on the Soviet Union—most recently in the April 1931
Resolution of the Eleventh Plenum of the Executive Committee of the
Cominterm. Accordingly, CCP statements from September 1931 on
had given undue attention to the Japanese threat to the Soviet Union
and the corollary slogans stressing its defense. These became all
the more necessary as Moscow's alarm over Japanese intentions grew
during 1932. While this concern for the Soviet Union in CCP propaganda may have limited its patriotic appeal to the Chinese masses
to some extent, I am unable to find that it seriously hindered either
the development or the defense of the Soviet Areas. Similarly, the

talk of direct imperialist intervention during the Fourth Campaign, while constituting a likely topic for discussion at Party conclaves in the summer of 1932, probably did not result in overweening complacency about the immediate KMT military threat.

22. Even the mysterious Ch'en Jan, whose personal recollections are so often used by Warren Kuo to fill in the gaps in documentary information, appears to reconstruct his story of the conference basically out of inferences from published Communist statements (such as those cited in the analysis above) rather than firsthand observations. Occasional suggestions of more direct knowledge are, on closer reading, usually inferable statements and many are less than convincing. Kuo, op. cit., II, pp. 441-48.

23. Hsiao Tso-liang, op. cit., I, pp. 210-11.

24. John E. Rue, Mao Tse-tung in Opposition, 1927-1935 (Stanford: Stanford University Press, 1966), p. 253.

25. Dieter Heinzig, "The Otto Braun Memoirs and Mao's Rise to Power," China Quarterly no. 46 (Apr.-June 1971): 279.

26. Han Suyin, The Morning Deluge: Mao Tse-tung and the Chinese Revolution, 1893-1954 (Boston: Little, Brown, 1972), p. 247.

27. Edgar Snow, Red Star Over China (New York: Random House, Modern Library ed., 1944), p. 185.

28. This was also implied in a biographical sketch of Mao published in Hong Kong in 1950, which dated his tenure as "General Political Commissar" of the Chinese Red Army as running from 1930 to 1932. Hsin Chung-kuo Jen-wu chih (Biographies of new China) (Hong Kong: Chou-mo pao-she, 1950), p. 5.

29. Hsiao Tso-liang quotes a KMT source to the effect that Mao left his post in the Red Army after the Ningtu meeting, pleading illness, in order to give way to Chou En-lai—who proceeded swiftly to take full control. See Power Relations, I, p. 211. More recently, Jerome Ch'en has quoted a "recollection" of Nelson Fu (Fu Lienchang) that in the autumn of 1932, after the Ningtu Conference, Mao fell ill and Fu ordered him to be hospitalized for four months. It is not clear whether Mao actually did this. See Jerome Ch'en, Mao and the Chinese Revolution (London: Oxford University Press, 1965), pp. 176-77.

30. Hsiao Tso-liang contends that Chou became political commissar of the Red Army only on May 8, 1933—while Chu Teh, by the same governmental decision, continued to be its commander-in-chief. Power Relations, I, p. 220. In fairness to his argument, however, it ought to be pointed out that the language of the governmental resolution appointing Chou is the same as that used to appoint Chu Teh. See Hung-se Chung-hua no. 78 (May 11, 1933): 1. In both cases the term jen-ming (to appoint) is employed, and in neither case does the term tsai-jen-ming (to reappoint) or an equivalent appear. Thus,

to judge from this document alone, that Chou—no less than Chu Teh—
could have not previously been identified as General Political Commissar in the available evidence (although he was a prolific writer
of signed articles) leads me to agree with Professor Hsiao that his
first appointment to the post probably did not occur until May 8, 1933.
The fact that no one else was identified as holding the position prior
to that makes it appear that Mao continued, at least formally, in tenure.

31. Mao had originally been elected to the Politburo in 1924
(Snow, op. cit., p. 166), but subsequently lost even alternate Politburo
standing in November 1927. He may well have won and lost Politburo
membership again in the period 1928-31; available evidence is in-
conclusive on this possibility. However, an official biographical sketch
published at Peking in 1951 stated: "Since 1932, he has been a member
of the Political Bureau of the Central Committee of the Communist
Party of China." It made no mention of either a Ningtu Conference
or Mao's prior membership in the Politburo. See "A Biographical
Note on Mao Tse-tung," People's China 6, no. 1 (July 1, 1951): 27.
While repeating the widely held view that, after Ningtu, Mao "yielded
real power" even in the Soviet Government to others, James P. Harrison notes the contrary indication of "three seemingly authoritative
reports of Mao's election to the Political Bureau in January, 1933."
See his The Long March to Power (New York: Praeger, 1972), pp.
229, 566 note.

32. Quoted in Harrison, op. cit., p. 230. Harrison, however,
notes evidence that Chang Wen-t'ien generally supported Mao against
Chou En-lai. Ibid., p. 566.

33. The Revolutionary Military Council (or "Commission"—
wei-yuan-hui), according to Braun, exercised the top direction over
military affairs in the Central Soviet Area, easily eclipsing in power
the Military Commission of the CCP Central Committee under Chou
En-lai, which remained impotent prior to the Long March. See the
account of Braun's recollections in Heinzig, op. cit., pp. 280-81.

34. SW, IV, p. 185; Mao Tse-tung hsüan-chi, III, p. 969. It is
even more difficult to reconcile Han Suyin's statement that "at Ningtu,
Mao Tse-tung was finally deprived of control over the Red Army,
right in the middle of the fourth campaign" (The Morning Deluge, p.
253 and, a few pages earlier that ". . . Mao was not deprived of control [over the Red Army] till the end of 1932" and, hence, the "erroneous" line of his opponents could not be applied until the following
year, after success in the Fourth Campaign. Ibid., p. 248.

35. A more recent example of somewhat parallel behavior,
in the face of frustration and difficulty in the objective situation, might
have been Mao's withdrawal to the less active "second line" of Politburo leadership (behind Liu Shao-chi'i's "front line") and relinquishment of his position as Chairman of the People's Republic in 1958.

The author has developed this hypothesis in greater detail in "Power, Policy, and Ideology in the Making of China's 'Cultural Revolution,'" in Thomas Robinson, ed., The Cultural Revolution in China (Berkeley: University of California Press, 1971), pp. 29-30.

36. Robert Payne's biography of Mao, while not generally recommended for its historical accuracy, provides an interesting insight here. He observes that after the Third Encirclement Campaign, despite the victory and continuing growth of the Communist movement, there was a loss of "original vitality" and development of "a curious sense of apathy, arising perhaps from the failure of the revolutionaries to solve the economic problems of the border regions." With the approach of winter in 1932, Payne continues (and the increasingly menacing KMT military threat as well as the loss of O-yü-wan and Hsiang-o-si, he might have added), "Mao decided that the time had come for a complete re-evaluation of policies; he abandoned his role as military commander and set about creating a new survey of conditions in the Soviet areas under his control." Robert Payne, Portrait of a Revolutionary: Mao Tse-tung (rev. ed.; London: Abelard-Schuman, 1961), p. 129.

In 1937 Chu Teh emphasized the critical impact of worsening economic problems on Communist preparations to meet the second stage of the Fourth Encirclement Campaign. By the spring of 1933, he recalled, "The Kiangsi economic situation for the army was not good because we had already expropriated all the landlords and had no further sources of revenue in this way." Quoted in Nym Wales, Inside Red China (New York: Doubleday, Doran, 1939), p. 256.

37. The most important command change after the Ningtu Conference appears to have been the appointment of Hsiao K'e, in September, to command the Sixth Red Army, operating in the Hunan-Kiangsi border region. This could hardly be interpreted as a returned student move against Mao, since Hsiao had served faithfully under Mao, Chu Teh, and P'eng Teh-huai since the formation of the old Fourth Red Army at Chingkangshan. Besides, the Sixth Red Army (new designation of the former Eighth Army) was badly in need of new leadership. In August 1932, both the commander, Li T'ien-chu, and the political commissar, Wang Chen, of this force had been wounded. It had suffered some 300 casualities in a futile attack on a KMT blockhouse near Fen-i. (See note 11 above.) Wang Chen later recalled, "The soldiers and political workers all had confidence in Hsiao K'e and Ts'ai Fei-wen [the new Political Commissar], since these two had been sent to us from the Central Soviet Government." Quoted in Nym Wales, Red Dust (Stanford: Stanford University Press, 1952), pp. 99, 138.

38. See SW, V (New York: International Publishers, 1962), p. 271.

39. Writing at Chingkangshan in 1928, Mao noted that Party committees were to be found at the army, regimental, and battalion levels, while each company had a Party branch. At the same time, soldiers' committees, under the leadership of officers, played an important role in hearing grievances and protecting the interests of the troops (for instance, seeing to their needs in food and clothing). SW, I (New York: (International Publishers, 1956), pp. 73, 83.

40. Ho Lung, "Democratic Tradition of the Chinese People's Liberation Army," Peking Review no. 32 (Aug. 6, 1965): 13-14. While Ho Lung did not give the exact date for the termination of the Party committee system in the Red Army, he maintained that it had occurred during the reign of the "third Left line," led by Wang Ming. The Party committee system was partially restored—in the form of military and political committees—during the war against Japan and fully restored on all levels with certain "improvements" about 1947. The soldiers' committees were restored at the company level at about the same time. See SW, I, p. 305; V, p. 271. To judge from Ho Lung's analysis, written nearly a quarter of a century later, the abolition of the Party committee system in the army opened the way for "individual arbitrariness" on the part of the leadership and undermined "collective leadership" and "democracy." However, no concrete manifestations of these ill effects were identified.

41. Ch'en, Mao and the Chinese Revolution, pp. 176-77.

42. The works cited are Hsiao Tso-liang, op. cit., I, pp. 220-21; and Ku Kuan-chiao, San-shih-nien lai ti chung-kung (The CCP in the last thirty years) (Hong Kong: Ya-chou ch'u-pan'-she, 1955), p. 76. Professor Ch'en admits (op. cit., p. 402) that the latter work was written as a rebuttal to Hu Ch'iao-mu's semiofficial CCP history published in 1951.

43. The works referred to are SW, I, p. 214 (Mao Tse-tung hsüan-chi, I, p. 200); and Hsiao Tso-liang, op. cit., I, p. 218. The latter source discusses documents published in mid-1933 that pertained to the Fifth Encirclement Campaign. The former source, a page from the revised edition of Mao's December 1936 military lectures, includes among a number of objectionable slogans for dealing with KMT attacks the phrase "Halt the enemy beyond the gate" (Yü ti yü kuo-men chih wai). It does not specifically relate the advocacy of this slogan to the Fourth Campaign, and says nothing about any Ningtu Conference. Assuming the authenticity of the passage as originally published (which is open to serious question), I am inclined to believe the objectionable phrase was intended to apply primarily, if not exclusively, to the Fifth Campaign. This was certainly the case when the slogan was mentioned again in a later passage. SW, I, pp. 220-21; Mao Tse-tung hsüan-chi, I, p. 205.

44. Kuo, op. cit., II, pp. 444-46. William Whitson offers a similar account of the military debate at Ningtu that portrays Mao as the target of attacks by both Party and army leaders (such as Liu Po-ch'eng, P'eng Teh-huai, and even Lin Piao) over a wide range of issues, from strategy and tactics ("adventurism," "guerrillaism," "escapism") to military organization and commander-commissar functions. William W. Whitson, The Chinese High Command (New York: Praeger, 1973), pp. 57-58, 147, 527.

45. Chou En-lai, "Yung-hu ch'uan-kuo hung-chün ti sheng-li, chien-chüeh chih-hsing chi-chi chin-kung ti lu-hsien" (Uphold the nationwide victories of the Red Army, resolutely carry out the positive offensive line), Shih-hua no. 5 (May 30, 1932): 1-4.

46. The official Maoist claim also runs counter to Whitson's contention that Mao "probably had little influence on defense planning against the Fourth Encirclement Campaign." See The Chinese High Command, p. 58.

47. Communist attacks in the late summer and fall of 1932, while smaller in scale than the Fukien expedition that culminated in the capture of Changchow, did permit a further consolidation and expansion of the Soviet base. However, the territory contested was remote from important population centers and lines of communication, and thus posed no immediate threat to the Nanking regime. The towns being stormed and seized tended to be small and rather insignificant; as Mao later acknowledged: "There was not a single medium-sized town among them." SW, V, pp. 17-18.

48. According to a CCP letter from Shanghai, the agrarian revolution in the West Fukien Soviet was proceeding in a correct manner after overcoming past landlord-kulak threats. It reported: "The Party organizations have increased their activity in drawing together the proletariat and the poor elements of the population." Moreover, they had "simultaneously thwarted kulak plots to foment excessive land struggle so as to cause an anti-Soviet reaction among the middle peasants." Inprecor 12, no. 15 (Mar. 31, 1932): 296. A Soviet report from northeastern Kiangsi about this same time noted that the "correct agrarian policy" carried out in that area had heightened the fighting enthusiasm of the poor peasants. Ibid., 12, no. 26 (June 9, 1932): 536-37.

49. Among them may have been Liu Shao-ch'i, whose pre-Cultural Revolution biography records that he went to the Kiangsi base in the autumn of 1932 and "took charge of the workers' movement in the Red areas." It also indicates that he was elevated to membership in the Politburo in 1932. This could have occurred at the Ningtu meeting, as was suggested above in the similar case of Mao. Any decision to add members to the Politburo, however, would have had to be made beforehand by that organ itself, and it apparently continued

to sit in Shanghai. For biographical details on Liu Shao-ch'i, see his On the Party, (3rd ed.; Peking: Foreign Languages Press, 1951), pp. 187-88.

50. According to a CCP report from Shanghai (which quoted Hung-ch'i of Jan. 18, 1932, as a source), the Central Soviet Government and various local Soviets dispatched these delegates to Shanghai shortly after the first National-Soviet Congress met. "All this clearly demonstrates the influence of the Soviet power as the spearhead of the anti-imperialist movement," the CCP report concluded. See Inprecor 12, no. 22 (May 19, 1932): 429.

51. In December 1933, Wang Ming told the 13th Plenum of the ECCI that CCP membership had reached a level of 300,000 in 1932. However, he admitted that only 30,000 of these were in the KMT areas and that half of even this number, some 15,000 members, had "no constant contact with the Party as a result of the White terror." Ibid. 14, no. 7 (Feb. 5, 1934): 199.

52. "Because of this," it continues, "the Party organs of the various Soviet areas must appoint Party members to mobilize the White areas which surround the Soviet areas. . . ." The resolution contained an exhortation to "build many guerrilla troops." If the Central Committee lacked a proper appreciation of the importance of guerrilla warfare, it certainly was not revealed in the resolution. For passages of the June 21, 1932, resolution quoted above, see Ko-ming yü chan-cheng (Revolution and war) no. 1 (Aug. 1, 1932): leaf 9.

53. Philip Bridgham, Arthur Cohen, and Leonard Jaffee, "Mao's Road and Sino-Soviet Relations: A View From Washington, 1953," China Quarterly no. 52 (Oct.-Dec. 1972): 672-75.

54. See text in John W. Lewis, ed., Major Doctrines of Communist China (New York: Norton, 1964), pp. 115-39; also Stuart Schram, "The Party in Chinese Communist Ideology," in John W. Lewis, ed., Party Leadership and Revolutionary Power in China (London: Cambridge University Press, 1970), pp. 185-86.

55. Solomon, op. cit., pp. 265-67, 431-32, 458-59.

56. See text of Constitution adopted by Ninth Party Congress in K. Fan, Mao Tse-tung and Lin Piao: Post-Revolutionary Writings (Garden City, N.Y.: Doubleday Anchor, 1972), pp. 529-36; and text adopted by Tenth Congress in Current Background no. 994 (Hong Kong: American Consulate-General, Sept. 20, 1973): 38-44.

CHAPTER

4

THE MAOIST MODEL:
APPEAL, RELEVANCE,
AND APPLICABILITY
George T. Yu

In this study, we are discussing a number of important aspects of "Maoism" in operation, under the general rubric of "Maoist model." They include, among other things, the Maoist mode of capturing political power (war of national liberation), a particular strategy of sociopolitical change and development, and a way of conducting China's diplomacy, in an age of great flux and fluidity, away from Cold War confrontation.

The term "Third World," used repeatedly in this study, denotes generally those nations in Africa, Asia, and Latin America that are consciously seeking (or at least are open to) an alternative ideology and/or sociopolitical system to that embraced by the Soviet Union or the United States. We use the term "model" in this case to suggest more than a static abstraction of a reality or body of experience because we take an incremental view of the essential strategies, tenets, and programs generally associated with, and made distinct, by its principal architect, Chairman Mao Tse-tung.

Since the coming to power of the Chinese Communist Party and the founding of the People's Republic of China in 1949, few issues have been subject to more discussion and controversy than the Maoist model. The model or specific features of it have been both condemned and praised. Consider, for example, the wars of national liberation or "people's war" formula. On the one hand, there have been those who have seen the formula as the key to China's foreign policy of subversion; on the other, some have accepted it as the salvation of the oppressed. In large part, the disagreement concerning the meaning of the Maoist model has been due to a complex array of factors, including the contemporary Chinese elite's image of themselves, their accomplishments and their self-proclaimed international mission, the interest expressed, directly and indirectly, by those groups and societies opposing or seeking change, and the attention that those of us who study China have given to the subject matter. These and other factors, it seems to me, have lent something to the "magic" of the Maoist model, which now constitutes one of the basic myths of contemporary China.

What is the magic of the Maoist model? There are various dimensions to this question, and I should like to examine one aspect of this complex problem: The model or specific features of it in an international context, with special reference to its symbolic role. The relationship between politics and symbolism requires no explanation.[1] For our purpose, this relationship within the context of the Maoist model in an international setting can be best understood by quoting from Murray Edelman.

> Practically every political act that is controversial or regarded as really important is bound to serve in part as a condensation symbol. It evokes a quiescent or an aroused mass response because it symbolizes a threat or reassurance. Because the meaning of the act in these cases depends only partly or not at all upon its objective consequences, which the mass public cannot know, the meaning can only come from the psychological needs of the respondents; and it can only be known from their responses.[2]

To translate Edelman's statement into our frame of reference, the Maoist model can be understood as a condensation symbol, evoking a threat, reassurance, or both. Furthermore, the meaning of the Maoist model, like other symbols, is only partly or not at all dependent upon "objective consequences." The important consideration is the need, psychological and otherwise, that the Maoist model evokes from the respondents (in this instance, non-Chinese societies). In this context, a primary point of this paper is to suggest that the international significance of the Maoist model lies neither in its appeal as a method to be emulated nor in the questions of relevance and applicability. Rather, a meaning is to be found in the Maoist model as a symbol promising the attainment of specific ends.

Before discussing the Maoist model from an international symbolic point of view, three factors deserve our attention. First, while claiming to be the model for others to emulate, the Chinese have been very careful about clearly defining what constitutes the Maoist model. This is not to suggest that China has not presented specific features of the model and offered them as examples to followed: Liu Shao-ch'i did this in 1949 when he made the famous statement that China's liberation war was the proper model for other emerging societies to follow. In most instances, however, the Maoist model has been only indirectly presented, and in piecemeal fashion. This means that for the most part, what constitutes the Maoist model has been left to the others to decide for themselves, depending upon the time, place, and needs.

Second, the Maoist model did not emerge full-grown but developed over an extended period. It therefore contains a dynamic element, in that the CCP's and the PRC's successes, real or perceived, become a part of the model. Thus the developmental experiences of the 1950s and the 1960s have become as much a component of the Maoist model as the people's liberation war formula of the pre-1949 era. Consequently, what the model may have represented in 1949 was vastly different from what it was in 1970; we can safely assume that in future years the Maoist model will acquire yet additional components.

Finally, in discussing the Maoist model from an international standpoint, we are of course adding a highly intangible factor. For one thing, the world is far too complex and diversified an entity to be subject to a single mold, with each world unit experiencing its own special stage of development and having its own special political, economic, and social needs. It must be stressed that the Maoist model does not operate in a void. Rather, the model has to be seen against the background of the internal polity and the environmental-situational context of each world unit. Neither does the Maoist model operate in a noncompetitive situation. A whole range of experiences and models for development and other dimensions of social change are present. In this context, a true meaning of the Maoist model is to be found in the relationship between the most pressing requisite— liberation, economic and social development—of a given world unit at a specific period in history and that unit's need, real and perceived, for the Maoist model or some feature of it.

Let us turn now to a discussion of the Maoist model. We shall focus on three primary dimensions: the struggle to capture power, international relations, and techniques for nation-building. These will be related to the appeal, relevance, and applicability of the Maoist model.

THE STRUGGLE TO CAPTURE POWER

The most often discussed, and certainly one of the earliest, components of the Maoist model has been the struggle to capture power. The "people's war" formula is well-known. Its major elements include the commitment to a comprehensive ideology, that the struggle must be led by a Communist Party, that the Party must control the army, that the Party and the army must secure the support of the masses, that the struggle must be basically self-reliant and headed by an indigenous leadership, and that the struggle should adopt a united front policy. Above all, the "people's war" formula calls for the salvation of the exploited and the oppressed through armed struggle. It was this formula that brought the Chinese Communist Party to power, after repeated failures and against great odds.

China has consistently expanded this feature of the Maoist model, including the extension of specific support, both verbal and material, to those who seek their liberation.[3] Consider, for example, China's support of the Algerian struggle for national liberation. In the early 1960s, Algeria was hailed as the living symbol of a successful armed struggle.

> The independence of Algeria is a great event in the contemporary African national liberation movement. It has set for other African people a brilliant example of daring to wage an armed struggle and daring to seize victory, and indicates to the oppressed nations throughout the world the correct road to win independence and freedom. . . .[4]

Since the early 1960s, China has supported diverse liberation struggles, including the Vietnamese movement, the Arab war against Israel, and the southern African struggles against Portuguese colonialism and the white minority governments in southern Africa. To be sure, the "people's war" formula has not always been fully emulated and successfully followed, though China has pointed to specific movements, such as the Liberation Front for Mozambique, that have attained a high level of "revolutionary struggle."

Chinese comments on the "people's war" formula have stressed several factors. First, revolutionary armed struggle can be learned only through practice. One's fighting ability increases through experience, and armed struggle further educates the masses. Second, the masses must be mobilized to insure the continuance of the struggle. Third, self-reliance and preparation for a protracted struggle must be expected. Finally, the liberation struggle should be conceived not merely in terms of opposing the immediate enemy—such as the Portuguese in Mozambique—but also in terms of opposition to "imperialism, colonialism and big power hegemony." China has supported the African liberation struggles in the context of the above themes.[5]

There can be no doubt that China's own successful national liberation struggle and its support of the "people's war" formula have caused others who seek liberation, for whatever reasons and in whatever environments, to look to China for support—material, moral, and otherwise. But it becomes equally important to point out that this feature of the Maoist model has its roots in the specific environmental-situational context of a given world unit. What I mean by this is that though it has an appeal to those seeking liberation, what in large part determines their interest is not so such China's self-proclaimed leadership or even China's militant posture and support, but the indigenous conditions in a given world unit and the goal of liberation.

Consider, for example, the Chinese Communist experience; a number of factors contributed to their successful struggle. Certainly the reasons for early Chinese receptivity to Communism constituted a vital consideration. The legacy of the early Communist efforts in the 1920s must also be taken into account. Neither can one ignore the contribution of the Long March mystique or neglect the influence on the struggle of China's war against Japan. The weaknesses and vulnerability of the enemy, the Kuomintang, must also be considered, especially during the final years of the struggle on the China mainland. Finally, the role of Mao Tse-tung cannot be ignored. The list of contributing factors can be lengthened, but the point is that the Chinese Communist experience must be understood within a specific milieu and time period. A question of obvious importance is to what extent we can expect other world units to duplicate the environmental-situational context and to have a similar series of experiences.

Here we are confronted not only with the basic question of the appeal of the Maoist model but also with the challenges or relevance and applicability. These questions, however, cannot be directly answered. Consider, for example, the case of the application of the "people's war" formula in southern Africa. We are assuming, of course, that some form of that formula, however imperfect, was being fought in southern Africa in the 1960s and early 1970s. Prior to 1964, the vast majority of the African colonies were being given independence by the European colonial powers. Consequently, there was limited interest (except in specific instances, such as Algeria) in the "people's war" formula. Indeed, for the most part the concept was unrelated to the environmental-situational context. Beginning only in the 1960s, when it became evident that the white minority governments of southern Africa and the Portuguese were not going to follow the pattern of "Africa for the Africans," did one begin to hear the cry for revolutionary armed struggle. What subsequently took place is history; southern Africa became one of the focal points for revolutionary armed struggle. It is to be noted that the changing environmental-situational context in large part determined the form of the final struggle. For many Africans, it was a case of either accepting the status quo or taking up arms; the national liberation movements of southern Africa and those African states that actively supported them felt increasingly forced to adopt methods more applicable to the situation. One African active in the liberation struggle has put it thus:

The African people have explored and exhausted all
peaceful avenues to political change. They find the whites
adamant and prepared to hold state power with the aid of
a gun. The Africans have been pushed against a wall.
They are human enough to feel the pinch of oppression
and exploitation; and they are natural enough to revolt,
using the appropriate means demanded by the situation.
They realize, as has been said, that political power
stems from the barrel of a gun. They have had to resort
to armed struggle as the only sure means of attaining
true freedom.[6]

Does this prove the applicability of the Maoist model?
     I am perhaps being unfair. There is obviously a general appeal
of the liberation war formula of the Maoist model in Africa and elsewhere, especially in those world units continuing to struggle against
colonialism. An argument can even be made for the applicability of
some form of people's war, especially in Mozambique, Angola, and
other areas where a war of national liberation or a version of it is
being fought. I am even willing to concede the relevance of the formula
within the context of "the appropriate means demanded by the situation." But the question must still be asked whether the "people's
war" formula in toto can be duplicated and whether others who seek
their own liberation do not experience different conditions requiring
different actions from those of China. Moises Moleiro, Secretary-
General of the Venezuelan Movement of the Revolutionary Left, discussing Lenin's and Mao's schemes for revolution, probably reflected
the attitude of many liberation fighters: One must assimilate foreign
schemes critically and abandon fluid acceptance of dogmas.[7]
     I would like to suggest that the international significance of the
"people's war" formula of the Maoist model lies neither in its appeal
as a method to be emulated nor in the questions of relevance and
applicability. Rather, the meaning is to be found in the people's war
as a symbol of liberation. To put it differently, a meaning of the
"people's war" formula is to be found in the symbolic function it
serves for China and for those seeking change.
     China's support of liberation-revolutionary struggles has long
since become a familiar policy. In essence, it promotes the idea of
a world revolutionary struggle against colonialism, imperialism, and
hegemony, that the primary enemies are the United States and the
Soviet Union, and that the struggle is "rising like the sweeping wind
and the waving cloud." However, China's policy is designed less to
provide direct assistance to liberation struggles than to establish
and maintain its revolutionary credibility. By supporting revolutionary struggles verbally, materially, and otherwise, China's

revolutionary posture is given credence. For those seeking liberation the "people's war" formula serves as not just a means to an end but as a proven scheme. It matters not whether the formula can be duplicated and executed; in the eyes of the beholder, the "people's war" formula represents the symbol of liberation. In short, its international significance is to be found in the example held out by the Chinese of what is possible for all who seek liberation.

PRINCIPLES OF INTERNATIONAL RELATIONS

The newest feature of the Maoist model relates to international relations; it is not new in terms of its content but in terms of the relative emphasis it receives. China has stressed its model of interstate relations especially since the conclusion of the Great Proletarian Cultural Revolution and China's "reentry" into the international arena. What is this "international relations" feature of the Maoist model? We need not repeat China's principles concerning its friendship, mutual assistance, and cooperation with other socialist states, its support of the people of Asia, Africa, and Latin America in their struggle for national independence, and its assertion of peaceful coexistence with countries having different social systems; nor need we restate China's arguments against the two superpowers. The principles and arguments are well known to anyone who has followed Chinese foreign policy and behavior.[8] The primary theme of these and other Chinese discussions governing China's relations with other states has been the stress on equality, mutual benefit, respect for sovereignty, and a desire to increase the political independence and economic and social well-being of all peoples. China has called this pattern of relationship "international relations of a new type."

Needless to say, China has no more followed a consistent pattern of relations in the conduct of foreign policy than have the United States, the Soviet Union, and other major world powers. But the question is not whether China has or has not followed its own pronounced principles. Rather, one should ask the following: What are China's principles? What has been done by China to live up to its principles? How have the others perceived its foreign policy and behavior? Again, given the different situations a state encounters and the diverse nature of the world, any generalizations about China's foreign policy and behavior must be stated with great caution. But several things can be said. First, China's military posture has been basically defensive; there has been little in the record to support the claims of aggressiveness and expansionist tendencies. China's two most overt instances of military involvement, Korea and India, seem to support this contention.[9] Second, China has offered uncompromising verbal support and some limited material aid to liberation struggles; this has not gone unnoticed. However, we should mention that China has made a very real differentiation between its direct support of liberation movements and the support of those governments with which China has entered into formal relations. Barring exceptional circumstances, China as a rule has not, by supporting liberation groups, engaged in direct subversion of governments that it recognizes. Generally speaking, China has confined direct and overt support to clear-cut cases of liberation struggles, such as the Arab-Israeli dispute and the situation in southern Africa. Indeed, China has been extremely discriminating in supporting liberation movements; and its direct support, verbal and material, has been much more symbolic than actual. Third, China has seemed to follow the Five Principles of Peaceful Coexistence, first proclaimed in the mid-1950s. For the most part, there has been a gradual expansion of the full application of the Five Principles, beginning with China's relations with the Asian states, followed by relations with other components of the Third World, the entrance into interaction with states in the "second intermediate zone" of Western Europe, Oceania, Canada, and other "capitalist countries", and finally relations even with states "which previously adopted a policy hostile to China."[10] Fourth, Chinese foreign policy and behavior have attempted to include a sense of positive internationalism. This has been manifested in China's record of foreign assistance, including the good conduct of China's aid personnel. The $401 million Tanzania-Zambia Railway, financed, built, and equipped by the Chinese, represents the best example of this internationalism. Taken together, China's foreign policy and behavior might well be considered as offering a new type of international relations.

On another level, the international relations feature of the Maoist model has stressed China's opposition to the domination of the international system by the two superpowers, the United States and the Soviet Union. In turn, China has defined its international role as that being in common cause with the world's small and medium-size states, or, as China puts it, with the Asian, African, and Latin American countries as well as with the countries in the "second intermediate zone." In the words of Jen-min Jih-pao, China joins with "the people of various countries to oppose the power politics and hegemony of the superpowers."[11]

China's "international relations of a new type" has been most vividly manifested in its relations with Third World countries, which have been singled out as "playing an ever greater role in international affairs," The basis of China's relations with Third World countries in general and with African countries in particular was succinctly stated on the occasion of the establishment of diplomatic relations with the Republic of Upper Volta.

93

The Chinese Government has always maintained that all
countries, big or small, should be equal. We are firmly
opposed to hegemonism and power politics as characterized by big nations bullying small ones and strong nations
bullying weak ones. Every country, regardless of its
social system, should handle relations between nations
in accordance with the following principles: mutual
respect for sovereignty and territorial integrity, mutual
non-aggression, non-interference in each other's internal
affairs, equality and mutual benefit, and peaceful coexistence. It is on the basis of these principles that China
has established diplomatic relations with many African
countries.[12]

China's position on international questions was also put forth
by Chou En-lai in his report to the Tenth National Congress of the
Communist Party of China.[13] He began by describing the contemporary
international situation as "one characterized by great disorder on the
earth." A major international event was "the awakening and growth
of the Third World," which had united against hegemonism of the
superpowers and was playing a significant role in international affairs.
But the struggle was not limited to the Third World; it included the
people of Europe, North America, and Oceania. Describing the world
situation, Chou repeated the now familiar phrase: "Countries want
independence, nations want liberation, and the people want revolution."
    Chou next commented on China's own international situation,
within the context of the contention for world hegemony by the superpowers. There was no question, he stated, that the United States and
the Soviet Union were vying and colluding with each another for world
hegemony. Chou cited the "Year of Europe" strategy, whereby collusion
in Europe allowed contention in the region to be reduced while urging
"the Soviet revisionists eastward to divert the peril towards China."
What was China's position on the strategy and past attempts by the
superpowers to devour China? Describing China as the victim of
superpower politics, but one that has stood up to the challenge, Chou
put it thus:

China is an attractive piece of meat coveted by all. But
this piece of meat is very tough, and for years no one has
been able to bite into it.[14]

But China was not the only victim of superpower politics. "The U.S.-
Soviet contention for hegemony is the cause of world intranquillity."
According to Chou, this was the source of resentment and resistance
by the Third World countries, Japan, and Western Europe. These

countries, like China, had refused to submit to the superpowers; the United States and the Soviet Union were finding "the going tougher and tougher." In effect, Chou was linking China's struggle against the superpowers with that of the Third World, Japan, and Western Europe. He also linked China's resistance, both as an inspiration and as a model, to the struggle of the other countries against the superpowers.

> They [the United States and the Soviet Union] want to devour China, but find it too tough even to bite. Europe and Japan are also hard to bite, not to speak of the vast Third World.[15]

The meaning of China's international relations feature of the Maoist model is highly intangible. However, a sense of the significance of China's "international relations of a new type" can be gathered from a sample of the speeches by the various members of the United Nations at the time they welcomed China into the organization. At a minimum, the statements provided the perceptions of specific states concerning China's international role.[16] We shall let the various countries, through their representatives at the United Nations, speak for themselves. Speaking for Tanzania, Salim Ahmed Salim welcomed China into the United Nations with the following comments.

> Those of us who have been fortunate, as I have been, to have lived with and known something about the people of China have good reason to admire their ancient and well-preserved culture, their heroic struggle for their own dignity and independence and their unflinching support for the liberation struggle all over the world. . . .
> . . . I have had the opportunity to learn firsthand of the great commitment of the Chinese people not only for the development of their own country but also and above all to support all just causes. . . . I was most impressed by the modesty and humility demonstrated by such a powerful nation. The respect accorded to us, as to many other African colleagues with missions in Peking, was indeed overwhelming. Perhaps I may just add that at no time were we reminded or ever made to feel that we represented smaller nations. . . . I am sure many of my colleagues will agree with me that such an experience of scrupulous respect for equality among nations, big and small, was a proper manifestation of the correct relations between sovereign states.[17]

Abdellatif Rahal, Algeria's representative to the United Nations, welcomed China's representation by stating that "a new spirit will dominate the organization." He continued:

> We are convinced that the hope that we have expressed is not a vain one. This hope is surely shared by the group of peoples which form what we call today the third world and which have been subjected, since their accession to independence, to international order that has maintained them, in fact if not in law, in a position of inferiority, against which their efforts have so far been of only slight usefulness. If an improvement in the international situation is to be achieved as a result of a better comprehension between the great powers, a radical redress will reside in the consideration of the claims—constantly renewed but still unsatisfied—of those peoples which form the overwhelming majority of humanity.[18]

Yugoslavia welcomed China's representation in the United Nations as "of far-reaching significance for the future work and development of the United Nations as well as for international relations as a whole." Lazar Mojsov, Yugoslavia's representative, put it thus:

> This decision, in addition to representing a recognition of the prevailing reality in the present-day world, also reflects the aspirations and desire of a growing number of states and peoples to promote international co-operation on the basis of equality and independence and to assert the right of each state to free and unobstructed development.[19]

Let us conclude this survey of China's international role as seen by others with the remarks of Jacques Kosciusko-Morizet, the French representative to the United Nations. He began by stating that China's representation signaled the end to a condition of "injustice and absurdity." France greeted China on the basis of friendship and hope.

> Friendship, because ever since General de Gaulle took the decision that his clear-sighted vision of the world's realities dictated to him, our relations, which are founded on age-old affinities and an equal desire for independence and security, have enabled us to understand each other better and be on good terms.

Hope, because the various dialogues which have already been started by so many nations will be enlarged and intensified within our organization.[20]

But the French welcome of China also echoed other thoughts. Kosciusko-Morizet spoke of the uniqueness of concepts and culture of each country, of the valuable contribution to the international community of "this diversity," and the desire for coexistence and cooperation. He concluded by stating, "We are convinced that the Chinese delegation will help us to seize this opportunity and will work with us to build a more peaceful, more just and more prosperous world."[21]

A number of significant meanings emerge from our dicussion of China's "international relations of a new type." We shall stress two factors. First, it should be stated that the interstate relations feature of the Maoist model does not lie in the application of China's foreign policy and behavior; except for the major powers, most states have neither the interest nor the resources to behave in such a manner as China. What this feature of the Maoist model does is to demonstrate China's good international behavior as a major power and to promise China's good conduct in its relations with other states. Second, China's "international relations of a new type" symbolizes China's new international role. By that I mean China's successful resistance against the domination of the superpowers and China's newly acquired international status. Put differently, an equally vital meaning of China's interstate feature of the Maoist model symbolizes to many other states the kind of relationship they are struggling to achieve vis-à-vis the superpowers, that of equality, mutual respect, and noninterference.

RELEVANCE OF DEVELOPMENT EXPERIENCE
TO THE THIRD WORLD

A final feature of the Maoist model is that relating to China's developmental experiences; the remainder of this dicussion will be devoted to this topic. We might inject an aside that only in very recent years has it become respectable to seriously discuss China as a model for nation-building. We are just beginning to emerge from a basically negative attitude toward China's developmental approach.[22]

There are a number of components to China's developmental experience inherent in the Maoist model. First, there is the overt record of China's development: given the level of development at the time of the founding of the People's Republic of China in 1949, China is seen as having achieved a degree of success in the economic

97

and social areas. For example, China has made bold experiments in a number of sectors, including education, public health, and factory management. Second, the time factor has been of great importance; that is, the relatively short period during which China has been able to achieve the present level of economic and social development. Finally, there is the theme of self-reliance, including the question of Chinese solutions, technical, organizational, and otherwise. Linked to the theme of self-reliance is the environmental-situational context of China's developmental experience—China as a rural society amid the process of modernization.

The developmental-experience feature of the Maoist model can best be appreciated from the viewpoint of those poor and small Third World countries seeking to develop their societies. It has been in those societies that China's experience has found the greatest appeal. Several reasons account for this. First, many Third World countries have become increasingly dissatisfied with their own national development patterns, based upon the liberal Western model, which either was imposed upon them by their former European colonial masters or was self-imposed at an earlier date in an effort to achieve modernization. This has led many of them to search for alternative forms of development. Second, the search for new approaches and solutions to nation-building has led many Third World societies to a closer examination of successful social systems similar to their own in historical and environmental-situational background. This does not imply a total rejection of things Western; rather, it means a desire to examine all approaches to development. Third, the Third World countries have been impatient with the pace of their own national development. Indeed, rapid national development has become the goal of almost every country in the African-Asian-Latin American world.

Yet another level of the significance of the Chinese developmental model has been the psychological appeal: the concern of Third World countries with the achievement of equality with the advanced West. We can explain this appeal as follows. The West has long held sway over much of the Third World with its technological and scientific advances. China, beginning as an underdeveloped society technologically, scientifically, and otherwise in the Western sense, has within a relatively short period achieved a meaningful level of development in these and other select areas, bringing to an end her total dependence upon and domination by the West. China's overall industrial and nuclear development can be seen in this light. The Maoist developmental experience, therefore, appeals to many Third World countries not only in the narrow economic and social sense but also in the broader context of equality with the West based upon developmental achievements.

Something can be said of the general appeal of China's developmental experiences; an example can be found in the case of Tanzania.[23] First, Tanzania was dissatisfied with its past developmental pattern, for the most part under British colonial influence. Since its independence in 1961, Tanzania has been seeking to create a new social system appropriate to its own historical and environmental-situational context. In building such a system, the Tanzanian elite has discovered that there is no one model to copy. Tanzania has to learn from both the East and the West; and it can learn equally from the Chinese and the Swedes. In short, the appeal of the Chinese model should be seen in the specific context of Tanzania's purposeful search for those a aspects of a given model best suited to its needs. The Chinese experience in nation-building constitutes one such model.

Second, Tanzania's deep concern with "success" has been an important factor contributing to the appeal of the Chinese model. Tanzania's rejection of the liberal Western model of development left the nation's elite increasingly attracted to examples of successful social systems similar to their own in historical and environmental-situational background. Within the African-Asian world, three systems have competed for attention: China, India, and Japan. Japan, which has been recognized as a developed and successful system, has been perceived primarily as a Western society in an Asian geographical context, and therefore not viable as a model for Tanzania. India, at least since the death of Nehru, has been regarded as in a state of stagnation, and thus of little interest to the success-oriented Tanzanian elite. China, on the other hand, with its perceptibly compatible historical experiences, similar environmental-situational background, and overall economic, political, and social achievements, has been seen as a successful developmental model that could answer Tanzania's needs.

A final factor of the appeal of China's developmental experience has been Tanzania's search for a proven strategy of rapid national development. Tanzania, like many Third World societies, is in a hurry and wishes conditions to change quickly; it sees China as having achieved rapid modernization in many sectors. China's appeal is best summarized in the following statement:

> . . . At the time of its liberation, China was a semi-feudal backward country. But today, New China has all the characteristics of a truly big power.
> . . . it is clearly seen that [China's] socialist system is the surest and quickest way to development.[24]

It is one thing to say that the developmental feature of the Maoist model has an appeal among certain Third World countries;

there can be no doubt that China's accomplishments have been impressive in specific areas and have so been regarded by others as well. But we must also examine the question of how relevant and how applicable the Chinese developmental experience is. Again, there are no general answers and the question cannot be answered directly. But let us examine two specific features of China's nation-building experiences for their relevancy and applicability to the Third World: structural change in health care and resource utilization in industrialization, especially with respect to importation of technology.

Let us first consider China's rural health care system. China was, and continues to be, a predominatly rural society. Yet, together with many other social services, rural health care was almost nonexistent before 1949. What health services were available, were confined chiefly to the urban centers, and mainly to those to who could afford them. Since the 1950s, China has sought to develop a comprehensive rural health care system, including both institution-building in terms of establishing rural health care centers, and the training of health care teams. Today almost everyone in rural (and urban) China enjoys some form of health care service.

Like China, the Third World countries are predominantly rural and lacking in rural health care. A root cause for the lack of rural health care has been attributed in large part to the Third World's imitations of the patterns of health care and medical-personnel training of the Western countries, patterns found to be seriously irrelevant for the Third World.[25] The emphasis has been for the most part upon highly skilled medical personnel and well-equipped health centers, usually clustered in the urban areas. But the most pressing need of most Third World countries, like China, is to provide health care for the rural population, requiring both the establishment of health care centers and the provision of medical personnel. What the Chinese approach to health care offers, therefore, is an alternative way of meeting the contemporary health care requisites most pertinent to the immediate conditions.

Another case of the relevance and applicability of China's experience in nation-building lies in resource utilization and technological level. Here one is faced with the problem of the extent of the labor resources available and the dilemma of capital-intensive technology versus labor-intensive technology. Though China has attained a high level of technological development in selected economic sectors, labor-intensive or semilabor-intensive methods continue to be utilized. Given the large reserve of untrained manpower, the developing nature of China's skilled manpower pool, and other constraints, the use of labor- or semilabor-intensive technology would seem to make sense. Such a strategy would also seem to apply to most Third World societies. The utilization of labor-intensive methods, as opposed to what has been called the overimportation of technology, would certainly accord better with their present level of national development and result in better use of their existing resources.

There were tangible and intangible elements of resource utilization. Consider, for example, the question in the context of self-reliance. We can best illustrate the point by using the case of the textile mills in Tanzania. One was built with Chinese aid and equipped with Chinese machinery; it relied on semilabor-intensive technology and employed nearly 3,000 workers. The other mill was built with French assistance and was equipped with modern machinery from the West; it was fully automated and employed only 1,500 workers. It may be argued that the Chinese-equipped textile mill provided a better utilization of Tanzanian resources, given the pool of available manpower and the skill level of the labor force. In addition, the mill provided employment for a larger working force and, because it relied on semilabor-intensive technology, the local labor force was able to master the machinery better. On the other hand, the French-built mill employed fewer workers and relied greatly on an expatriate labor force because of the capital-intensive, technological nature of the machinery. In the case of the French mill, there have been an over-import of technology. In the context of self-reliance and national development, it can be argued in this instance that China's level of technology was "correct" for Tanzania, not only making better utilization of existing resources but also providing a greater sense of independence by allowing the Tanzanians themselves to operate the machinery.

The health care system and resource utilization should not be taken as examples of the full relevance and applicability of the Maoist developmental experience to Third World societies. Nation-building is far too complex a process, as we have all learned and witnessed. It entails, for example, not merely learning certain skills and adopting specific approaches but also instilling a certain spirit. It is not a piecemeal undertaking, but a total effort. Thus, as certain reformist groups in the Third World have discovered, it becomes difficult to even begin to apply selected features of China's developmental experience as long as that effort is not total in nature, however good and related to their own environmental-situational context the model may be. Most Third World countries have been either unwilling or unable to apply China's nation-building features in total.

This brings us back to the question of the meaning of the developmental feature of the Maoist model. If the Maoist model of nation-building is not applicable to the Third World, speaking in total terms, then the question must be asked wherein its significance lies. There can be many answers, but I should like to suggest one: The significance of China's developmental experience lies in the hope it provides, because in general terms the goals are seen as within reach of most Third World societies. In short, it holds the promise that certain developmental goals can be attained, because it has been the case in China. This should not be confused with the questions of relevance and/or applicability, which, though important, are insignificant in relation to the symbolic meaning of China's developmental experience.

This discussion of the Maoist model has greatly stressed the symbolic factor. I should like to conclude on this note. First, it seems to me that the true meaning of the significance of the Maoist model lies in the understanding of the contemporary world's environmental-situational context: the revolutionary nature of the present world. What I am saying is that every human phenomenon, in this instance the Maoist model, takes place in a specific setting; one cannot separate the scene from the action. The Maoist model at this stage in man's development process seems best to represent some of man's hopes and needs. The model may not accurately describe the situation, but it tells what others want to hear. Thus the meaning of the Maoist model is not to be found in its relevance or applicability—though specific features of the model may be relevant and applicable—but it is to be sought in what others look for in it and what the model symbolizes.

Second, in stressing the symbolic value of the Maoist Model, I do not wish to belittle the substantive contributions of the model. Consider, for example, the $401 million-plus Tanzania-Zambia Railway. The project can be taken as the operationalization of the interstate relations feature of the Maoist model. China's support of selected liberation struggles constitutes another example of what can be done with the model in an operational sense. I would suggest, however, that the meaning of the Maoist model lies not in the building of railways or in supporting liberation struggles (China could not build enough railways or support enough liberation struggles). Rather, the meaning of these and other Chinese substantive endeavors is to be sought in what they lend to the symbol of the Maoist model. In a real sense, these and other operations reinforce the symbol of the Maoist model and further enhance its appeal.

Finally, it should be evident from our discussion that the Maoist model as an international symbol is as much determined by what the model represents as by the needs of the model seekers. What it seems to have achieved is that it has successfully captured the aspirations of many in the Third World; it has created a common bond between them and the Chinese. To reiterate, it is not what the Maoist model says that is potent, but the meaning given to it by others. The "magic" of the Maoist model lies in the communication of an idea, a promise, and a hope.

NOTES

1. See Murray Edelman, The Symbolic Uses of Politics (Urbana: University of Illinois Press, 1964).

2. Ibid., p. 7.

3. For an account of China's support of the "people's war" formula, see Peter Van Ness, Revolution and Chinese Foreign Policy (Berkeley: University of California Press, 1970).

4. "Premier Chou En-lai's Speech at the Meeting of Cadres of the Algerian National Liberation Front," Ya-Fei jen-min fan-ti ta-t'uan-chieh wan-sui (Long live the great solidarity of the Asian-African people against imperialism) (Peking: Foreign Languages Press, 1964), pp. 57-58.

5. George T. Yu, "China's Competitive Diplomacy in Africa," Jerome Alan Cohen, ed., The Dynamics of China's Foreign Relations (Cambridge: Harvard University Press, 1970).

6. Chenhamo Chimutengwende, "Zimbabwe and White-Ruled Africa," Donald C. Hodges and Robert Elias Abu Shanab, eds., National Liberation Fronts, 1960/1970 (New York: William Morrow and Co., 1972), pp. 192-93.

7. "Interview with Comandante Moises Moleiro," in Hodges and Shanab, op. cit., p. 241.

8. For a recent Chinese statement, see "Congratulations on the Successful Conclusion of the 4th Summit Meeting of the Non-Aligned Countries," Jen-min Jih-pao (People's Daily), Sept. 13, 1973, p. 1.

9. See, for example, Allen S. Whiting, China Crosses the Yalu, the Decision to Enter the Korean War (New York: Macmillan, 1960).

10. "Strive for New Victories," Jen-min Jih-pao, Oct. 1, 1972, p. 1.

11. Ibid.

12. "On Greeting the Establishment of Diplomatic Relations Between China and Volta," Jen-min Jih-pao, Sept. 16, 1973, p. 1. The English translation is taken from the press release, People's Republic of China, Mission to the United Nations, no. 69, Sept. 16, 1973.

13. Chou En-lai, "Report to the 10th National Congress of the Communist Party of China," press release, People's Republic of China, Mission to the United Nations, no, 57, Aug. 31, 1973.

14. Ibid.

15. Ibid.

16. Speeches Welcoming the Delegation of the People's Republic of China by the U.N. General Assembly President and Representatives of Various Countries at the Plenary Meeting of the 26th Session Session of the U.N. General Assembly (Nov. 15, 1971) (Peking: Foreign Languages Press, 1971). Hereafter referred to as Speeches.

17. Speeches, pp. 54-55.

18. Speeches, pp. 78-79.

19. Speeches, p. 73.

20. Speeches, p. 22.

21. Ibid.

22. Michel Oksenberg, ed., China's Developmental Experiences New York: Praeger, 1973.

23. George T. Yu, China and Tanzania: A Study in Cooperative Interaction (Berkeley: Center for Chinese Studies, University of California, 1970).

24. "New China," The Nationalist (Dar es Salaam), Oct. 2, 1969.

25. John Bryant, Health and the Developing World (Ithaca: Cornell University Press, 1969).

5

MAO'S "UNITED FRONT"
AS APPLIED IN
CHINA'S DIPLOMACY
Vincent Chen

From his experience in the Chinese Communist revolution, Chariman Mao Tse-tung has concluded that the "united front" is one of the three vital instruments with which to win victory over the enemy (the other two being the Communist Party and the Red Army).[1] Together with armed struggle, the united front is also considered by Mao to be one of the two important revolutionary weapons.[2]

The united front is, among other things, a political strategy. During the insurrectional years, when the CCP was relatively weak, the united front was used to rally the support of the discontented classes in order to isolate and weaken the Kuomintang adversary. The Communist rise to power can be largely attributed to Mao's prudent implementation of this strategy. Insofar as diplomacy is a means of making up for insufficient power by winning over friends and dividing the enemy, the united front is also an instrument of diplomacy. In its application in the international arena, the united front is sometimes described as the right hand, in contrast with armed struggle (or armed revolution), the left hand. The right hand signifies a mild posture and the left hand a radical posture.

This paper attempts to analyze the theory and practice of Mao's united front as applied in China's diplomacy. First, we shall address the nature of the united front by examining its origin, operational code, and class composition. Second, in the light of the united front strategy, we shall examine the PRC's relations with countries in the Communist world, the Western world, and the Third World. Third, we shall discuss the tactics used in the Maoists' efforts to establish and consolidate an international united front.

We shall, finally, compare Mao's concept of the united front with William H. Riker's theory of political coalitions. Although Mao's united front is a form of political coalition and, like Riker's, belongs to the politics of maneuver, we shall see that the Maoist class distinction and the ideological variable mark off the united front from Riker's political coalitions. The uniqueness resulting from the requirements of the Maoist concept of revolution presents problems unanticipated in Riker's general theory.

THE NATURE OF THE UNITED FRONT

Origin of the United Front Strategy and Tactics

Mao did not originate the "united front" concept but, as its foremost applicator, he has so enriched its theory and practice that it has become a major weapon of the Chinese Communist revolution. Lenin first introduced the idea and Stalin, in his Foundation of Leninism, elaborated on the importance of the united front as political strategy and tactics in the revolutionary process.

Strategy and tactics are primarily military concepts concerned with winning, and this military frame of reference pervades the Communist ideology. Stalin defines Lenin's political strategy and tactics as follows:

> Strategy is the determination of the direction of the main blow of the proletariat at a given stage of revolution, the elaboration of a corresponding plan for the disposition of the revolutionary forces (the main and secondary reserves), the fight to carry out this plan throughout the given stage of the revolution.[3]

> Tactics are the determination of the line of conduct of the proletariat in the comparatively short period of the flow and ebb of the movement, of the rise and decline of the revolution, the fight to carry out this line by means of replacing old forms of struggle and organization by new ones, old slogans by new ones, by combining these forms.[4]

> Tactics deal with the forms of struggle and the forms of organization of the proletariat, with their changes and combinations.[5]

Thus, strategy is generally understood as longer patterns and sequences of moves, and tactics as single moves and short sequences of moves that are components of a strategy.

Since the Chinese Communist revolution was aimed at the overthrow of the Nationalist government and the establishment of a

Communist regime, Mao built a number of political strategies and tactics around the concept of the united front. The inherent premise is that various social forces, though opposed to each other, should be united against a common enemy. The classical Communist statement dealing with the united front can be found in the Communist Manifesto:

> The Communists do not form a separate party opposed to other working class parties. They have no interests separate and apart from those of the proletariat as a whole. Instead they are to ally themselves with all progressive parties: now with Social Democrats, now with Radicals, now with the party of agrarian reform, and even with the bourgeoisie when the latter are fighting against the old regime, and support every revolutionary movement against the existing social and political order of things.[6]

In Marx's address to the Central Council of the Communist League in 1850, he urged the German Communists to work together with the peasantry and the bourgeois Democratic Party in the face of the common enemy. Once the enemy was conquered, the Communists should then strive for a monopoly of state power, even by conspiratorial methods. To this end, Marx propounded that the proletariat should form their own workers' party whose nucleus was the Communist League.[7]

The Russian Revolution of 1905 can be said to be the first united front ever organized by the Communists as an organized force. In that revolution and then in the Revolution of 1917, Lenin upheld the alliance between the peasantry, petite bourgeoisie, and the proletariat, with the latter leading the alliance. He believed that utilizing the petite bourgeoisie and the peasantry would be an effective way to prosecute the proletarian revolution. The petite bourgeoisie and the peasantry, after their wavering nature had been resolved, could be recruited to help break the general resistance of the bourgeoisie.[8] Although he did not use the term "united front" at that time, his view did anticipate the later fuller development of the concept.

It was not until after World War I that the idea of the united front became a well-known policy. After the war, the Communists felt that the prospect for world revolution was too remote, and they were somehow isolated from the leftist workers and their parties. The Comintern designed the united front to keep contacts with them.[9] The proletarian revolution in the West would be linked with the national movement in the East. In the colonial and semicolonial countries of the East, all social forces were to be rallied to an anti-imperialist movement—not only the proletariat and the peasantry, but also the

petite bourgeoisie and the national bourgeoisie.[10] The Comintern
thus conceived the united front as a way for the Communists to unite
with these forces, as called for by the Third Congress of the Comintern held in 1921.[11] Stalin later elaborated the strategy in an attempt
to advance the revolutionary movement in the colonial and semicolonial
countries.[12] Since then, the united front policy has been an essential
part of the Communist doctrine.

In 1935, when the Fascist aggression was rife, Georgi Demitrov,
General Secretary of the Comintern, introduced at the Second Congress
of the Comintern the strategy of a popular front in the developed
countries and a national "united front" in the colonies and semicolonies,
so that various political groups, including even those with outright
bourgeois leadership, might participate in a coalition government to
defeat Fascism.[13] This idea of a popular front and a national front
had been either advanced or sanctioned by Stalin. During World War
II, Soviet alliance with the Western powers against the Axis powers
was a diplomatic application of Stalin's concept of the united front.
Since its scope transcended the class line, it definitely went further
than Lenin would have gone in 1905 and 1917. From this background,
Mao introduced the strategy of the united front to China. He seems
to owe more to Stalin and the Comintern than to the remote sources
of Marx and Lenin.

To the extent that the Communist Party strives for power, its
constant concern is how to unite the various social forces for the
power struggle; and the "united front" is a device to create power
for the party. As the term "united front" indicates, the Communist
Party gains legitimacy by posing as a partner in an alliance of political
partners. Attainment of legitimacy is essential for gaining access to
mass organizations and ultimately to winning over the masses. In
its rationale, the united front is basically aimed to offset the strategic
weakness of the Communist Party. Through the united front, the
Party can utilize other forces as well as provide legitimacy to the
promotion of the proletarian revolution. This is why Lenin stated:
"In my opinion, 'utilizes' is a much more accurate and appropriate
word than support and alliance."[14]

In December 1937, Chang Hao (alias Lin Yü-ying), a Chinese
Communist delegate to the Comintern in Moscow, who had brought
back to Yenan the "Comintern Resolution on the Question of Anti-
Imperialist 'United Front,'" gave a lecture entitled "Tactical Line
of the Chinese Communist Party":

> All classes in China including some warlords are willing
> to stop all civil wars and to join the resisting Japanese
> national salvation movement. . . . When we appeal to the
> whole nation by the tactics and slogans of the resisting

national salvation, no one can oppose it. . . . Under the pretense of stopping all civil wars in favor of the whole nation's war against Japanese, not only can we stop and eliminate Chiang Kai-shek's attack on our Red army, but our Red army in the Soviet [Chinese Communist] area will be able to regroup, tidy up, resupply ourselves and thus expand. If we can stop Chiang's attack one day, we can gain one day to strengthen ourselves. . . . In the name of resisting Japanese tactics we can control and utilize the contradictions among the parties, the factions and the armies so as to divide them, neutralize them, entice them and win them over to the side of revolution. While pretending to appeal to the people's sentiments of resisting Japan and national salvation, we can divide, weaken and eliminate anti-revolutionary forces. One day when the revolutionary sentiments reach its high pitch, we with speedy measures realize the proletarian dictatorship and complete the socialist revolution.[15]

Chang's words clearly revealed the nature of the united front.

Operational Code of the United Front

From its underlying rationale the united front derives its operational code. First, the Communist Party, by all possible means, should maintain its organizational and policy independence in a united front coalition with other political forces. Second, it may employ the "united front from above" tactics by coming to an agreement on some specific programs with the leaders of the other parties within the united front, which may involve a pledge by the Communists of full cooperation and a reduction of militancy.

Third, through the "united front from above" tactics, the Communist Party may be able to create its peripheral organizations or to infiltrate the groups and communities considered to be the power bases of the other political parties. In so doing, the Communists apply the "united front from below" tactics to win over the rank and file. This is done by dividing the members into leftists, neutralists, and rightists; the Communists make efforts to unite with the leftists, to pull in the neutralists, and to isolate and attack the rightists. Gradually, the Communists and their newly acquired followers create a faction and thus set up a dual power in the organization.

Fourth, the dual-power process is applied to the united front as a whole, as is shown in the independent existence of the Communist Party in the united front. After it has succeeded in expanding its power by means of the united front from above and from below, the Party can easily monopolize power, even to the point of ousting other partners from the coalition. Therefore, compared with the open revolutionary struggle, the united front is a general term for the roundabout forms of struggle by which the Communist party enhances its power during the insurrectional stage of the revolution.

The relationship between independence and unity in the united front poses a continual dilemma. Insistence on Communist "independence" would alienate the other coalition partners, and an indiscriminate emphasis on "unity" with the other partners would be incompatible with the Communist revolutionary aims. To steer the united front on a correct course thus requires adroit maneuvering.

Class Alliances

From the above discussion, the united front can be briefly defined as the organizational form of uniting various social classes for the prosecution of class struggle. It is important to understand the principles governing organization and struggle in the united front.

Class Organization

Class organization in the united front is the class alliance contrived to promote the interest in the proletarian revolution. It is the existence of various classes in a society that necessitates the united front. Mao's initial concept of the united front is found in his 1926 article "Analysis of the Social Classes in China":

> Who is our enemy? Who is our friend? This is the
> foremost question of the revolution. If our revolution
> is to have an unmistaken direction and to hold the promise
> of success, we must pay our attention to uniting our
> friends in order that we can attack our true enemy.[16]

Mao provided a differentiation of the enemy, friends, and the proletariat on the basis of their economic interests and political attitudes:

> All the imperialist-supported warlords, bureaucrats,
> compradores, big landlords and their affiliated intel-
> lectuals are our enemy. The proletariat and the petty
> bourgeoisie are our close friends. The right wing of
> the wavering middle class may be our enemy, and its
> left wing our friends.[17]

This division of Chinese social classes into enemy, friend, and the leading force of the proletarian revolution contained Mao's inchoate concept of the united front in China, which later helped define the participants as well as the objects of class struggle. Stalin developed the point regarding the class character of the united front in his "Brief Comments on Current Events" in 1927, when he spoke of the need for the proletariat to make alliance with other social classes:

> The Communist party in every country must at least
> give possible assurance that the proletariat is able
> to make use of its numerous allies, even though they
> are temporary, wavering and unreliable allies.[18]

With regard to the "revolutionary problem in China," Stalin's counsel required that the success of the Chinese revolution depend on the formation of an alliance of various social classes:

> The question of the proletariat's alliance is the
> fundamental question of the Chinese revolution. In
> front of the Chinese Proletariat stand powerful enemies:
> greater and lesser feudal lords, the military and bureau-
> cratic machines of the old and new warlords, anti-revo-
> lutionary national bourgeoisie as well as Western and
> Eastern imperialism which controls Chinese economic
> life, and which entrenches its own position to exploit
> Chinese people with its navy and land forces.
> In order to defeat the enemies, the proletariat
> apart from all others must have its considered policy
> and take advantage of every gap existing in the camp of
> the enemies, for the purpose of looking for its allies who
> may be wavering and unreliable, so long as they provide
> the alliance with a great number of people.[19]

In a similar vein, Mao rationalized the extreme necessity of making alliance among different social classes for successfully carrying out the Chinese revolution. He noted the weaknesses of the Chinese proletariat, such as their "small number (in comparison with the peasantry), their new emergence (in comparison with the proletariat in the Western capitalist countries), and their low cultural level (in comparison with the Chinese bourgeoisie)."[20] He then went on to say:

> The Chinese proletariat must understand: Although they
> are an awakened class amenable to organization, they
> cannot win victory by the strength of their class alone.

For the sake of victory, they must under different possible circumstances unite with all revolutionary classes and strata and organize them into a united front. Among the various classes in Chinese society, the peasantry can be the proletariat's solid ally, the urban petty bourgeoisie can also be a reliable ally, and the national bourgeoise can be an ally only to certain degree in certain periods. This is the basic law which the history of modern Chinese revolution has proved.[21]

Clearly, both Stalin and Mao considered the united front to be an organizational form of the necessary alliance among various social classes in the process of the proletarian revolution. But the Chinese united front comprised the proletariat, the peasantry, the petite bourgeoisie and the national bourgeoisie, the inclusion of the last being a peculiar characteristic.

According to the Chinese Communists, there are two kinds of class alliances within the united front. First, the working people's alliance consists of the proletariat and the peasantry, which provides a solid foundation for the united front in both the stage of the democratic revolution and that of the socialist revolution. Second, the alliance between the working people and the nonworking people—that is, the alliance between the working classes and the bourgeoisie, is the key factor that determines the success or failure of the united front in the stage of the democratic revolution. Mao believes that in such a united front, the proletariat must unite with the bourgeoisie while at the same time struggling against it.[22]

Class Struggle

Since the united front is the unity of class contradictions, it is not only an organizational form of class alliance but also a special form of class struggle. Class struggle is a central theme in Marxism-Leninism. Mao has further developed the theme by stating that every man's ideology is without exception imprinted with a class mark because he lives according to his class status in a class society.[23] And even in a socialist society, classes, class contradictions, and class struggle continue to exist.[24] In Mao's view, class struggle will continue throughout the history of mankind until the full realization of Communism—and possibly even beyond that.

Because contradictions exist among all the classes, the proletariat must not forget class struggle inside and outside the united front. It is easy to carry out class struggle outside the united front, for the enemy or the object of class struggle is clearly defined from the very beginning. But the class struggle within the united front is a complicated matter. As previously mentioned, the united front intends to utilize the other classes in the proletariat's bid to power. Once this goal has been achieved, all the class partners in the alliance will be vulnerable to liquidation through an extension of the class struggle. Lenin described the situation as "the rope [that] supports a hanged man."[25]

As noted above, the inclusion of the national bourgeoisie as an ally in the united front was Mao's innovation.[26] Fundamentally, Mao's united front was built on the alliance of the proletariat and the peasantry, with the former taking the leadership. Thus the proletariat, through the Communist Party, could extend its influence in many directions. The Communist Party, as well as other parties in the united front, was to maintain its independence. Rather than jeopardizing unity, this independence was to be subordinate to unity.[27] In Mao's formula to balance the two, independence was "to be hard to the point that it will not break unity, but soft to the point that it will not lead to the loss of independence."[28] Following this principle, Mao stressed greater independence for the CCP throughout its wartime united front alliance with the Nationalist government. He was opposed to the idea, held by Chen Shao-yu and others, that all policies must go through the united front and be agreed upon by the Nationalist government.[29] On this point, Mao's view was closer to the Leninist-Stalinist line than those of Chen Shao-yu and the other Chinese Communists, for both Lenin and Stalin had insisted on independence.

At the heart of Mao's united front was a simple but fundamental formula: "unity and struggle at the same time," whether the struggle was peaceful or violent.[30] He condemned either "all unity without struggle" or "all struggle without unity." Since the Chinese united front was characterized by alliance with the bourgeoisie, the CCP under Mao was confronted with simultaneous alliance and conflict with the bourgeoisie. When breaking with them, the Communist would have to resort to violent struggle. But, in time of alliance, they should undertake "peaceful struggle" with the bourgeoisie ideologically, politically, and organizationally.[31] In other words, they should engage in propaganda and organization work among the masses, in order to convert them to Communism. This does not seem to differ from the Leninist-Stalinist idea that the Communists should expand their power among the masses under the cover of a legal framework, but Mao explained it in terms of class struggle.

Also in ways reminiscent of the teachings of Lenin and Stalin to seek all possible allies—even the smallest, the temporary, or the most wavering—Mao limited the targets of the class struggle to the smallest possible number at any given time and place, and considered all the others to be Communist allies. For this reason, the makeup of the allies in the united front shifted from time to time.[32]

Furthermore, in what was known as "beating in and pulling out," the Communists would infiltrate the target parties and then divide the leaders, as well as the rank and file, into allies, sympathizers, and enemies. By concentrating attacks on the latter and winning over the former two, they would succeed in weakening the target parties.[33]

Broadly speaking, the CCP's united front has been introduced in five different stages: the democratic united front in 1923-27; the proletariat-peasantry united front in 1927-37; the anti-Japanese national united front in 1937-45; the patriotic democratic united front in 1945-49; and the democratic-dictatorial united front from 1949 to date. While Mao has criticized the failures of the first and second united fronts, respectively for "unity without struggle" and for "struggle without unity," the other three were great successes because of an unswerving implementation of the principles of class alliance and class struggle.

CHINA'S UNITED FRONT IN DIPLOMATIC RELATIONS

If their domestic revolutionary experience can be projected into the world arena, the Maoists seem to consider the capitalist and imperialist Western nations as the bourgeoisie, the Communist nations as the proletariat, and the underdeveloped nations as the peasantry.[34] In accordance with the united front principles, a distinction is made between friends, neutrals, and enemies among nations; and the tactics of "unity and struggle" can be applied once the target nation is identified. Since the target may change from time to time, it may be said that there are no permanent friends, neutrals, and enemies; and the application of the "unity and struggle" tactics also shifts accordingly. But the shifting tactics is not expected to compromise the interests of the proletariat. We shall examine whether these principles apply to the PRC's diplomatic relations with Communist, Western, and Third World nations.

In his article "On People's Democratic Dictatorship" (1949), Mao explained the united front at home and abroad:

> The Communist party of China, internally, should unite
> with the working class, the peasantry, the urban petty
> bourgeoisie and the national bourgeoisie and form a
> domestic united front under the leadership of working
> class; externally, it should ally ourselves with the Soviet
> Union, the people's democracies, the proletariats and
> the broad masses of the people in all other countries,
> and form an international united front.[35]

Mao was looking ahead to the possible extension of his united front tactics to China's diplomacy. On the premise of solidarity of all Communist nations and the unity of the world's proletariats, Mao's idea of an international united front was initially to guide China's diplomatic relations with other countries. But the actual course of China's foreign relations later changed somewhat as new international situations developed.

Relations with the Communist Nations

From the beginning, China's relations with the Communist nations were predicated on an international united front to defeat imperialism. The cardinal principle governing the relations among the Communist nations was "proletarian internationalism," calling for unity within the Communist bloc on the basis of equality, respect of independence and sovereignty, and fraternal mutual assistance. Given the socioeconomic and political affinity and a commonality of purpose, a lasting and friendly relationship was expected within the "socialist camp." In his Internationalism and Nationalism, Liu Shao-ch'i, however, added nationalism to proletarian internationalism, advocating that each Communist nation may follow its own road to socialism without interference from any other fraternal Communist nations. In other words, independence within unity was emphasized for the international united front, just as it had been for the Chinese domestic scene. In the initial stage, however, China acknowledged the leadership of the Soviet Union not only because the latter was the first Communist nation but also because China would need support from the Soviet Union.

As a rule, the PRC's relations with other Communist countries are maintained on both the party and the state levels. The communication and consultation between the parties is aimed at securing unity on doctrinal matters and on strategy and tactics affecting the larger concerns of the Communist bloc, while the interstate relations concern coordination in policy and power. After the Moscow Conference of the Communist Parties in 1960, following the deterioration of the relationship between the PRC and the Soviet Union, their party relations were drastically curtailed and at one point even nonexistent, but normal state relations were continued. Increasingly, the Communist Party of China has claimed to be the exponent of true Marxism-Leninism and has labeled the Soviet Party from Khrushchev to Brezhnev as the agent of "modern revisionism."

Within the "socialist camp," the PRC has launched its attacks at the state level on Soviet "revisionism," which, in the Maoist view, has resulted from bourgeoisization of the Soviet system. As the self-appointed upholder of true Marxism-Leninism, the Chinese seem to suggest that they ought to play a leading role in the "socialist camp" and in the international Communist movement. In supporting their claim to ideological leadership, the Maoists have pronounced on three often-used Marxist-Leninist concepts—unity, solidarity, and leadership.[36]

Unity

True unity, according to the Maoist view, can be achieved only on the basis of Marxism-Leninism and should include not only the parties, states, and people within the "socialist camp" but also the peoples in all other countries. The Soviet revisionists, according to the Maoists, show only a sham concern for unity and are in fact alienated from a great number of the Soviet Party membership and people, the parties and people of other socialist countries, and the people of the world. Red Flag, the CCP's theoretical journal, raised the following questions in 1963:

> Are the ranks of the International Communist movement to be united or not? Is there to be genuine unity or sham unity? On what basis is there to be unity—is there to be unity on the basis of the Moscow declaration or the Moscow statement or unity on the basis of Yugoslav revisionist program or on some other basis? In other words, are differences to be ironed out and unity strengthened, or are differences to be widened and a split created?[37]

The implicit accusations seem to have been intended to rally a "united front from below" against the "revisionist" leadership of the Soviet Communist Party (Khrushchev and, after him, Brezhnev?). The PRC, it may be noted, has always clung to the principle of independence in its relations with states within the socialist camp and has insisted on unanimity through consultation. The Chinese endorsement of a united international Communist front does not mean their willing submission to Soviet domination; instead it offers them a weapon with which to compete with the Soviets for leadership within the Communist world.

Solidarity

In the same vein, solidarity is required for the international Communist movement, but it must rest on complete independence and equality so that the PRC can exercise a veto power. Only through unanimous consensus can a genuine solidarity be generated.

Leadership

To the Maoists, proletarian internationalist leaderhip connotes
a responsibility to aid and support fraternal socialist countries and
nations still struggling for national liberation, but not to control them.
Because the Soviet Union has violated this principle, she has forfeited
her leadership in the international Communist movement; and this
leadership logically fell upon the shoulders of the CCP.[38]
The Chinese have taken steps to consolidate the international
Communist movement in their own way. But, thus far, their relations
with the other Communist countries vary according to whether they
are pro-Soviet Union or pro-China. At present, the PRC has closer
relations with Albania, North Korea, and North Vietnam than with
other Communist countries. She has been endeavoring to strengthen
her relations within the socialist camp in general by means of trade,
aid, propaganda, cultural exchange, and friendly visits—in other words
at both the "united front from above" and "united front from below"
levels. On balance, however, the PRC seems to stress "united front
from below" in her effort to subvert the Soviet leadership, as she did
before to undermine the Yugoslav position within the camp.

Relations with the Capitalist Nations

Imperialism, which according to Lenin is the highest stage of
capitalism, is the target of the struggle of the international united
front. In general, according to the Maoist view, the government in
any capitalist country only represents the interests of the bourgeois-
capitalist class and is opposed by the proletariat and the broad masses
of the people. The latter, therefore, ought to be recruited into the
international united front. To achieve this purpose, both the "united
front from above" and the "united front from below" tactics are to be
employed. With regard to those countries having diplomatic relations
with China—for example, Britain, France, Italy, Canada, and other
Western European nations—normal diplomatic intercourse is conducted
between governments (the "united front from above"). With regard
to those countries having no diplomatic relations, close contacts with
government and parliamentary leaders who are ideologically sympathetic to China are promoted, but resort is also made to the "united
front from below." By 1973 practically all the capitalist countries
in Europe, Canada, Australia, New Zealand, and Japan, had recognized
the PRC. Of course, the United States is in a somewhat legally ambiguous position.
China's relations with the capitalist countries is based on the
assumption that friendship exists between the peoples of China and

the capitalist countries and that they should work to change the "reactionary policy" of their governments or even to change the "reactionary governments" themselves.

Relations with the Third World

On the basis of their domestic experience in the Chinese revolutionary process, in which the peasantry was the true and reliable ally of the proletariat, the Maoists seem to have a peasantry image of the underdeveloped world, in the sense that the latter should be brought into the international united front under the leadership of the proletariat in its struggle against imperialism. If this analogy is true, it recalls Lenin's "grand design" that sought to defeat capitalism in Western Europe by way of Asia and Africa, since these formed the lifelines of European imperialism. Now that the United States is the strongest imperialist representative, Latin America—the back door of American imperialism—seems to merit inclusion in Lenin's "grand design." The PRC has been making great efforts to win friends among the Asian, African, and Latin American countries. Having suffered under the past imperialist oppressions, the underdeveloped countries are expected and urged to join the anti-imperialist struggle.

Many of the underdeveloped countries, however, follow a neutralist course, steering clear of the "socialist camp" and the "imperialist camp" when they deem it beneficial to do so. The Maoists first disapproved neutralism on the ground that it merely disguised the continued control by local bourgeoisie acting for the interests of Western imperialism. Later in the Korean war, when the neutralists extended their sympathy to China, the latter began to realize the utility of neutralism either as an ally in the struggle against imperialism or as a political deterrent to imperialist aggression. In 1954, the PRC signed an agreement with India setting forth the five principles of peaceful existence, which read: "mutual respect for each other's territorial integrity and sovereignty, mutual nonaggression, mutual noninterference in each other's internal affairs, equality and mutual benefit, and peaceful coexistence." These principles were intiially intended to apply to some Asian and African countries, such as India, but eventually extended to all non-Communist countries, including the United States.

To the Maoists, between the "world proletariat" or the "socialist camp," on the one hand, and the "world bourgeoisie" or the "imperialist camp," on the other, lies the "vast intermediate zone"—the underdeveloped countries that will eventually determine the outcome

of the struggle between the two antagonistic camps.* The Maoists
endorse Lenin's view that the proletariat alone in the capitalist
countries cannot win its struggle against the bourgeoisie unless it is
united with the anti-imperialist forces in the colonies.[39] From the
standpoint of the united front, the Five Principles of Peaceful Coexistence may serve to link China with the underdeveloped countries. But,
in reality, the simultaneous use of the "united front from above" and
the "united front from below" may cost the PRC dearly when its
support for local revolutionary movements clashes openly with the
local governments it also supports, as in Burma, India, and Indonesia.

---

*The term "intermediate zone" is a modification of the term
"intermediate force," which was often used in the Chinese domestic
united front in the past. According to the Maoists, as a consequence
of the operation of the united front tactics, certain anti-Communist
social groups and individuals may be changed into the intermediate
forces or even pro-Communist forces. The term "intermediate
force" refers, socially and economically, to the petite bourgeoisie
in a society and, politically, to those wavering social groups and
individuals who may become either rightists or leftists.

The same tactics may be applied to international relations.
Those nations that are not anti-Communist diehards but, for fear of
Communism, take a defensive position against the Communists, or
that have been traditionally related with strongly anti-Communist
policy can be transformed into the neutral or even pro-Communist
intermediate forces. Therefore, the Third World—Asia, Africa, and
Latin America—can be termed the first intermediate zone and Western
Europe, Canada, and Japan the second intermediate zone. In recent
years, in opposition to the hegemony of the two superpowers, almost
all the nations in the two zones are expected to take a neutralist
position.

This neutralism would fit well into the Maoist united front
framework. By encouraging neutralism, the Maoists hope to divide
and weaken the anti-Communist camp and even to draw these neutralist nations closer to China. The concept of the "intermediate
zone" is created for the purpose of neutralizing the allies of China's
main enemies and other nonaligned nations. Once China succeeds in
her neutralization effort, her main enemies will become isolated.
As a result, the countries lying in the intermediate zones will soon
find it easier to loosen their ties with the superpowers or even shift
their loyalty to China. This is known as the dialectic process by
which the Maoists would be able to fragment the opposing camp into
disjointed units.

As in the other cases, trade and exchange of friendly visits have been important means by which the PRC seeks to improve her relations with the underdeveloped countries in anticipation of diplomatic relations. As soon as diplomatic relations are established, aid may become an additional means for cultivating friendship. Treaties and agreements on political, economic, military, technical, and cultural cooperation are instruments solidifying the PRC's friendly relations within the "vast intermediate zone" (the Third World).

United Front Diplomacy After the Cultural Revolution

During the Proletarian Cultural Revolution, when the spilled-over militancy jeopardized the PRC's relations with both Communist and non-Communist countries, Peking isolated itself by turning inward. Its diplomatic contacts with the outside world became nearly non-existent. Since the Ninth Party Congress of the CPC in 1969, however, the PRC has turned around and cultivated a détente with the United States. Its foreign policy seems to be aimed at an all-out international united front. In the face of the relentless Soviet political and military pressures, the Soviet Union has replaced the United States as the PRC's number-one enemy. Because of its defensive needs, Peking has intensified its efforts to win as many allies as possible. In this regard, the Maoists seem to divide the world into five power constellations: the United States, the Soviet Union, China, the first intermediate zone (or the Third World—Asia, Africa, Latin America, and the small nations around the Mediterranean, extending even to such anti-Soviet Communist states as Albania and Yugoslavia), and the second intermediate zone (Western Europe, Australia, New Zealand, Canada, and Japan). The PRC appears to be endeavoring to recruit countries of the Third World as allies in the united front that it is promoting, and those of the second intermediate zone as indirect and temporary allies.[40] If necessary, the United States should be enlisted or at least neutralized in the event of a Chinese showdown with the Soviet Union. But the professed long-standing policy of Peking is a common struggle by all oppressed nations against the hegemony of the two superpowers, as was reiterated by the Red Flag:

> The past year witnessed great change in the world situations and the new development in revolutionary struggles of the people in various countries. In Indochina, the Middle East, and throughout Asia, Africa and Latin America, the people's struggle for national liberation and for the preservation of national independence deepened and rose higher. It has become the common demand of the people

in various countries to oppose power politics and hegemony of the superpowers. Not only in the first intermediate zone but also in the second intermediate zone,
more and more countries unite in different forms and
scope in their joint effort against the two superpowers.
The Third World has been playing an increasingly important role in international affairs. Those countries
which have been relatively under rigid control of the
Soviet revisionism and American imperialism strive
to change their position of being commanded. Egypt's
announcement of sending back the Soviet military experts
and part of men and officers, the enlargement of the
Western European common market and the formation of
seventeen countries' free trade area, and the new diplomatic moves of Japan and some countries, all indicate
that the international relations are undergoing new adjustments and changes.[41]

Although adjustments have been made to meet the changing world
situations, the PRC seems to continue to conduct its diplomacy according to the "unity and struggle" principle underscoring the united front.
Unity with the secondary enemies and temporary allies will be promoted
in a common struggle against the main enemy, so long as China's
independence is not compromised. Struggle against the secondary
enemies and temporary allies, on the other hand, may continue simultaneously, but only up to a point where the united front will not be
jeopardized.

In the present world, according to the Maoist analysis, there
are four great contradictions: (1) those between the oppressed peoples,
on the one hand, and the imperialists and socialist-imperialists, on
the other; (2) those between the proletariat and the bourgeoisie within
the capitalist and the revisionist countries; (3) those between imperialism and socialist-imperialism as well, as between the imperialist
countries; and (4) those between socialist countries (China and other
Communist countries), on the one hand, and the imperialists and
socialist-imperialists (the Soviet Union), on the other. The existence
and development of these purported irreconcilable contradictions is
believed to lead to revolution. For example, the Americans and the
socialist-imperialists collude with, but also struggle against, each
other in their competitive bid to dominate the intermediate zones and
to consolidate their own spheres of influence. Their aggressive
designs, the Chinese claim, have led to their collusion in suppressing
the aspirations of the Third World peoples, as well as to their mutual
struggle, with increasing intensity, for the control of the Middle East,
and the Mediterranean. The simultaneous collusion and struggle

between the two superpowers will, in the Chinese view, only deepen the strong resistance of the oppressed peoples of the whole world.[42]

Such an assessment of the world situation lends theoretical justification to the united front activities that the PRC seems to be pursuing in its campaign to win supporters in the two intermediate zones. The common cause to weld together this broad union is the struggle against the hegemony of the two superpowers and the threat of both of them, although the answer to the question as to which superpower is a greater threat varies with specific time and specific issues.

THE TACTICS OF CHINA'S UNITED FRONT DIPLOMACY

In the PRC's united front diplomacy, a number of commonly employed tactics—such as propaganda, trade and aid, exchange of friendly visits, cultural exchange, and international meetings and organizations—may be noted. Each will be discussed separately.

Propaganda

The Maoists are known to be able to use propaagnda with great effect. In their united front diplomacy, they can be expected to intensify their "exposure" of the evils of capitalism and imperialism, and simultaneously to present the merits of a Communist system. In this regard, two principal themes—peace movement and antioppression movement—are likely to be heavily emphasized.

Peace Movement

Recalling the Leninist view that imperialism with its overwhelming force would launch a war against Communism, the Maoists have developed the peace-movement thesis out of a defensive need. Their standard slogan is "All the peace-loving people in the whole world, unite!" Those countries that show support or sympathy for the present Chinese Communist ideals are considered the "forces of peace" and the opponents, the "forces of war." The common desire for peace has made it possible for the Maoists to broaden the base of their international united front among the two intermediate zones and to arouse hostility to the two superpowers.

During the Vietnam war, the Chinese were not left behind or outdone by the world's critics in condemning the senseless U.S. bombings and killings of the helpless Vietnamese people. The main thrust of PRC propaganda was to turn the war into a moral issue and to capitalize on the widespread desire for peace both within the United States and throughout the world. While the Chinese were not alone in this effort, they have, like the Vietnamese Communists, continued to use the "defeat" of U.S. imperialism in Vietnam as an irrefutable example of the triumph of the "forces of peace" over the imperialist "forces of war." As events in the 1970s demonstrate, they have reaped tremendous propaganda gains from manipulating the peace aspirations of the Americans at home and of people in other parts of the world.

Anti—oppression Movement

The Maoists have been consistently striving to unite all the oppressed nations and peoples against their oppressors. The "oppressed nations" are those nations in Asia, Africa, and Latin America that are under Western influence or domination and certain minority groups, such as the blacks in the United States and in South Africa and the Indians in Latin America. The "oppressed peoples" include the Communists and their sympathizers in the anti-Communist countries. In the former case, the oppressors are the Western imperialist countries and the revisionist Soviet Union; and in the latter case, the "reactionary" governments of the resident countries. All the oppressed nations and peoples who have been under dehumanizing "economic exploitation" and "political oppression" by their oppressors, the Chinese argue, properly belong to the broad international united front directed against all oppressions.

Aside from its comparable developmental aspirations, the PRC has shared a similar experience with many of the underdeveloped countries under imperialist, colonial, or neocolonial domination. The Chinese are very aware of the nationalistic bond that unites China with many of the Third World countries, an advantage denied not only to the Western powers but to the Soviet Union as well. In an important editorial, the Peking press put it squarely:

> The countries in the Third world have been playing an increasingly positive role in international affairs. All the nations and people who are suffering from the two superpowers' aggression, subversion, control, interference and bullying are forming a broad united front.
> . . . Together with the people of other countries, we are opposing imperialism, expansionism, colonialism and neo-colonialism. We are opposing the hegemony and power politics of the two superpowers.[43]

While propaganda holds an intangible significance for the international "united front," trade and aid provide a material bond. Assistance to the "oppressed" nations and peoples has been explained according to the Marxist-Leninist ideology. On the question of capitalist deprivation in the world, Lenin long ago observed:

> . . . the toiler should not forget that capitalism has divided the nations into a smaller number of oppressing, powerful, privileged (imperialist) nations enjoying full rights, and an overwhelming majority of oppressed, dependent and semi-dependent nations.[44]

In order to eliminate imperialist exploitation and develop their own productive forces, underdeveloped countries are urged by Peking to develop their own independent national economies through mutual trade and aid among themselves (including China). Since the split between China and the Soviet Union, the two Communist giants have carried their fight to the areas of foreign trade and foreign aid.

Foreign Trade

In contrast with the usual Western concept of trade, the PRC believes that politics and trade are inseparable and makes no bones about its own attempt to expand its contacts with the non-Communist countries by combining trade with politics. The political motivations in Peking's trade relations become particularly pronounced when it uses trade to finance a failing economy in an underdeveloped country. It may buy up surplus goods that may not be needed in China's domestic economy, or it may decide to supply certain Chinese goods and manufactures even when these are in short supply in China.[45]

China's foreign trade has been carried out through a network of trade agreements that specify types of goods, target quotas, and terms of delivery and payment.

Foreign Aid

The PRC's foreign aid program, including financial, technical, and military aids, seems to have had greater impact than trade upon the underdeveloped countries. Chinese aid is known to be more welcome in these countries than that of the West and the Soviet Union, because Peking has a reputation for offering aid to a recipient in times of crisis—usually offered on very generous terms, bordering on altruism, under the well-known "eight principles." These principles, first enunciated by Premier Chou En-lai in 1964, stress (1) equality and mutual benefit; (2) respect for sovereignty; (3) long-term interest-free and low-interest loans; (4) promotion of recipient's self-reliance; (5) aid to capital-generating projects; (6) quality equipment and material from China; (7) assurance of mastery by native personnel of necessary techniques; and (8) no special accommodation and amenities for Chinese experts.[46] At least in Tanzania, these favorable terms have ingratiated the Chinese with the local population.

Financial Aid. Financial aid is extended in the form of either grants or loans, all long-term. The Chinese prefer low-interest loans to outright grants, because a grant could arouse suspicions of ulterior motives; and low-interest loans, on the other hand, would serve to encourage self-reliance on the part of the recipient countries and to show up the greed of the Western granters who charge a high interest rate. The long-term loans not only make it easier for the recipients to pay back, but also allow the good relations between China and the recipient countries to continue over the prolonged period of repayment and possibly beyond.

Technical Aid. Technical aid is closely related to trade and financial aid. China sends out a great number of engineers, agriculturalists, doctors, advisers, technicians, skilled workers, and experienced farmers to the underdeveloped countries, where they help take charge of planning, supervision, management, farming, skilled labor, medical care, and on-the-job training of native personnel in the projects financed by the Chinese. The Chinese personnel are paid out of the aid funds or through agreed trade in which the recipient is obliged to import certain goods from China.

By sending its aid personnel to the underdeveloped countries, the PRC is able to come into contact and to influence the native co-workers and the population at large. The spread of Chinese influence in this manner is not so much through person-to-person communications as through the exemplary behavior of the Chinese personnel and their demonstration of the merits of the collective system in carrying out the projects. The Chinese personnel selected by Peking are undoubtedly committed to Communism. Not only do they live a puritan life during their tour of duty in the host countries, but their collective sense of dedication, discipline, and hard work are generally impressive. The collective system introduced into the factory, farm, road-building, and other projects is modeled on the Chinese system. The achievements made in the projects speak for the superiority of the Chinese collective system and approach, and their relevance o to the modernization and social transformation of the recipient countries. Also, the native personnel sent to China for training under the aid program are physically exposed to the Chinese collective way of life and the ideology behind it. Technical assistance thus speaks a political language in ways very familiar to all similar aid programs dispensed by other granter states.

Military Aid. Chinese military assistance to the underdeveloped countries is by and large provided for in the economic and technical aid agreements. Loans and grants are extended to cover expenses for the purchase of arms and training services from the PRC. Various arms and equipment—rifles, machine guns, tanks, trucks, patrol boats, and communication equipment—are supplied from Peking. Chinese officers are sent to train native officers and men, and the native governments also send their own personnel to China for special training. Circumstances permitting, the Maoists are known to have covertly trained and equipped guerrilla forces in some countries.

Usually the PRC extends military aid to countries in clear political trouble with their neighbors or considered strategically suitable for helping to promote or spread national liberation movements. Massive military aid has been given to Tanzania because it feels threatened by the white regimes in Rhodesia, South Africa, and Portuguese Mozambique, and also because Tanzania has the potential of providing a base for the national liberation movement in Africa.[47]

Success of the PRC's aid program depends not only on the Chinese economic capabilities but also on the receptiveness of the recipient country. Peking's relative economic weakness has made its bid to compete with the United States and the Soviet Union for influence in the Third World a very precarious fight. On the other hand, it has scored a big victory in Tanzania because the latter is very responsive to the Chinese model as well as what they have to offer in terms of aid.[48]

It is understood that the PRC's foreign aid programs have often strained its meager resources, sometimes at the expense of domestic development and the welfare of its own population. But the Chinese policy in the economic field probably can be better understood in the light of their ideological motivations. A grateful recipient country would bring incalculable returns to the international "united front" that the PRC is promoting. To the extent that trade and aid programs can be translated into power and influence, in the long run the Chinese pursuit of a united front diplomacy is nothing less than a rational endeavor.

Exchange of Friendly Visits

Exchange of visits is another aspect of the Chinese united front diplomacy. When a country is considered a potential ally, invitations to visit China are extended to governmental leaders, influential individuals, and leaders of political parties and civic groups (labor, business, youth, women, science, medicine, education, religion, journalism), especially to those who are ideologically not hostile to Peking. Elaborate "guided tours" are conducted in factories, communes, hospitals, schools, public works, and armed forces installations to impress the visitors with the achievements made under Chinese Communism. Special care is taken to ensure that visitors from big and small nations are treated equally.[49] Successful visits by foreign government leaders sometimes are highlighted by the conclusion of nonaggression and friendship pacts.

The exchange of visits between governmental leaders made on the state level is known as formal diplomacy, conducted when there are diplomatic relations. The exchange of other, less formal visits is known as "people's diplomacy." While the individuals and groups visiting China from non-Communist countries act in their private capacity, the Chinese visitors to foreign countries are mostly selected by Peking. The "people's diplomacy," therefore, is an extension of China's formal diplomacy. For countries that have no diplomatic relations with China, "people's diplomacy" is a substitute for state diplomacy. While the Chinese state diplomacy is a form of the "united front from above," both the "united front from above" and the "united front from below" fall within the framework of the "people's diplomacy." The application of this type of the united front has shown its effectiveness in the PRC's relations with Japan and many underdeveloped countries, where diplomatic and friendly relations have often followed a period of less formal contacts.

Cultural Exchange

Closely related to the exchange of friendly visits is cultural exchange, under which visits by cultural groups are made. The Maoists encourage cultural exchange programs because of their conviction that the Communist system is superior to feudal, capitalist, and other systems. Exposure to the PRC's accomplishments is believed to be the most effective way to spread the word about Communism.

To facilitate cultural contacts, the PRC has concluded cultural agreements with foreign countries, some with the "people's organizations" of countries with which there are no diplomatic relations. The agreements provide for the circulation of publications, films, and exhibitions; airing of radio broadcasts; exchange of scholars and students; presentation of operas and concerts; and exchange of athletes, acrobats, and ballet and drama troupes.

International Meetings and Organizations

Both the Soviet Union and China have sponsored or taken part in international meetings and organizations that may be considered as part of their respective united front diplomacies. Since their split, Moscow and Peking have been competing for leadership at many international meetings and international organizations.

International Meetings

The first and foremost international conference that helped launch the PRC's united front diplomacy is the Asian-African Conference held at Bandung in 1955. Attended by many Asian and African countries, the Bandung Conference provided a forum in which Premier Chou En-lai emphatically urged Asian-African solidarity against colonialism and imperialism. Because of the shared grievances of economic deprivation and political oppression and the common hatred for racial discrimination practiced by the Western countries, Chou was in an advantageous position to appeal to the prevailing anti-Western sentiments. He also reminded the delegates of the insidious danger of neocolonialism, which threatened to subvert their countries' newly won independence. Friendly cooperation among Asian and African nations would, therefore, be necessary for safeguarding peace and preserving national independence. Chou also presented the Five Principles of Peaceful Coexistence, as outlined above, which were favorably received by the conference. The image of moderation and conciliation that Chou projected helped to dispel the fear on the part of some delegates of alleged Chinese expansive designs and revolutionary rashness. As a follow-up, the First Afro-Asian Solidarity Conference was held in Cairo in 1957; this time China shifted her attention to Africa and the Middle East. A permanent Council of Afro-Asian Solidarity was created as one of the international organizations in charge of coordination and cooperation among these nations.

Related to the national independence movement is the world peace movement. The Maoists took a stand on the peace question at a meeting of the Council on World Peace, held at Stockholm in 1961. In contrast with the Soviet view that disarmament would be a prelude to world peace, the Maoists favored the arming of the national independence movements against imperialism and colonialism, because in their view, world peace could be secured only after the defeat of imperialism and colonialism—the causes of war. The controversy was surrounded by the then-heated ideological dispute between the Chinese and the Soviets over the question of the inevitability of war. The controversy was but another indication of the intensity of the Sino-Soviet split and the struggle between Peking and Moscow for leadership in Communist-sponsored international meetings and organizations. Although Peking did not win all the stakes, a good number of the Afro-Asian nations did come out in support of the Chinese position on the peace question.

International Mass Organizations

The PRC has been involved in a number of international mass organizations, one of which is the Council on World Peace, the executive body of the Congress for Safeguarding World Peace. The Council consists of both individual and group members without discrimination on the basis of race, religion, or political ideology. Its membership includes representatives from Western countries, among them parliamentarians, scientists, writers, professors, religious leaders, and civic leaders. The PRC is expected to increase its activities in international mass organizations like this one because their general orientations toward peace, anticolonialism, and anti-imperialism will make them responsive to Peking's united front diplomacy.

Communist Parties and Affiliated Organizations

Owing to their ideological and organizational affinity, Communist parties and their affiliated organizations in various countries may be mentioned in our discussion of international organizations that are susceptible to Peking's "united front" appeals. Aside from the local Communist parties, the affiliated organizations include those made up of labor, youth, women, students, and cultural groups. The Sino-Soviet ideological division has also divided the local parties and affiliated organizations, some of which accept Soviet leadership and some, Chinese leadership. But, in the long run, the local Communist parties and their affiliated organizations may play a mediating role in the relations between Peking and Moscow, a role no less important than their possible support for the Chinese-sponsored international united front.

The United Nations

From the very beginning, the Chinese recognized the vital importance of the United Nations as an international forum and a possible channel for China's united front diplomacy. They also came to realize that the PRC's entry into the United Nations would depend to a large extent on the support of the Afro-Asian countries, which had the numerical superiority in the world body. Gaining the

Afro-Asian support was therefore a high-priority goal in the PRC's united front diplomacy in the 1950s and early 1960s.[50] In 1971, with the overwhelming support of the Afro-Asian nations, the PRC was finally seated in the United Nations.

Scarcely had the PRC taken its seat in the United Nations when she began her attacks on the two superpowers, focusing on their collusion for the domination of the world. To counter what they believed to be an attempt by the United States and the Soviet Union to divide the world into their own spheres of influence, the Chinese have applied the Maoist theory of the two intermediate zones to their united front diplomacy in the United Nations. In the first place, the PRC considers herself to be one of the underdeveloped countries and thus a member of the Third World. Second, she joins forces with the spokesmen for nationalism, anti-imperialism, and anticolonialism. Third, she concentrates her fire on U.S. imperialism and the Soviet socialist-imperialism, but eschews any direct attacks on other industrial countries. The purpose is obviously to seek to establish a "united front" in the United Nations with nations in both intermediate zones.

When Ch'iao Kuan-hua, who led the first PRC delegation to the United Nations in November 1971, paid a courtesy call on Adam Malik, the Indonesian delegate who was the session's President of the General Assembly, he explicitly evoked the Bandung spirit. As we have noted, it was at Bandung in 1955 that the Chinese had first promoted Afro-Asian solidarity on the basis of the Five Principles of Peaceful Coexistence. In his policy speech to the General Assembly, on October 3, 1972, Ch'iao attempted to champion all the favorite causes of the nations in the two intermediate zones, particularly those in the Third World.[51] As the voting records on the issues in the Security Council and the General Assembly demonstrate, the PRC's influence in the United Nations has been steadily on the increase. The Maoist united front diplomacy is expected, therefore, to continue as the PRC's participation in the United Nations becomes more active.

The five "united front" diplomatic tactics discussed above have the common "unity" and "struggle" dimensions in their practical application. The Five Principles of Peaceful Coexistence provide the common theoretical basis for the united front diplomacy. While peaceful coexistence undersocres "unity," the "struggle" dimension never diminishes in its importance. Peaceful coexistence and national liberation exist side by side, just as the "united front from above" and the "united front from below" mutually complement each other.

In all fairness, the "united front" is not peculiar to the Maoists or to the Communists in general. The West employs the same tactics in attempts to influence the government and people of the Communist and other countries. The United States' "bridge building" and West Germany's Ostpolitik exemplify the same methods and goals as the "united front." The difference, however, lies not only in emphasis and priorities but above all in the ideological "god" that the united front strategy is employed to serve.

CONCLUSIONS

Out of both "crusading" and unusual defensive needs—because of earlier U.S. containment and later Soviet threat—and also normal national interests, the PRC has developed a global "united front," modeled after Mao's original strategy employed in domestic politics. The international extension of the strategy was first conceived to include Asian, African, and Latin American countries (comparable to the domestic peasantry) and the Communist states (comparable to the domestic proletariat). As the Sino-Soviet conflict intensified, however, the Chinese international "united front" was modified to allow for the inclusion of Western European nations and other industrially developed nations (comparable to the domestic petite bourgeoisie and national bourgeoisie), so that a broad, informal alliance could be formed to counter the United States and the Soviet Union.

The Maoist united front diplomacy is a strategy of political coalitions applied in the international arena. The next question is whether Mao's united front has anything in common with current coalition theories, such as developed by William H. Riker.[52] To answer this, we shall examine Riker's coalition theory briefly and make a comparison. According to Riker, in the competitive system of the political world, it is a common phenomenon that an n-person, zero-sum game is invariably transformed into a two-person, zero-sum game. In that situation, a political actor must organize a coalition that will enable him to win decisively. This may explain why the Maoists resort to the "united front" at home and abroad to garner a winning coalition.

Riker warns that coalition leaders cannot overreach and over-spend just for the sake of winning, because they would weaken themselves by overpaying the allies with their assets, which would exceed the value of eventual victory. On the other hand, adds Riker, rational leaders inevitably attempt to increase their capabilities and in the end need no support from their allies. Both tendencies would work toward disappearance of the coalition, and this disequilibrium is an inherent weakness of any coalition. The Maoists seem to be fully aware of this instability, for they have refrained from overreaching and overspending on allies because they are limited in resources. Unlike the United States and the Soviet Union, the PRC in practice (as distinct from theory) concentrates her efforts on a few target countries of strategic importance at a given time, when substantial payoffs are involved. Further, Mao is not a pure opportunist but a man of high principle. In his application of the united front, he openly and honestly calls attention to the coexistence of "unity and struggle" and of Communist "leadership and independence." In other words, "unity" is balanced by "struggle," and the "united front" euphoria never purports to undermine Maoist "leadership and independence" in the alliance. Mao considers the united front a temporary winning strategem, not something to be kept for its intrinsic value. Therefore, both Riker's coalition and Mao's united front belong to the politics of maneuver.

Apart from these similarities, however, Riker's political coalition and Mao's united front have some significant differences, which will become more evident if one examines the four principles Riker has formulated in regard to political coalitions.

The rationality principle. In Riker's view, rational political actors join or organize a coalition in order to win. Whether potential participants will join it, depends on the spoils they can share after victory. In Mao's concept, however, other parties or nations are expected to join the united front not merely for material payoffs but also for reasons of ideological affinity.

The size principle. According to Riker, political rationality requires political actors to form a "smallest winning coalition," in which each participant is likely to receive a large amount of spoils. On the contrary, Mao's theory (if not necessarily practice) looks to the widest possible united front, because if revolution is a "redemptive" process, the more people are involved in it, the better for mankind. The enlarged Maoist definition of payoff thus justifies the ideal of a maximal (as opposed to Riker's minimal-winning) coalition.

The strategic principle. A small participant contributing most to the coalition's winning, Riker notes, may be rewarded a larger share of the spoils, in proportion to the value of his strategic position in this particular winning process. For the Maoist maximal coalition, however, the intangible reward from the very fact of participating in the "redemptive" process of revolution should be added to the contribution-spoils equation. Riker further notes that toward the final stage, the coalition leader may drop some of the partners in order to maximize the spoils. In the Maoist united front, on the other hand, if any partners are to be so dispensed, they will probably be dropped from the coalition as a result of the simultaneous "struggle" that accompanies "unity." In both cases, it is true, there is a comparable element of disequilibrium, but the causes are different.

Side-payments. According to Riker, aide-payments, such as a bill or treaty to be enacted or commitments to future policies and appointments beyond the immediate victory, may be offered to prospective coalition partners so as to buy their support. To the extent that they pander to opportunism, such payments would present a moral-ideological dilemma to the ideologically conscious Maoists, unless they were in dire need of the support of the potential partners— in which case the opportunist partners would eventually be purged in the "struggle" process of the united front.

The Maoist united front coalition differs from the traditional international coalition in that it is more than an alliance between or among states, because it is also an alliance among social classes across national boundaries that is aimed at changing the policies or governments of the various states, in pursuit of certain goals considered to be "redemptive" to mankind. The class character and the allegedly "redemptive" goal of world revolution combine to distinguish the Maoist united front from the traditional political coalitions that have been the empirical referents for Riker's theory.

NOTES

1. Mao Tse-tung, "Kung-ch'an tang jen fa-k'an t'zu (Remarks on the publication of 'The Communists')" (1939), Hsüan chi (Selected works) (Peking: Jen-min ch'u-pan-she, 1960), II, p. 597. Hereafter cited as HC (Peking, 1960).

2. Mao, "Lun jen-min min-chu chuan-cheng (On people's democratic dictatorship)" (1949), HC (Peking, 1960), IV, p. 1484.

3. Joseph Stalin, Foundations of Leninism (London: Lawrence and Wishart, 1942), p. 79.

4. Ibid., p. 81.

5. Ibid., p. 82.

6. Karl Marx and Friedrich Engels, The Communist Manifesto, quoted in Henry B. Mayo, Democracy and Marxism (New York: Oxford University Press, 1955), p. 107.

7. Ibid., quoted in Mayo, pp. 107-08.

8. Nikolai Lenin, Lieh-ning ch'üan-chi (Lenin's collected works) (Peking: Jen-min ch'u-pan-she, 1953), VIII, p. 96.

9. Philip Selznick, The Organizational Weapon: A Study of Bolshevik Strategy and Tactics (New York: McGraw-Hill, 1952), p. 129.

10. Mao, "Chung-kuo ke-ming yü chung-kuo kung-ch'an-tang (The Chinese Revolution and the Chinese Communist Party)" (1939), HC (Dairen: Ta-chung shu-tien, 1946), I, p. 183; Lun jen-min min-chu chuan-cheng (On people's democratic dictatorship) (Dairen: Hsin-hua shu-tien, 1949), pp. 13-14.

11. The Central Reform Committee of the Chinese Nationalist Party (KMT), ed., Fei-tang ti tsu-chih yü t'se-lüeh lu-hsien (The

organization and tactical lines of the Chinese Communist Party) (Taipei, Taiwan: Chung-yang wen-wu kung-yin she, 1952), pp. 80, 82.

12. Stalin, op. cit., pp. 70-71, 73.

13. See Georgi Dimitrov, The United Front, the Struggle Against Fascism and War (London: Lawrence and Wishart, 1938).

14. Quoted in Selznick, op. cit., p. 128.

15. Chang Hao, "Chung-kuo kung-ch'an-tang ti t'se-lüeh lu-hsien (The tactical lines of the Chinese Communist Party)," unpublished paper, 1937, at the Institute of International Relations, Taipei, Taiwan.

16. Mao, "Chung-kuo she-hui ko chieh-chi ti fen-hsi (Analysis of various classes in Chinese society)" (1926), HC (Peking, 1960), I, p. 3.

17. Ibid., pp. 8-9.

18. Joseph Stalin, "Shih-shih wen-t'i chien-p'ing (Brief comments on current events)" (July 28, 1927), Ch'üan-chi (Collected works) (Peking: Jen-min ch'u-pan-she, 1954), IX, p. 298.

19. Ibid., p. 305.

20. Mao, "Chung-kuo ke-ming yü chung-kuo kung-ch'an-tang" (The Chinese Revolution and the Chinese Communist Party), HC (Peking, 1960), II, p. 607.

21. Ibid., p. 608.

22. Mao, "Remarks on the publication of 'The Communists,'" HC (Peking, 1960), II, p. 599.

23. Mao, "Shih-chien lun" (On practice) (1937), HC (Peking, 1960), I, p. 272.

24. Mao, "Tsai chung-kung pa-chieh shih-chung ch'üan-hui shang ti chiang-hua (Address at the Tenth Plenary Session of the Central Committee of the CPC's Eighth Congress)" (Sept. 1962), quoted in Lin Piao, "Chung-kuo kung-ch'an-tang ti-chiu-ts'u ch'üan-kuo tai-piao ta-hui shang ti pao-kao" (Report at the Ninth Congress of the CPC) (Apr. 1969), Hung Chi (Red flag), May 1969, no. 5: 12. Hereafter cited as HCh.

25. Quoted in Selznick, op. cit., p. 144.

26. Mao, Lun hsin chieh-tuan (On new stage) (also known as The Chinese Communist Party's position in the national war) (1938) (Chungking: Hsin-hua jih-pao kuan, 1939), p. 52; "Remarks on the Publication of 'The Communists,'" HC (Peking, 1960), II, pp. 565-77.

27. Mao, On New Stage, loc. cit., "T'ung-i chan-hsien chung ti tu-li tsu-chu wen-t'i" (The question of independence in the united front) (1938), HC (Peking, 1960), II, pp. 485-501.

28. Quoted in the Central Reform Committee of the KMT, op. cit., p. 86.

29. Mao, "T'ung-yi chang-hsien te tu-li wen-t'i" (The Question of Independence in the United Front) HC (Peking 1960), II, pp. 502-5.

30. Mao," 'Kung-ch'ang tang-jen' tang-k'an tzu" (Remarks on the Publication of 'The Communists'), <u>HC</u> (Peking, 1960), II, pp. 573-76.

31. Ibid., p. 575.

32. Mao, "Nung-ts'un t'iao-cha ti hsü-yen ho pa (Prologue and epilogue to 'The rural investigation')" (1941), <u>HC</u> (Peking, 1960), III, pp. 747-52.

33. The Central Reform Committee of the KMT, op. cit., p. 163.

34. Lin Piao, "People's War," New York <u>Times</u>, Sept. 3, 1965, p. 2.

35. Mao, "On People's Democratic Dictatorship," <u>SW</u> (Peking: Foreign Languages Press, 1961), IV, p. 415. Emphasis added.

36. Harold C. Hinton, <u>Communist China in World Politics</u> (Boston: Houghton Mifflin Co., 1966), pp. 98-99.

37. Ibid., p. 98 n., quoted from "More on the Differences Between Comrade Togliatti and Us: Some Important Problems of Leninism in the Contemporary World," <u>HCh</u>, Mar. 4, 1963, p. 3.

38. George T. Yu, <u>China and Tanzania: A Study of Cooperative Interaction</u> (Berkeley: University of California Press, 1970), p. 73.

39. Hinton, op. cit., pp. 101-03.

40. Editorial, "Ch'uan shih-chieh i-ch'ieh fan-tui mei ti-kuo chu-i te li-liang lien-ho ch'i-lai (All the anti-American-imperialist forces in the world: Unite!), <u>JMJP</u>, Jan. 21, 1964, p. 1.

41. <u>HCh</u> editorial, Oct. 1, 1972, no. 10, pp. 5-9. Emphasis added.

42. Writing Group of the Hupei Provincial Committee of the CCP, "T'uan-chieh jen-min chan-sheng ti-jen te ch'iang-ta wu-ch'i—hsueh-hsi 'lun cheng-ts'e'" (A powerful weapon to unite the people and to defeat the enemy—study "On Policy"), <u>HCh</u>, Aug. 1971, no. 9 pp. 10-17.

43. Joint editorial by <u>HCh</u>, <u>JMJP</u>, and <u>CFCP</u>, Jan. 1, 1972.

44. Lenin, <u>Collected Works</u> (Russian ed.), XXX, p. 269.

45. In 1956 arrangements were made for funding the $16.2 million Indonesian trade deficit with Communist China, making it repayable over several years. Under an $11.2 million credit repayable in 10 years at 2.5 percent interest, China delivered to Indonesia rice and textiles, which were in acute shortage in China at that time. U.S. State Department, "The Nature of the Offensive in Less Developed Areas," in Devere E. Pentony, ed., <u>Soviet Behavior in World Affairs</u> (San Francisco: Chandler Publishing Co., 1962), pp. 216-17.

46. Yu, op. cit., pp. 46-47.

47. Ibid., pp. 64-65.

48. Ibid., pp. 47-51, 58-59.

49. China redeemed her pledge to treat all nations equally on the evening of Oct. 5, 1972, by throwing a banquet in celebration of her friendship with San Marino. Three hundred guests sat down in

the Great Hall of the People to a sumptuous, nine-course dinner in honor of Gian-Carlo Ghironzi, Foreign Secretary of San Marino. Foreign Minister Chi Peng-fei, speaking for the 800 million people of China, lauded the 20,000 citizens of San Marino as "an example to all people who love independence and freedom." "Peking Sets a Banquet for San Marino," New York Times, Oct. 7, 1972, p. 3.

50. See Nan-hua Morning Daily News, November 14, 1971, p. 5.

51. "Excerpts from Policy Speech by China's Representative at UN Assembly," New York Times, Oct. 4, 1972, p. 4.

52. See William H. Riker, The Theory of Political Coalitions (New Haven and London: Yale University Press, 1968).

6

SOVIET CRITIQUE
OF THE MAOIST
POLITICAL MODEL
George Ginsburgs

From the outset, the Soviets seem to have felt a bit uneasy about some of the novel institutional experimentations made by their Chinese partners in the political organization and management of their newly won domain. While relations between the two capitals remained cordial, these doubts were carefully kept in check and the suspicious innovations were officially ascribed to the imperative need to take into account "objective local conditions" (as the stock expression goes), China's historical antecedents and cultural heritage, and the specific features of the revolutionary struggle that brought the CCP power, and were wrapped in other vague and innocuous circumlocutions. As the rift between Moscow and Peking widened, the dialogue took on a more frank tone and many of the hitherto hushed-up or muted opinions as to virtues and shortcomings emerged into the open, including Soviet views critical of the constitutional mechanism developed on the mainland since 1949 and its modus operandi.

To appreciate the thrust and tenor of the comments encountered in Russian literature today on this subject, it must be remembered that, according to the latest Soviet thesis, the record of current events on the China scene in the politico-juridical sphere is neither the inevitable product of historical evolution nor a momentary aberration sparked by honest misperception or miscalculation, but the result of conscious and persistent deviation by the present leadership of the PRC from the corresponding maxims of Marxism-Leninism, a

---

Since this synthetic account of the Soviet critique was put together by the author from a wide range of primary sources, no individual notes are used. The reader however, is referred to the Russian-language sources given in the bibliography at the end of this volume.

course deliberately pursued over many years by all sorts of camou-flaged and devious means and only now fully unveiled. To be sure, the Russians concede that the national milieu played a definite role in facilitating the genesis and development of the complex of elements that constitute the Maoist phenomenon. With regard to the latter's political and jural dimensions, they cite environmental factors re-sponsible for the general backwardness of political life in the PRC and the absence of sufficiently strong traditions and mores of socialist democracy capable of countering the Maoist machinations: the his-torical past of the country and the suppression of the popular masses who suffered not just from semifeudal forms of exploitation but were also deprived of minimal rights and freedoms, and had to bear the yoke of the militarist clique and foreign intervention. However, had China's revolutionary leadership, once victory was won, maintained a correct line and followed sound and proper policies, these obstacles could have gradually been overcome and the business of building a socialist society in China placed on a firm footing. Instead, the Rus-sians claim, the growth of the Party and state apparatus in China proceeded in such a way that at times it not only did not contribute to the consolidation of the ethos and customs of socialist democracy, but directly impeded progress in this area.

In a nutshell, what the Russians are saying is that the strands of the Maoist syndrome run through the entire fabric of the PRC's political experience. Evidence of its fractious influence can be dis-cerned at every stage of the PRC's constitutional career, from its very inception; and the so-called Cultural Revolution simply capped Mao's clandestine struggle against the ensemble of Marxist-Leninist principles of government, laying bare his determination to circumvent the established constitutional regime and replace it with a military-bureaucratic dictatorship subservient to his personal wishes and designs. The central theme in this analytical approach, then, is the continuity and consistency of the Maoist agenda; the methodical nature of Mao's efforts to shape the PRC's political system to his own ends, in opposition to the pertinent norms of the Marxist-Leninist canon; and the organic link between the early symptoms of heresy, the im-pulses behind and the subsequent practices of the Cultural Revolution, and its institutional legacy, which merely represents the logical culmination of the whole pernicious trend.

THE NATIONALITY QUESTION

A prime target of Soviet criticism of the Chinese leadership's political record to date is the latter's manner of handling the nation-ality question. On the logistical side, the Russians note that, given

138

their figures (even accepting the artificial statistics the Chinese have created in order to conceal their real numbers) and the size of the territory that the non-Han ethnic elements occupy, their ability to preserve a separate identity, their cultural, linguistic, and religious distinctiveness from the Hans, and their history of independence until quite recently, a policy was called for that would duly reflect the heterogeneous quality of China's population and safeguard equal status and self-rule for its major components. Only thus, in the Soviet estimate, could a harmonious multinational community be built in China and the loyalty of the non-Han peoples to the cause of the revolution, laboriously won in the course of domestic strife and foreign war, retain its primordial strength and vitality. What is more, Marxism-Leninism and the experience of the Soviet Union had already demonstrated (to the Kremlin's satisfaction) that a formula geared to the key concept of the right of nations and peoples to self-determination—which ultimately also means liberty to dispose of their own fate to the point of secession and the establishment of a separate state—was the sole solution under the circumstances, especially in the light of China's past, where the postulate of racial superiority was endemic to the successive dynasties.

Prior to 1949, the Chinese Communist Party had behaved orthodoxly enough in this respect; and the voluminous documents, statements, and declarations issued in its name over the years repeatedly endorsed the proposition that the future state would function on the federal principle based on the voluntary union of the different nationalities living within the physical frontiers of China, together with a guarantee to the non-Han entities of a right to national state existence (as was done in the Soviet Union). To the Russians, this approach seemed best calculated to combine practical and ideological virtues, in terms both of meeting the pragmatic exigencies of China's geopolitical reality and of complying with the tried and tested prescriptions of Marxist-Leninist dogma. At the same time, parenthetically, it would confirm once again the universal relevance and validity of the Soviet model, to which must go the credit for having pioneered and refined these methods. In short, judging by external evidence, the CCP leaders then appeared firmly wedded to the staple commandments of proletarian internationalism, as interpreted by their Russian mentors.

However, we are now told, after accession to power, Mao and his cohorts surreptitiously began pushing their own brand of political philosophy that, inter alia, profoundly affected the projected program of action on the nationality question. The federalist scheme was abandoned; the notion of national statehood was replaced by that of regional autonomy and, instead of being treated as peers, the non-Han elements were demoted to the inferior status of "national minorities"; the PRC was proclaimed a unitary state of which the territories inhabited by people of non-Han stock formed an integral part, with no mention anywhere of a right of secession. Thus, in the Russian view, the Han nucleus alone is at present vested with the right of self-determination and the rest of China's nationalities are denied it.

Today, Soviet spokesmen describe this situation as a crass betrayal of the central tenets of Marxism-Leninism, quintessentially incompatible with the cardinal norms of Marxist-Leninist theory and practice; as an overt repudiation of the Marxist-Leninist credo and a gross manifestation of big-power chauvinist proclivities. In these circles, Maoist attempts to explain the innovations by seeking to prove that the conditions prevailing in China were not propitious to the adoption of national self-determination and a federal structure fall on deaf ears. The main reason given—that the non-Chinese peoples lack territorial integrity—is rejected as utterly opposed to the facts and a bare falsification of the true state of affairs. Nor do they assign much value to Peking's assertions that from ancient times, China had evolved as a unitary state where in all historical epochs eternal friendship reigned between the Hans and the other nationalities, or that the Chinese comprise the overwhelming majority of the population, forming the core of the country and its political, economic, and cultural spearhead. None of this, according to the Russians, can justify condemning all demands for self-determination and a federal system as unlawful, counterrevolutionary, nationalistic, and subversive. On the contrary, they warn, any bid to impose unity and cohesion without equality or national freedom, through the absorption and compulsory assimilation of non-Han peoples, by depriving them of the right of national self-determination and by supressing their independence, is bound to be fragile and short-lived.

If the Russians find the Maoist blueprint intrinsically defective, their attitude toward the manner of its subsequent application is still more negative. The list of offenses imputed to the Maoist regime is long. Unsatisfactory though it may be, even regional autonomy has been granted in just five cases—with Tibet having to wait 14 years to make the grade—and the units involved coincide in rank with mere provinces. Autonomous chou and counties do not count, for the Russians dismiss the possibility of genuine exercise of autonomy on that minute scale—derisively labeled "microautonomy"—as sheer nonsense. Hence, only five out of China's more than 100 non-Han constituencies are possessed, at least on paper, of what the Russians are prepared to accept as a minimum charter of self-government, while all the others are stripped of that right.

Add to this the charge that the Chinese authorities have intentionally kept the old provincial divisions and have refused to redraw their boundaries, so that the minority groups remain fragmented. Instead of revising the boundary lines so as to gather the people of a particular stock in a closely knit mass residing within a compact and contiguous territorial area, the traditional spatial arrangement was left intact, with the result that isolated pockets of minority settlement are scattered throughout several provinces. Within the confines of these provinces the most these enclaves can hope for is to be elevated to the rank of an autonomous chou or county. For example, to cite Russian authors, the Chinese aimed at preventing the territorial unity and consolidation of the population of Tibetan nationality living in the provinces adjoining Tibet, and thus created a constellation of nine autonomous chou and counties around Tibet's perimeter. Analogous measures were taken with regard to the Chuang nation, which was dismembered in such a way that half of it constitutes the Kwangsi-Chuang Autonomous Region and the other half is dispersed among the neighboring provinces without any rights of territorial autonomy. As a consequence, the once cohesive Chuang nationality now accounts for less than a quarter of the total population of its own autonomous region.

Another phenomenon to which the Russians have voiced objection on similar grounds is the technique of merging territories inhabited by non-Han elements with surrounding areas containing a dense Han population. For instance, that fate befell the Inner Mongolian Autonomous Region, which was augmented with two provinces of solidly Chinese ethnic composition, turning the Mongols into a minority in their designated "homeland"—a mere 10 percent of the resident population. A comparable experience lay in store for the Tehung autonomous chou organized in Yunnan in 1953 to accommodate a local concentration of Thai and Chingpo peoples. To increase the proportion of the Chinese contingent in the autonomous chou, its territory was expanded by incorporating nearby districts in which the Chinese element predominated, whereupon the town of Paoshan became the chou administrative center in place of the Thai town Mangshih (Luhsi).

Even symbolic concessions to native sensibilities were fiercely resisted by the Chinese hierarchy, which saw in the bid to rename Sinkiang Uighuristan a threat to its authority, vetoed the suggestion, and instituted a wild witch-hunt against its proponents for harboring "bourgeois-nationalist" sentiments.

Incidentally, in connection with some of these episodes, the Russians seem to be operating with obsolete data. Thus, as far back as 1956, the Tehung Thai-Chingpo autonomous chou reverted to its original territory, with a non-Chinese majority; and the diaspora of the Chuang was significantly alleviated when Kwangsi annexed the Kwantung panhandle in 1965 and, in the process, absorbed the Yamchow Chuang autonomous county that had been inaugurated in Kwantung in

1963. By contrast, the relative position of the Mongols in Inner Mongolia has in the meantime deteriorated further than Soviet sources would indicate: following the loss of the Manchurian leagues in 1969, the Mongols numbered only 600,000 out of the Inner Mongolian Autonomous Region's population of approximately 9 million, or 6.6 percent of the total.

The institutional aspects are, of course, but one facet of the general problem. The Russians are quite ready to concede that, at the initial stage, appreciable progress was indeed registered in China in the fields of culture, public health, and education; that, thanks to land reform and industrial development, the minority areas had started to move forward and overcome their traditional economic lag, and that a corps of native cadres had been trained and had assumed a growing share of local governmental and managerial responsibility. The 1954-56 period marked the high point of this trend. The Constitution contained much that was new regarding the regulation of the legal status of the national autonomous units: they were empowered to create their own organs of self-government, staffed by representatives of the native population, that were authorized to draft statutes concerning the exercise of autonomy and to pass special laws applicable only to the particular territory and diverging in detail from national legislation; to recruit local public security forces; and to administer local finances. This "correct line" found its clearest expression in the decisions of the Eighth Party Congress. Had these directives been properly carried out, the Russians say, favorable conditions would have arisen for the early transformation of the non-Chinese peoples into modern socialist nations.

This was not destined to happen, for Mao's group simply cast aside the Party's resolutions and ventured along an entirely different track. As a consequence, all of the previous achievements were virtually wiped out during the late 1950s and 1960s in the convulsions of the Great Leap Forward and the commune campaign and the ensuing social tremors that finally reached a crescendo in the events of the Cultural Revolution. In the process, native cadres and intellectuals have been purged wholesale (the hardest hit, according to Russian accounts, were those individuals in Sinkiang who were born in the Soviet Union) and the elected organs of government have been liquidated and replaced by Revolutionary Committees in which, contrary to the provisions of the Constitution, power is concentrated in the hands of Chinese appointees, mostly military figures. A flood of Chinese settlers has descended on the non-Han areas, where they are assigned all the directorial and technical jobs, leaving the menial tasks to the local people (mass forced-labor conscription is a routine feature). A determined drive has been mounted to sinify the language, literature, and culture of the national minorities; and economic development is either neglected or harnessed to the needs of the Chinese heartland, primarily as a source and purveyor of raw materials, while industry is allowed to stagnate.

Proximate assimilation is the current refrain and the acknowledged goal, a concept that the Russians assail as anti-Marxist and doomed to failure, citing such extravagances as attempted resort to compulsory marriage between Chinese males and native women, and attacks on indigenous cultural and religious mores, which in turn have spawned widespread resistance that occasionally spills over into open rebellion and armed hostilities. No wonder, then, the Russians note, that the vaunted Revolutionary Committes were set up last in the non-Han areas, only after a prolonged pacification campaign backed by the military had assured Mao's minions tenuous control over the local inhabitants, after the native leaders had been suppressed for exhibiting "bourgeois-nationalist" tendencies, and after all signs of national autonomy had been systematically uprooted. In 1964, we are reminded, in the first session of the Third National People's Congress, while the size of the delegations from the national minority areas was increased, many of these representatives were of Chinese origin. In the top echelons this policy has since become more pronounced; for example, very few non-Chinese were included in the membership of the Central Committee of the CPC formed at the Ninth Session in 1969.

Today, the Russians claim, national autonomy in the PRC is dead even as a mere theoretical proposition. The Chinese reign supreme everywhere; and the other national groups are simply striving to survive in the face of Mao's great Han chauvinism, which is bent on submerging them under the weight of China's masses and erasing them from the historical scene. How bleak their prospects look can be judged from the glaring omission from the programmatic portion of the new Party statutes adopted at the Ninth Congress of any reference whatever to the nationality policy of the PRC, as if the nationality question no longer existed and the impending fusion of the non-Han nations and peoples (their mandatory assimilation) was a matter taken for granted.

THE CONSTITUTION AND ADMINISTRATIVE APPARATUS

Soviet criticism of the Chinese performance in assembling and operating the PRC's constitutional and administrative apparatus is more complex and pervasive. Central to the Soviet analysis of the PRC's experience in this domain is the proposition that, pursuant to the 1954 Constitution, a state mechanism of a socialist type was established and functioned in China. A system of representative institutions—the congresses of people's representatives and their executive organs, the people's committees—formed the political foundations of the PRC. The organs of the judiciary and the procuracy envisaged by the Constitution were entrusted with the task of maintaining legality and order. The people's regime recognized a wide spectrum of democratic rights and civil liberties. To be sure, the Soviets now admit, the organization and activities of the Chinese state displayed certain shortcomings stemming from both the backwardness and the ignorance of the masses and Maoist distortions that crept in from the start. These could have been successfully mastered, the Russians insist, if the CCP had followed a bona fide Marxist-Leninist line. Up until the late 1950s that seemed to be the case: Soviet experience was extensively utilized in China and reportedly contributed much to the progress then recorded by the Chinese people. Intense cooperation with the socialist camp guaranteed the PRC a rapid pace of development; and the decisions of the Eighth Party Congress confirmed the correctness of the path already traversed, and projected a further strengthening of democracy, order, and legality in the country, as well as the steady promotion of the role of the state in resolving problems of economic, political, and cultural growth.

What happened next destroyed these expectations and, in fact, marked the gradual ascendancy of Mao's views on the subject, the influence of which could, in attenuated form, be sensed from the very outset. The "deviationist" impulses finally triumphed in the wake of the Cultural Revolution, which, in the Soviet interpretation, consummated a political putsch aimed at nothing less than to weaken and undermine the mainstays of the people's power, shattering the sociopolitical and especially the state-juridical institutions that impeded the execution of Maoist plans and, in essence, repealed the effect of the Constitution and the rest of the laws promulgated after 1949. But, the Soviets take care to stress, the roots of the latest phenomena lie deep in the events of the past and, while there had been a net escalation of heretical conduct on the part of the Maoist clique in recent years, a definite continuity links the initial traces of apostasy and its current virulent manifestations.

Again, the Russians do not minimize the importance of various objective conditions in fostering the urge to excessive centralization at the expense of democratic principles and the militarization of the entire tenor of state and social life that they perceive as the chief insignia of the Maoist political blueprint. Throughout its recent history, China has suffered from local separatism accompanied by the concentration of enormous political, economic, and military power in the hands of provincial governors. After the 1911 revolution China was, to all intents and purposes, split into several regions, each a state within the state, ruled by a particular militarist group. The inauguration in 1927 of the KMT central government did not result in the establishment of a centralized authority. Determined to stamp out the Communist movement, Chiang contracted alliances with the local militarists, buying their cooperation in exchange for guaranteeing their extensive rights in the provinces they controlled. The Japanese invasion of Manchuria and China proper accelerated the process of decomposition and encouraged the drift toward national fragmentation.

All of this meant that after the victory of the people's revolution on the mainland, a concerted effort at centralization emerged as a top-priority item and that some of the tactics characteristic of the period of struggle against the KMT continued to be used to that end. In addition, prior to 1949 China had had little experience with democratic methods of government: feudal traditions of dictatorial absolutism still held sway over the minds of the common folk, the protracted civil war had stunted the growth of democratic centralism within the Party and the mass organizations, the leading Party cadres lacked a Marxist tempering, and Mao's doctrinal works made the situation worse by spreading primitive versions of the key theories of scientific socialism. Thus, instead of neutralizing and overcoming the adverse effects of these historical stimuli—which, according to the Russians, could have been achieved with the proper attitude and desire—Mao and his collaborators let themselves be diverted from the right track and began actively defending and disseminating their own revisionist views. Rather than eradicate the noxious influences of the past, the Maoist regime now sought to legitimize these blemishes by a liberal application of pseudo-Marxist cosmetics.

A closer look at these controversial formulations is imperative, since they have allegedly left a sharp imprint on the complexion of domestic political practices in the PRC. The Maoist concept of the persistence of the class struggle for an indefinite duration, even after the overthrow of the bourgeoisie and the assumption of power by a people's democratic regime, for example, is pilloried for having served as a justification for lavishing inordinate attention on the instruments of repression, principally the army and the secret police, and for elevating resorting to bald coercion to a cardinal precept of political action while scorning the value of ordinary legal tools. To be sure, the Soviets concede that the proletarian state, too, requires an adequate supply of institutionalized means of compulsion and cannot survive without recourse to organized violence against its internal and foreign enemies. Yet, the Russians argue, this is a transient phenomenon that is a departure from the norm and not a fixed feature of a socialist society. It is one thing to acknowledge the exigency of an occasional exertion of physical force in special circumstances, and quite another to glorify such a procedure as routine.

When, in the 1950s, the new regime had to fight against counter-revolution, the resistance of the exploiting classes, the vacillations of the bourgeois stratum, and the criminality of the déclassé elements, the use of administrative repression and outright military suppression, often on a considerable scale, was doubtless warranted, even though it provoked numerous errors and abuses and often entailed harsh punitive measures. Unfortunately, the Soviets complain, many of the PRC's leaders acquired the habit and fell victim to the illusion that, because they had mastered coercive, military and semimilitary methods of resolving problems, compulsion, administrative fiat, and "commandism," coupled with mass campaigns, were the most efficient and dependable way of handling any political, economic, or other business. The Eighth Party Congress bitterly inveighed against these tendencies but, as subsequent events demonstrated, its efforts were in vain. In the end, the Cultural Revolution sanctioned the supremacy of the military machine and turned the PRC into a full-fledged military-bureaucratic state.

As evidence of the persistent nature of this predilection, the Soviets remind us of how, for instance, the Common Program had perpetuated the system of government that had crystallized during the war of national liberation, with its accent on military-control committees and powerful military-administrative organs to head the large administrative regions, the absence of elected representative organs, and the concentration in the same institutions of both administrative and judicial functions. The subsequent gradual transfer of administrative responsibility to civilian agencies only signified a reduction in the staff of the military-control commissions and not a diminution of their competence, which included the right to draft and enact local legislation. Indeed, they continued to operate even after the adoption of the Constitution, when military control was already deemed abolished. In similar vein, the State Administrative Council, unlike the Cabinets in the other socialist states (or, one might add, its own successor, the State Council), did not comprise all the ministers and its jurisdiction did not extend to matters concerned with the organization of the armed forces.

True, the 1954 Constitution restored a semblance of proper perspective on this score. Nevertheless, certain disquieting aspects remained. Typically, the armed forces retained their privileged status and were allocated a specified quota or representatives in the National People's Congress and the lower congresses above the county level. By the time the Great Leap Forward and commune campaigns had ground to a halt, the military establishment had resumed much of its former prominence as a regular component of the PRC's governmental and administrative apparatus. The Cultural Revolution finished the process and propelled the army into the open glare of the footlights:

the imposition of "military control" over Party and state organs, and later over economic organizations as well, was publicly announced early in 1967. The organs of the judiciary were replaced by military justice, while Party and government organs were put under direct army control. The emergence of the Revolutionary Committees gave the army virtually free rein: behind the official facade of triumvirate rule that these new agencies projected, the men in uniform continued to wield absolute power. To this day they serve as the backbone of the bureaucratic structure to which the Maoist regime has seen fit to entrust the management of domestic affairs in the aftermath of the recent upheavals.

From the first, the heavy emphasis on administrative media also meant a corresponding atrophy of the organs of representative government. A historical precedent was set when the Central People's Government Council was vested with plenary powers to run the country. The interim legislature, the Chinese People's Political Consultative Council, met just once to constitute the top state organs; it never convened again, and its committee did not exercise any state functions. This arrangement lasted until 1954, when a more familiar format, calling for separate executive, legislative, judicial, and administrative branches, was introduced.

Normalcy prevailed for a while, but then the Cultural Revolution turned the clock back with a vengeance, although in fact things began to go seriously awry before that. The work of the highest organs of central government was repeatedly disrupted, and with increasing frequency it proceeded behind closed doors. The Second National People's Congress missed its annual convocation in 1961, and its third session, in April 1962, was shrouded in secrecy. During its term, much of its normal business was transacted at preliminary sessions; contrary to precedent, the assembly did not pass a single major law and even failed to endorse the state plan and state budget every year. The meetings of its Standing Committee and of the State Council were not publicized, except for laconic communiqués released to the press that merely mentioned the items reported on or discussed on those occasions. The Third National People's Congress, elected in 1964, was summoned to meet between December 21, 1964, and January 4, 1965, to hear a report on the work of the government and approve the state plan and the state budget for 1965. It has not scheduled a session since. (The Party Congress suffered a parallel decline after 1956, notwithstanding the statute's stipulation that no more than five years shall elapse between sessions.) Today, key directives that fundamentally alter the provisions of existing legislation emanate from organs lacking the necessary juridical authority, despite the fact that the Constitution has never been formally repealed or amended in order to impart to the present procedure a tinge of legality.

In the lower echelons, the Soviet critics continue, the situation over the long haul proved equally unsatisfactory. The debut was inauspicious. The tight intertwining of the organs of the United Front and the state organs of comparable level slowed the development of a robust and dynamic local government. Minor functionaries associated with the previous regime kept their posts, often for many years; and their conservative style of performing their prescribed duties helped rob the primary units of the new governmental organism of some of their vitality. An appreciable delay in staging local elections meant that, for an extended period of time, a congeries of appointed executive committees monopolized the field. None of this was calculated to invigorate the nascent institution of popular self-government in the bottom and intermediate ranges and, according to the Russians, the latter's effectiveness was gravely impaired by the circumstances surrounding its infancy. As a result, the organs of representative government never really fulfilled their assigned role: they exercised no tangible control over the executive departments, the political activity of the voters and the deputies boiled down to a few ritualized motions, and substantive political power coalesced in the hands of the executive state agencies that shared a large proportion of their personnel with the Party apparatus, along lines strangely reminiscent of the standard modus operandi in the initial period of the PRC's constitutional experience.

On yet two other counts Chinese conduct in this sphere has elicited adverse commentary. First, the Soviets note that the well-intentioned move in 1954 to broaden the base of local government by instituting committees of the urban population that were organizationally connected with the street bureaus did not have the desired effect because the committees very soon degenerated into administrative appendages of the bureaus and lost their quality of independent organizations of the population. To be sure, in 1956 a strenuous effort was made to arrest and reverse this drift; but in light of what happened next on the internal political front, the bid came to naught, the previous trend gained fresh momentum, and, in the Soviet view, the end product shortly took on most of the reprehensible attributes of the ill-famed pao-chia system.

Second, a serious breach of the Constitution is seen in the widespread use in the PRC of the ad hoc device of "special districts" and analogous artifices characterized by the absence of corresponding elective organs of government and Party and the concentration of all power in these territorial divisions in the hands of appointive administrative bodies accountable solely to their superior parent agencies. Moreover, whereas the apparatus of representative government of comparable rank steadily shrank, the opposite tendency could be observed in the "special districts" and kindred units: here, the organizational chart continued to expand and so did the office staff. To the Russians, the whole phenomenon was illustrative of the slow but constant shift of the center of gravity in the PRC from the domain of representative popular government to that of the career bureaucracy.

COMMUNE, PEASANTRY, AND THE MASS LINE

The commune venture dealt the constitutional system of local government a further blow. The project was neither discussed nor ratified by the National People's Congress, as was required by law, since the scheme entailed a fundamental revision of the established pattern of village government. The hsiang congresses of people's representatives were in practice liquidated. The congresses of commune representatives that displaced them were now indirectly elected and slated to meet twice annually (by contrast, hsiang congresses were expected to meet at least once in three months). They were occupied with production questions but paid no attention to public services, culture, education, or public hygiene, matters to which the hsiang congresses had hitherto devoted much time and energy. With the collapse of the communes, even these congresses stopped convening. Their administrative branches alone functioned throughout and continued to operate (a thoroughly familiar state of affairs, the Russians say), and the deliberations concerning production questions were transferred to brigade meetings.

Hamstrung and gelded, the government-Party edifice proved incapable of mounting a significant defense against the onslaughts of the Cultural Revolution and succumbed, completing the job of destruction: all the old organs of representative government and Party committees have been disbanded and their shoes filled by Revolutionary Committees whose members, mostly military figures, are appointed from the top and consist entirely of those owing personal loyalty to Mao. A generic feature of the whole episode, the Russians claim, is that while all the democratic institutions in the PRC—state, Party, social organizations—were smashed in the process, the army took the organs of public security and the nonelective branch organs of administration under its protective wing and, apart from the changes in the directorial quarters, the dismantling of the professional bureaucratic apparatus was never seriously contemplated. Whether or not the experiment succeeds remains to be seen. Soviet analysts point out that many of the government employees who had lost their positions in the purge have since been rehabilitated and restored to office, and that sporadic attempts to organize "Congresses of Revolutionary People's Representatives" may foreshadow an eventual return to the earlier model.

The dangers inherent in the above dicta, according to the Soviets, are compounded by the confusion Mao has deliberately wrought in the Marxist-Leninist theory of the dictatorship of the proletariat. For an equation predicated on the neat dichotomy of an irreconcilable confrontation of antagonistic social classes, he has substituted the bastard formula of a dictatorship of all classes, or of the masses, or of the people. In place of concrete, objective criteria and a scientific definition of social classes, he has espoused a vague, hybrid conception designed, the Soviets allege, to secure him maximum freedom and flexibility in intramural political maneuvers. Indeed, the Russians contend, what has been achieved thereby is to let Mao identify his allies and his opponents, to reward the former and to punish the latter, not by reason of whether or not they fall within the empirically verifiable categories of workers or working peasants or working-class intellectuals, but strictly in terms of their willingness to render absolute allegiance to Mao and his personal creed.

In extremis, the Soviets do not object to recourse to harsh measures against genuine "class enemies." However, in the absence of sound ideological appreciation of that phenomenon, they insist, the weapon of coercion is bound to misfire or hit the wrong target. In Mao's China, according to the Russians, that is precisely what has occurred in recent years. True Marxists, who have loyally opposed Mao's deviationist course, have suffered brutal persecution as "enemies of the people" (read "enemies of Mao himself") in a climate of mounting national hysteria that has swept away all legal guarantees and procedural safeguards, and has treated its victims without any sense of justice of decorum. By contrast, people of dubious social extraction have been handled with kid gloves in return for their ostensible devotion to the Maoist regime.

Failure to abide by the Marxist-Leninist canon in this respect has either lured Mao into the trap of subjectivism or he has voluntarily chosen that slippery path. At any rate, the net result has been the progressive abandonment of the correct axiom of putting primary reliance on and trust in the proletariat and a switch to the expedient of operating with a contrived assemblage of random pro-Mao groups that are distinguished not by their innate ideological complexion but by a pragmatic display of readiness to cooperate temporarily with the prevailing Maoist line. Within the framework of a string of ramshackle, floating coalitions—so runs the Kremlin's thesis—the peasantry and the national bourgeoisie have gradually emerged as decisive forces whose own class views have left an indelible imprint on the policies currently implemented in the PRC, to the detriment of the real business of building socialism in the country. To show how far the erosion has advanced, the Soviets point to such anomalies as the widespread excesses committed during the "three-anti" campaign, which was aimed mainly at government cadres, compared with the leniency that, during the "five-anti" campaign, was afforded the national bourgeoisie (mass summary executions versus fines and, on rare occasion, imprisonment), or the minority position occupied by the workers in all organs of local government, even those serving the large industrial centers.

Interestingly enough, the Soviets are quite prepared to acknowledge the wisdom and propriety of the PRC leadership's original resort to united front tactics in the historical context of the Chinese scene. This stratagem, by Russian account too, made possible the mobilization of mass support under the banner of the revolution, greatly facilitated its ultimate victory, and paved the way for the successes achieved during the seminal years in overthrowing the pillars of the old order and laying the foundations of a socialist community. The right approach under the circumstances would have been to harness these populist instincts, to steer them in the proper direction, and thus at one and the same time to neutralize potential sources of hostility and to attract fresh recruits to the cause—meanwhile vigilantly guarding against the perils of capitulating to the insidious spell cast by alien-class elements and vigorously pushing for an early transition from the presocialist phase of the "democratic dictatorship of the people" to the next stage of the "dictatorship of the proletariat." In sum, a heightened awareness of the risks incurred in pursuing this delicate game was called for, prompting the application of suitable antidotes to preserve the hegemony of the proletariat in the partnership and restrain the pressures emanating from the peasantry and the petite bourgeoisie that might otherwise deflect the revolutionary movement from its true objectives and lead it astray.

Mao not only neglected to take the necessary precautions but, the Russians now charge, openly catered to these subversive impulses and actively connived at their present ascendancy over the authentic norms of socialist behavior. The influence of the peasant factor, the importance of which Mao premeditatedly exaggerated, to the extent of equating the political structure of the new democracy with the peasantry's accession to power, proved especially fatal. On the one hand, it posed a major stumbling block in the path of the socialist transformation of China. On the other hand, with Mao shopping around for means of attaining his private ends, he soon perceived that the unique mores of China's rural heartland could furnish him with a convenient vehicle to promote his interests if he managed to adapt his modus operandi to it and to exploit its peculiar ethical outlook. The cult of his own personality was Mao's response to the challenge. The choice was dictated by the dual realization that the instrument fitted the Chinese peasant's universe of semifeudal traditions of deification of the country's rulers and the ingrained habit of passively obeying the commands of the overlords and that these traditions lent themselves perfectly to the achievement of the goals he had in mind: the perpetuation of the political submissiveness of the masses, the establishment of a system of stringent bureaucratic control, and the sole exercise of supreme political power in deciding on all questions of the PRC's social and political life. Hence, for Mao, the peasants were both a ready excuse and rationalization for proceeding in a certain way and a welcome tool to further his ambitions.

By going that route, however, Mao also inevitably committed himself to a specific political style. To sway the ignorant masses, he has had to rely on crude demagoguery and crass emotionalism, to fan primitive passions and to appeal to the basest human appetites, and to fashion an institutional mechanism that would personalize the regime and dramatize the personal dimensions of power in China today. This would explain one of the sins the Russians impute to him—his marked indifference to matters related to the building of the state and to the routine doctrinal and practical aspects of state-craft. The attitude is understandable enough if one sees Mao, who at this juncture is accused of always having been an authoritarian at heart, as absorbed from the first in the task of creating a monolithic, pyramidal structure run at every level by men whom he has appointed to executive office and who are vested with a broad range of powers and allowed considerable room for local initiative—in short, a system inspired by the spirit of hierarchical autocracy, a form of adminis-tration in which the plenitude of power in a given territory rests in the hands of an individual who, to all intents and purposes, is answer-able only to the person standing on the next higher rung of the bureau-cratic ladder. At the apex, Mao himself once epitomized the principle of interlocking directorates by concurrently discharging the functions of Chairman of the Central People's Government Council, Chairman of the People's Revolutionary Military Council, and Chairman of the Party's Central Committee.

All of this, as already mentioned, worked against the develop-ment of responsible government in China. Effective power was wielded by the executive agencies at each level of authority. Prior to the Cultural Revolution, the situation was further aggravated by frequent resort to the device of letting Party personnel serve in government posts and encouraging constant Party interference in government affairs, via the executive branch. Except, to make matters worse yet, within the Party proper, the first secretaries of the correspond-ing Party committees were extolled as commanders in chief during the 1950s and 1960s and so felt impelled to issue orders unilaterally: this, in turn, spread distrust of collegiality and formalism in the operation of the state institutions, which sank deeper into apathy and impotence. Thus, whereas the rest of the socialist states ostensibly

strive to increase the degree of popular participation in the organs
of local government, China is pictured as the lone maverick in this
respect, for, we are told, the aim of all the activities of Mao and his
confederates since 1958 has been to telescope the process of democratization of state organs, limiting and then preventing the mass of
the working people from occupying posts in those organs. These efforts
have succeeded in virtually depriving the regular mass organizations
of the opportunity to play a role in the management of society.

Still other steps were taken to make sure that the performance
of the complex bureaucratic edifice set in motion by a rigid vertical
chain of command would be adequately insulated from outside checks
of its record by autonomous sister media—which is why the Committee of People's Control was first demoted to the rank of an ordinary
ministry and, later, all central and local control institutions were
abolished; why the formula of "direct subordination" within the organs
of the procuracy and its job of general supervision withered away;
why the rule of the independence of the judges was never promulgated
and the rule of the independence of the courts enunciated by the Constitution was never observed; and why the PRC eschewed a law on
procedures for the recall of deputies from the congresses of people's
representatives—for a long time, this situation basically suited many
local leaders and the Mao group, which considered them the most
reliable and docile implementers of any plans it might concoct.

Today, the Russians bitterly note, Mao's fondest dreams have
been fulfilled. Political power in China has been seized by a tiny
clique, dominated by Mao himself. This group determines the direction of the country's social and political life and has completely usurped
the functions of the highest organs of Party and government. From
the standpoint of the PRC's constitutional law, this entity fits none
of the recognized components of the political system and, more than
anything, resembles the semiconsultative/semidecision-making institutions of monarchies and regimes of absolute dictatorship. "Mao's
headquarters" is a vague concept that is not backed by any legal or
other document: it lacks a precise structure, a special apparatus,
a clearly defined and permanent staff. The various Revolutionary
Committees at the lower echelons are no better: they likewise ignore
the principle of the separation of functions and instead symbolize
the theme of the universality of official rights and duties, in that their
jurisdictional circuit spans every field of public endeavor.

In an operational sense, the cult of the personality found its
purest expression in the method of the "mass line." Again, the Soviets
do not seem to object to the concept as such and, indeed, earlier they
had many complimentary things to say about certain aspects of that
approach. To the Russians, however, the formula has a specific
meaning and conveys the notion of large-scale popular involvement,

either directly in the affairs of local government or in an ancillary capacity thereto—that is, ample civic initiative within the established institutional matrix. What shocks them about the Maoist script is that, in the name of this principle, the regime has precipitated a series of deliberate confrontations between segments of the population and various state and Party organs, pitting the common folk against the government and Party officialdom. Lenin, the Soviets emphasize, never confused socialist democracy with the arbitrary behavior of faceless crowds, nor did he visualize the grass-roots activities of the masses as a counterweight to the job performed by the representative institutions of the proletarian state. Hence, the effect of Mao's perversion of Marxist practice in this regard has been to undermine the authority of representative government; to drive a wedge between the government and the Party, on the one hand, and the citizenry, on the other; to foster among the workers an image of the state organs, laws, and even Party and state cadres as a force opposed to the people; and to resurrect the darkest traditions of the feudal age by inflaming unhealthy passions and instincts among the shadier elements in the community. For, the Russians insist, the phenomenon lacks a scintilla of spontaneity, vociferous Chinese claims to the contrary notwithstanding, and represents a carefully orchestrated and manipulated mise-en-scene that owes its success to the regime's skill in exploiting the gullibility of a host of ignorant peasants, a flock of opportunistic members of the petite bourgeoisie, and a fraction of the working class that it has managed to deceive concerning its true objectives.

ADMINISTRATION OF JUSTICE

Though the whole apparatus of government suffered as a result, the agencies associated with the administration of justice fared worst of all, which is quite understandable, given that the style of the "mass line" is inherently incompatible both with the normal spirit of the law and with the judiciary's standard modus operandi. According to the Russians, several mistakes were committed in this sector from the very beginning. For example, the 1951 provisional regulations on the organization of the courts retained the arrangement pursuant to which each court formed an integral part of the people's government of equivalent rank and was put under the twin jurisdiction of the corresponding people's government and the next higher court. Other novel features included letting cases be heard by single judges, except especially complicated ones, which were tried by a panel of judges, and limiting the status of the people's assessors in the proceedings to a consultative role. The structure of the organs of the procuracy was supposed to parallel the pattern of territorial distribution of the courts; but much time elapsed before offices could be installed in every chosen location, and meanwhile their assignment to carry out investigations and press charges in court were entrusted to the organs of public security.

By and large, these technical defects that experience might be expected to cure. A more permanent and dangerous ingredient was introduced when the regime began experimenting, with increasing scope and frequency, with the instrumentality of extraordinary courts in connection with mass political campaigns. The activities of the military tribunals attached to the military-control committees assumed alarming proportions during the campaigns to suppress counterrevolutionary elements that raged from 1950 to 1952. Land reform then brought into existence an array of people's tribunals: these acted independently of the regular courts, their verdicts were subject to administrative confirmation but were not open to judicial appeal, and their manner of conducting business often departed from the accepted norms of procedure and turned their sessions into trial meetings. In fact, the Russians maintain, they were given a fixed quota of death sentences to meet and, like as not, would merely rubber-stamp previous instructions without worrying much about how licit were the sentences they dispensed.

During the "three-anti" campaign, launched in 1951 and waged through most of the first half of 1952, the growth of special tribunals reached truly hypertrophic dimensions. They were authorized to impose capital punishment and, the Russians write, the way these units were set up meant that every administrative and military leader of any significance exercised judicial rights that left ample room for virtually uncontrolled arbitrariness. The country was plunged into an orgy of trial meetings; and the accused was often executed on the spot in the presence of a large crowd, without ever having had a chance to defend himself: he could only stand there with a poster around his neck that listed his crimes and listen to the various speeches denouncing him, interrupted by frequent cries from the audience demanding his death. The "five-anti" campaign was more subdued in tone and avoided the excesses of its predecessor. Although special tribunals were also created during the election campaign of 1953-54, they did not preside over the ceremonies but, rather, served as watchdogs to cut short any attempt to disturb the official program.

Inevitably, these phenomena had a profound negative effect on the development of the law and the regular judicial system of the PRC. They bred a contemptuous, not to say nihilistic, attitude toward the role of law in the new society and relegated the ordinary judicial organs to a secondary position while calling on the agencies of administrative repression to tackle the top-priority items. All the fanfare, publicity, and credit went to the army, the organs of public security, and the state and Party bureaucracy, which emerged as the folk heroes in these marathon spectacles, while the law and the judicial institutions waited backstage or dealt with common matters that brought them neither glory nor popular recognition. To be sure, they were kept busy too, especially in connection with the drive initiated in 1951 to implement the marriage and family law and, ironically, in 1952-53 were thrust into the limelight as the target of the mass campaign for judicial reform. Neither episode, however, attained the pitch and intensity of the preceding incidents; soon after, the storm began to subside, and by 1955-56 things had to a considerable extent returned to normal, although, the Russians point out, even as late as 1955 the regime unleashed a routine campaign to suppress counterrevolutionaries that struck primarily at the broad peasant masses and an appreciable number of Party members who advocated adherence to the slower pace of rural cooperativization decided upon earlier and opposed the whirlwind tempo of collectivization sanctioned by the latest instructions.

In the Soviet frame of analysis, the events of the Eighth Party Congress mark a historical watershed in the outspoken criticism voiced at that forum of the manner in which legal issues had hitherto been neglected and the ensuing recommendations that the work of the juridico-political institutions be strengthened, particularly through the rapid promulgation of the necessary codes, the elaboration of indispensable procedural safeguards, and the enforcement of strict control measures over the legitimacy of the acts of the bureaucratic apparatus. These steps, in the opinion of the assembled speakers (and current Soviet commentators), would help put the system back on the right track by eradicating the trend toward administrative irresponsibility and legal anarchy characteristic of the record of past years. To achieve these goals, the immediate problem was to strengthen all the organs supervising legality, especially the procuracy; to establish offices of defense counsel, notary public, and economic arbitration; to curb the use of capital punishment; and generally to improve the quality of the PRC's legal fabric.

Instead of heeding these wise injunctions, Mao lashed out at those who thus expressed tacit criticism of his pet theories. Under the pretext of combating "rightist bourgeois elements" unmasked during the "Hundred Flowers" campaign, Mao ordered a veritable pogrom of loyal Communists who had taken the lessons of the Eighth Party Congress to heart, concentrating his fire on the juridico-political departments (the courts, the procuracy, and the organs of state control) and educational institutions (the law faculties and the political science and law institutes). The ranks of the Ministry of Control, the Supreme People's Court, and the Supreme People's

Procuratorate and their local offices underwent a thorough purge for urging direct subordination of the control agencies and their independence from local state organs in fulfilling their duties, genuine independence of the courts, judicial monopoly over the trial of cases, presumption of innocence, centralized control over the procuratorial organs and the insulation of their functions from local influences. The plans for codification were scrapped.

Thenceforward the road ran relentlessly downhill, declare the Soviet antagonists. August 1, 1957, witnessed the passage of the infamous regulations on labor education that let the administrative organs, without benefit of trial or investigation, send practically any Chinese citizen to a special camp for an indefinite duration for such vague reasons as the individual's refusal to accept a different job, or constant change of employment, or a long list of other manifestations of antisocial behavior. According to Soviet estimates, hundreds of thousands of people, including countless technical specialists, were caught in the monster dragnet; and the magnitude of the successive waves of repression may be gauged from reports that in the province of Kwangtung alone, at the beginning of the 1960s roughly 1 million souls languished in assorted concentration camps. The sorriest aspect of this whole business, the Russians lament, is that it victimized principally the working strata of the population and not the exploiting classes (the national bourgeoisie). Today, the China watchers in the Soviet Union see a close similarity between this project and the provisional regulations of August 26, 1954, on the procedure for freeing inmates after they had served their sentences and finding them work, that empowered the administration of the corrective-labor camps, in consultation with the organs of public security, to hold the prisoners at the place of detention for an indeterminate period.

The Great Leap Forward and commune ventures accelerated the process: penal sentences and other reprisals again skyrocketed. Roving brigades, consisting of officials from the public security bureaus, the courts, and the procurcies, were organized to mete out summary mass reprisals, a practice that has attracted particularly vehement attacks from Soviet quarters as a fundamentally incorrect merger, in the hands of single "operative groups," of unidentical functions previously performed by separate institutions. In a number of places, public rallies were staged to watch the execution of death sentences. In all provinces increasingly extensive use was made of convict labor.

All pretense at the independence of the courts and their subordination only to the law and the nature of the relations between the Party organs and the courts was dropped. The essence of Party control of the courts was distorted and, in the Maoist lexicon, became synonymous with the right of local Party organs to give the court instructions in deciding specific cases, coinciding with the court's obligation to "coordinate" its decision in a specific case with the appropriate Party committee, a proposition flatly contrary to the cardinal principles that, according to Soviet legal experts, animate truly socialist justice. Soviet authors scoff at colorful vignettes, for instance, of judges who, in the course of the commune campaign, utilized the rest periods and lunch breaks during three days of work in the fields to hear 35 criminal cases—on top of which, during these three days, they finished deep-plowing 23 mou of land. Or, to cite a second sample of the kind of episode that goaded Soviet commentators to grim sarcasm, there is the story of the judge who one day fell ill in the middle of a trial. It so happened that the secretary of the district Party committee dropped in for a visit; the latter advised the judge to rest well, personally took over the case, applied his ideological training, and soon fully resolved the matter.

The ignominious collapse of these radical economic reforms and their companion legal innovations brought a momentary pause in the regime's enthusiasm for experimentation. A corollary of the ensuing partial stabilization in the economic sphere was the gradual sobering of the Party-political and administrative cadres. Competent judgments on the role of law in economic administration and the organization of management reappeared in the professional journals. Sensible voices were raised once again on the need to reinforce legality and intensify propaganda to that end. Even Mao's instructions at the 1962 Party Central Committee Plenum to step up the struggle against internal enemies seemingly did not yield the desired results. In this sense, 1964 represents a vintage year: by local account, too, the number of counterrevolutionary and other cases, as well as the number of persons arrested in 1964, was less than in any other year of the PRC's existence.

The rectification drive pushed to the fore the more moderate elements within the local Party and government leadership. As a consequence, the gap between the lower echelons and the top Maoist hierarchy widened and power slowly slipped between the fingers of Mao and his friends, trickling down to the amorphous bulk of the junior and middle officialdom with a realistic appreciation of the Chinese scene who emerged as a passive and unconscious, yet stubborn, bulwark against Mao's grandiloquent dreams. Obviously, this development did not suit Mao's purposes and, to reverse the trend and reassert the supremacy of the Maoist credo while it was still possible to do so, a campaign for "socialist education" was instigated on a scale that, the Russians contend, ranked with or even surpassed such monster movements as the agrarian reform, the extermination of counterrevolution, and the struggle against the "three evils" and the "five evils."

Advertised as a universal medium for eradicating the embryos of "revisionism" and "embourgeoisement" in all strata of the population, the operation was extended into every village, into every enterprise and every municipal organization by brigades composed of Party officials, officials of the public security organs, the courts and the procuracies, officers, soldiers, and students assigned to the task by the competent Party committee. One of their functions was to ferret out the "enemies of socialism . . . who were trying to follow the capitalist road." The Russians claim that a directive from the center stipulated that, in the final analysis, these enemies were to comprise approximately 5 percent of the particular locality's population. The politico-juridical cadres recruited for the job were admonished to discard all purely juridical precautions and unnecessary ceremony that fettered the masses and did not conform to the revolutionary struggle, to understand that all requisite standard regulations and procedural methods were intended to facilitate the struggle against the enemy but not to bind them, to apply the revolutionary viewpoint of the class struggle, and not to take a metaphysical approach to the various institutions of the law.

The scheme was aimed, the Soviets insist, not at the punishment of criminals but at general intimidation and, inter alia, proposed to radicalize the politico-juridical personnel and turn them into obedient implementers of Mao's will. The bid was less than a total success, despite the heavy pressure exerted on the recalcitrant cadres. Thus, as a last resort, Mao and his entourage fell back on their stock in trade—the purge. In the course of the 18 months directly preceding the peak of the Cultural Revolution, the Soviets allege, there was an almost wholesale replacement of senior officials of the Supreme People's Court and the Supreme People's Procuracy, of their branches in Tibet, and of the judicial and procuratorial officials of Peking, Shanghai, and all the provinces.

Since even these extreme measures failed to satisfy the grandiose aspirations of the Maoist clique to exercise absolute control over every facet of the PRC's life, the "socialist education" campaign escalated into the Cultural Revolution, which spelled the doom of the PRC's former legal universe. From the first, the Maoist faction reportedly concentrated on extrajudicial summary reprisals; in many places the judicial organs virtually ceased to function and, where they did survive, the regime soon reduced them to tools of reprisal and intimidation. Show trials multiplied, often followed by summary public executions. The judicial reprisals against "Mao's enemies" were backed by military squads and, according to Russian spokesmen, judicial criminal practice in the PRC henceforth ran flagrantly counter to the democratic principles of justice inherent in socialist communities. The climax of the Maoist assault on the country's constitutional system coincided with the complete abolition of the organs of the judiciary, the procuratorate, and public security and the establishment of "single, unitary committees for the eradication of counterrevolutionaries," whose competence and authority derived from the support they received from the armed forces. The morale of the legal staff wilted in the cross fire of perennial criticism and self-criticism, and its professional integrity crumbled. All procedural safeguards were now abandoned, and naked power reigned unchallenged.

In short, the Russians paint China today as a land blanketed with prisons and corrective-labor, labor-reform, and compulsory-labor camps. The army is firmly in charge of every aspect of public activity, ordinary forms of repression have been joined to the technique of mass exile of city dwellers to remote rural regions, and common crime prospers—all the normal and indispensable attributes of a regime of military-bureaucratic dictatorship of the sort, Moscow says, that Mao has always craved and has finally achieved.

CONCLUSIONS

An inventory of the contents of Moscow's indictment of Mao's political record to date reveals several interesting articles that can be briefly summarized as follows:

First, it is clearly not enough for the Russians to denounce Mao for individual current peccadillos. They feel impelled to prove that these transgressions have a long history, are part of a methodical plan, and lie at the very core of the Maoist phenomenon. The natural inference is that superficial treatment will not cure the condition, and drastic surgery is called for if recovery is to occur. By that token, of course, Mao attains the status not of an occasional minor heretic but of a central devil-figure whose numerous sins are due to conscious failings and not to simple error, and whose whole personality is the source of the poison with which he has managed to infect the Chinese revolutionary movement.

Second, the features of the Maoist experience that have attracted Soviet criticism are not random items picked just because they seemed available and looked convenient. Rather, Soviet analysts have had to grapple with them from the very beginning, in an attempt to explain and vindicate the PRC's novel contributions to the socialist political repertory and the reasons for these departures from the Soviet model and its East European adaptations. Earlier, however, these inventions had been lauded as specimens of original, albeit orthodox, creativity that accommodated the tenets of classical Marxism to the unique objective circumstances of Chinese society; subsequently, these "improvements" earned the sobriquet of deliberate perversions of Marxian categorical imperatives. The point, though, is that these

160

issues have always been a topic of discussion among Soviet experts in the field, whether in positive or negative tones. This would tend to confirm the notion that from the start they drew attention and generated a certain amount of controversy, even if only in a genteel sense and with complimentary results.

Third, quite logically, the China watchers in the Soviet Union now focus on those aspects of Chinese behavior that represent genuine shortcomings in the PRC's political system, either in absolute or in relative terms. For example, Mao's handling of the nationality question frankly invites adverse comment, both because the Russians realize that the recent pattern of relations between the Hans and the local ethnic minorities is inherently apt to breed tension and conflict that automatically casts the Chinese in a bad light and because, by contrast, the formal picture in the Soviet Union is so much superior to the quality of the PRC's performance on that score. On a purely theoretical plane alone, the Soviets can expect to win sympathy abroad for their strict adherence to the principles of national self-determination, to which the federal structure of the Soviet Union pays ample lip service, whereas the Chinese would have a harder time establishing a good credit rating in this field.

Fourth, from the way Soviet academic people have flailed at some of the latest Maoist formulas, one often gets the impression that in condemning the PRC's practices they may well be indulging in vicarious castigation of various disturbing tendencies closer to home. In discussing, say, the Chinese rejection of the concept of presumption of innocence or the principle of independence of defense counsel, Russian legal specialists go further in support of these propositions than they do in their own literary pastures. In roundabout fashion, then, Chinese excesses in the legal realm may offer the liberal wing of the Soviet legal profession an opportunity to warn against possible reversion to Stalinist methods in the Soviet Union itself and, by this circuitous means, to fight against any perceived attempt to restore some of the older devices to favor in the domestic areas.

Last, it is curious how "Western" most of the Soviet tirades against Chinese "legal nihilism" sound. Nothing could illustrate better the vast disparity between the two countries than the law-and-order theme that dominates Soviet thinking in this sector versus the slogan of revolutionary improvisation that the Communist Chinese keep chanting. The emphasis on formal legality, the authority of the state, and the majesty of the courts may convey a positive image to a status quo-oriented Westerner; but how relevant these exhortations are to a society trying to give itself a radical face-lift is an altogether different matter. On balance, the Soviets seem to be denying the Chinese the freedom to engage in revolutionary experimentation, on

161

grounds that such conduct no longer squares with the Soviet archetype of the Marxist political model, is unnecessary and, in fact, only causes irreparable harm to the urgent business of building a viable socialist community. The Chinese, on the other hand, see the Soviet preoccupation with these incidental details as a betrayal of the Marxist-Leninist canon, a stark sign of abject Soviet surrender to the bourgeois code of ethics. How, if ever, the former partners will manage to bridge these differences remains a key issue: from all the foregoing evidence, the prospects of reaching a practicable solution within the near future are dim indeed. Meantime, Soviet attribution to the Maoist leadership of a rabid determination to promote an alternative political blueprint, matching comparable bids in the doctrinal and economic domains, further exacerbates an already hypersensitive situation while illuminating the depths to which their past association has sunk.

7

THE LOGIC OF
MAOIST POLITICAL
COMMUNICATION
Arnold B. Urken

During the Great Proletarian Cultural Revolution, informal and formal channels of political communication were exploited in the effort to form a coalition to defeat anti-Maoist forces. The competition for control of channels of information involved extensive innovation in the forms of mass mobilization—such as the ta-tzu pao (big character poster), radio broadcasts, Mao Tse-tung Thought Propaganda Teams, and newspapers. Although Peking has emphasized the important contribution of these developments in mass mobilization to the "victory" of Mao Tse-tung thought, foreign analysts of the Great Proletarian Cultural Revolution have not agreed on their significance. Generally, one group of analysts maintains that Maoist reliance on the manipulation of human emotions will backfire and lead to the overthrow of the Maoist regime. In contrast, another group of analysts suggests that the Great Proletarian Cultural Revolution has strengthened the Maoist cause in China.

These conflicting predictions about the effects of the Cultural Revolution on the viability of Maoist leadership of China's modernization prompt one to try to analyze the basis for these claims. The purpose of this work is to provide such an analysis.

These goals guide my analysis. First, I distinguish those predictive statements about Maoist political communication and modernization that are based on tested scientific theory from those predictions whose basis is speculative or motivated by ideological concerns. Second, I investigate the relationship of assumptions and conclusions about the logic of Maoist political communication in scientific and non-scientific explanations; in particular, I focus on the validity of the

This study is based on an analysis of the same title presented at the 1973 Annual Meeting of the American Political Science Association, New Orleans, Louisiana. I should like to thank Professors James C. Hsiung, James D. Seymour, and J. Gruender for their comments on an earlier draft.

general causal inferences that are derived from assumptions in ostensibly scientific explanations of the logic of Maoist political communication. The third goal of my analysis is to illustrate the use of "rational choice models" in creating theoretical explanations of political behavior in nonelectoral political systems such as the People's Republic of China.

In order to achieve these goals, I first provide an interpretation of the phenomena of the process of Maoist political communication that highlights its possible contructive role in the modernization of China. Next I demonstrate the necessity for reconceptualizing the logic of political communication in Chinese politics by pointing out an analytical limitation of current interpretations common to different ideological perspectives. This reconceptualization leads to an explanation of the analytical significance of the Maoist model of political communication. Finally, I consider the explanatory usefulness of a simple model in analyzing political communication in the People's Republic of China.

PROPAGANDA AND DECISION-MAKING

The constructive aspect of Maoist political communication in the modernization of China may be illustrated by referring to two models of decision-making. Reference to these models does not mean that individuals or groups are necessarily conscious of the goals and constraints found in either model. However, one may assume that actors behave as if they acted according to a model's postulated goals and constraints in order to explain political behavior. Through a process of trial and error, it is possible to refine models so that hypothetical inferences are consistent with observed outcomes.[1]

"Rationalist" Decision-Making

The first model, rationalist decision-making, postulates that individuals may verify their knowledge by relying on facts or logic or a combination of both. In an electoral political system, for instance, the behavior of voters may be interpreted as if they used information to determine which party or candidate would maximize the policy utility of their vote. Suppose, for example, that in a two-party system a voter is located at point M along the left-right policy continuum in Figure 1 and is faced with choosing between candidates or parties located at X and Y. In this simple example, if a voter's goal is to maximize the policy utility of a vote, it would be rational to vote for X rather than Y. That is, if a voter's preference were located at M, then party X would deliver policy benefits closer to the voter's preference. Moreover, if the voter could choose a candidate or party at point M, his preferences and utility would be in equilibrium.

FIGURE 1

Hypothetical Policy Space

	M		
Left	X	Y	Right

"Propagandistic" Decision-Making

In contrast with the model of "rationalist" decision-making, one may assume that an individual's knowledge will be circumscribed by actions that preclude reasoning and suppress evidence inconsistent with the purpose of a political leader or party. Although these postulates do not rule out "rational" behavior in the instrumental sense of acting to achieve a goal, the postulated conditions do suggest that a voter would not have perfect information about the implications of his choices and would have to resort to probabilistic calculations. In order to emphasize the contrast with the rationalist model, let us refer to this set of goals and constraints as the propagandistic model.

In the discussion below on whether current explanations are "scientific," I will elaborate on the significance of ambiguity in political decision-making and also suggest that some analysts of the logic of Maoist political communication write as if individuals in a "democracy" could maximize the utility income from their votes according to the rationalist model. At this point, however, it is important to note that the analyses of party competition by Anthony Downs and others suggest that the propagandistic model is more descriptive of political behavior in electoral systems. Specifically, these analyses indicate that political parties or candidates may find it advantageous to be ambiguous about their position in policy space in order to attract voters. Consequently, voters may be prevented from finding an equilibrium choice.[2]

The concept of voter equilibrium is an abstraction, but it is interesting because it suggests that voters do not revolt simply because they do not obtain everything they want. In fact, we do not know precisely how much dissatisfaction voters will tolerate.

Similarly, we do not know how much dissatisfaction individuals in nonelectoral political systems can tolerate. Yet the fact that national elections are not a mechanism for choice in such systems does not necessarily imply that it is logically impossible to achieve an equilibrium between individual preference and governmental policy. (Downs notes that normal conditions in an electoral system make it unlikely that an equilibrium will be viable even if attained.)

165

In other words, it is logically possible for a regime in a nonelectoral system like the People's Republic of China to succeed as a viable government. Moreover, it follows that to some degree, the government of the PRC might remain in power even if it deviates from an equilibrium position for many people.

This discussion of equilibriums is important because it highlights the type of statement that causes distress among some analysts of Chinese politics. Specifically, unless one can offer an explicit theoretical justification for statements about what is possible in a political system, it is not clear whether one is making propaganda that bolsters a particular policy position or is offering intuitive assessments. If, in fact, one's statements are not propagandistic, it becomes imperative to offer a rationale for an assessment, because such reasoning helps clarify the purpose of communication.

Ellul's Functional Analysis of Propaganda

The general problem of distinguishing fact from intuitive opinion is discussed by Jacques Ellul.[3] His analysis not only clarifies this distinction but also relates it to Maoist political communication.

For Ellul, propaganda is a sociological phenomenon associated with the process of modernization. He defines propaganda as

> . . . [a] set of methods employed by an organized group that wants to bring about the active or passive participation in its actions of a mass of individuals psychologically unified through psychological manipulation and incorporated in an organization.[4]

Ellul maintains that propaganda works by preparing men gradually through education, and then using agitation to mobilize them to achieve a particular goal. By exploiting all media to "surround man by all possible routes,"[5] continuous propaganda can exceed the attention capability of the individual and gradually overcome his capacity for resistance. Propaganda does not aim at changing beliefs or ideas, but strives to provoke action. For Ellul, this action can take the form of active or passive "participation."[6] He asserts that among human beings there is no necessary connection between conviction and action. Consider the morale of a military unit as an example of human conviction. Bad morale in a military unit may contribute to decreased fighting efficiency, but the necessities of combat may conceal a unit's low morale. In this case, fighting efficiency would not be minimized. In general, then, no necessary direct causal connection can be drawn between the single factor of a unit's morale level and fighting efficiency when the unit must fight.[7]

If the aim of propaganda is to render men mobilizable, then the propagandist must rely on exploiting the "internal characteristics" of propaganda.[8] For example, by knowing the "psychological terrain" of his audience, the propagandist can obtain action without demanding consistency in the manner or content of his communication. Although the propagandist cannot create new mechanisms of psychological manipulation by fiat, he can exploit human needs to achieve his goals. For instance, opinions detrimental to the interests of a regime may be diverted from their accepted course by means of education.[9]

Moreover, by being aware of fundamental social currents, the propagandist can insure the timeliness of his themes and the likelihood that they will create a mobilized audience that will be powerful enough to achieve the desired goals. Propaganda may lie about intentions or the interpretations of facts, but it must also be accurate enough to create long-term credibility in the target audience.

According to Ellul, Mao Tse-tung's greatness as a propagandist is that he propagandized without being held directly responsible for accomplishing the goals he advocated. To paraphrase Ellul, Mao learned the advantages of formulating a slogan to mobilize people in order to obtain goals and not being the one to fulfill the slogans.[10] This technique has facilitated the Maoist task of the continuing re-molding of the Chinese population.[11]

From this viewpoint, Maoist political communication can be interpreted as a dialectical process of subversion and integration. It is subversive in the sense that Maoist propaganda appeals to the "most basic feelings in order to arouse revolt" and eventually leads to combat by conditioning people and relying on slogans.[12] Nevertheless, Maoist political communication is integrative, because a person is subjected to political education as soon as he is mobilized.[13]

Propaganda, then, is a necessary phenomenon of all states, regardless of their stage of modernization. The governments of states need propaganda to determine what people want and to gain compliance with official actions. Similarly, the individual needs propaganda to achieve a vicarious sense of participation in his political system. Moreover, even in a technological society, the individual's sphere of effectiveness is limited by dislocation and tension, which are dissolved by the rationalizations of propaganda.[14]

EXAMPLES OF CURRENT ANALYSES

An argument for the necessity of reconceptualizing the role of "political communication" in Chinese politics may be based on the fact that some current analyses of the subject do not yield conclusions that are rigorously derived from general assumptions. Instead, predictions are based on sets of statements that are not systematically related. As a consequence, the implications of these analyses for policy-making are ambiguous, regardless of one's ideological viewpoint. In order to clarify this ambiguity, it is useful to begin by classifying analyses as "scientific" explanations or official explanations, according to their treatment of ambiguous situations. This classification will be based on an evaluation of the goal of an explanation. It may seem unusual to treat "scientific" and official explanations of Chinese "political communication" as parts of a common intellectual genre. However, there is a common concern with two mutually dependent variables that affect the persuasiveness of an explanation: the complexity of an event and public information about an event. These dependent variables depend on each other rather than on a third variable. Currently it is not possible to determine whether they are directly or inversely related.

"Official" Explanations

Let us consider the significance of these variables for the political actor whose goal is to create effective official explanations, or "propaganda." If the complexity of an event is great, a propagandist will find it easier to select facts to produce a credible and persuasive explanation so long as the information possessed by the audience is not sufficient to contradict official statements. Some contradictions may be tolerated, because suppression of information and repetition of the official line can eliminate any evidence of contradictions. However, an event may be so inherently complex that people are naturally skeptical about an explanation. This may be the case with many political events that breed skepticism of official explanations regardless of the relationship between the two variables. Moreover, if an event is relatively simple and the amount of public information is great, a propagandist will find it more difficult to sustain a particular explanatory viewpoint.

Despite ideological differences, there is a tendency for opposing propagandists to use the same formula in dealing with these mutually dependent variables. For example, in explaining the Great Proletarian Cultural Revolution, Peking and Taipei both tend toward an optimal combination of the variables: a simplified explanation to minimize doubt about official accounts of events and minimum public information about the Cultural Revolution. This combination simultaneously allows Kuomintang observers to portray the Cultural Revolution as another indication of impending doom for Maoism and permits Chinese Communist commentators to hail the event as a great victory for Mao Tse-tung thought.

In both cases, it is important to note that the official treatment of events implicitly rules out the possibility of encountering a a refutation.[15] The goal of the explanation is to mobilize facts in order to support a particular political outlook. Achieving this goal makes it possible for the target of a propaganda message to sustain his beliefs by finding that the operation of his environment is consistent with his expectations.

"Scientific" Explanations

Since all explanation involves some degree of simplification of events, it is not surprising that assumptions are found in scientific explanation. But the function of these assumptions is quite different from those found in official explanations. Specifically, there is no necessary logical relationship between scientific assumptions and ideological viewpoint. In order words, the justification for making scientific assumptions depends on empirically verified consequences derived as part of the trial-and-error process of improving our knowledge.[16]

Ideally, scientific explanations may be judged by how much they explain and how well they explain it. Consequently, scientific explanation thrives on maximum information and consideration of the full complexity of events—the opposite of the propagandist's optimal combination of variables.[17] In practice, however many scientific analyses of "political communication" in China do not fulfill the conditions included in the "scientific" definition of the optimal combination of variables. This state of affairs may be illustrated by considering four analyses that relate Maoist propaganda or political communication to the operation of the Chinese political system.[18]

Liu's Critique of Cultural
Revolution Propaganda

"Political communication" may be approached as one factor in the process of modernization or one element of political culture.[19] Alan P. L. Liu selects the former approach in focusing on the breakdown of the Maoist political communications system during the Great Proletarian Cultural Revolution.[20] He says that the cinema and urban press were attacked because they played up ideas that were incompatible with the Maoist line. For instance, during the "blooming and contending" of 1957, urban media staff openly criticized party control. As a consequence, radio became the "vital channel of communication" for the Maoist line. Normal functioning of the broadcast networks enabled Mao Tse-tung to mobilize support by using radio transmissions from Peking to lend legitimacy to coercive action and create a sense of coherence. In addition, People's Liberation Army (PLA) Thought Propaganda Teams were given the "important political task" of increasing the range of wired networks. Some of these networks were constructed with remnants of wire attached to tree branches. In October 1969, a new radio station began operating Yunnan Province to facilitate the timely and accurate targeting of minority audiences.[21]

While it is true that broadcast networks "functioned normally," it should be noted that they functioned normally in comparison with the disruption that occurred in other media. For example, during the Great Proletarian Cultural Revolution, it was common practice for Radio Peking to substitute direct transmissions from Peking for provincial broadcasts when the revolutionary situation in a particular area was threatened by "a handful of capitalist-roaders." In general, the duration of this practice varied with the seriousness of the threat. In Inner Mongolia, Ulanfu's anti-Maoist movement captured the transmitter and it became necessary to dispatch an armed forced to return the provincial station to Maoist control.[22]

Moreover, there is some evidence to suggest that anti-Maoist elements may have used the provincial stations to advantage without actually taking them over. For example, during the Cultural Revolution, it was general practice for Maoist propaganda to play up the activities of the PLA Thought Propaganda Teams. Peking and provincial broadcasts invariably would extoll the power of Mao Tse-tung thought and report examples of how a group had struggled to become good Maoists. Normally, the broadcasts omitted any mention of popular reaction against the Thought Propaganda Teams. In particular, reports of attacks on the teams and resulting casualties were not mentioned.

In one instance, however, a provincial station broadcast a report that deviated significantly from the accepted format for this subject. The report extolled the power of Mao Tse-tung thought and said that the activities of a particular Thought Propaganda Team illustrated that power. According to the report, the team had been attacked by anti-Maoist elements and suffered two killed and several wounded. The report ended without the proverbial example of group progress in the study and application of Mao Tse-tung thought. This report may be an example of a case in which anti-Maoists subtly inplanted doubt about the power of Mao thought. Nevertheless, it should be noted that the statistical significance of this example is unclear and that this deviation might be attributed to the confusion and relative lack of professionalism of a provincial propaganda operation or intra-Maoist competition.[23]

While Liu is correct in calling radio the "vital channel of communication" for the Maoists, he does not give sufficient emphasis to Red Guard publications that were used to mobilize the masses to intimidate followers of the "capitalist road." If radio had a vital general strategic role, it is also true that the Red Guard publications played an important tactical role in stemming the tide of anti-Maoist opposition by motivating activists to mobilize support for Mao.[24]

In appraising Maoist propaganda during the Cultural Revolution, Liu defines three crucial issues. First, he notes that ideology seemed to give way to reality and "secularization." Generally, Maoist propaganda seemed to undermine its own legitimacy by appealing to Chinese to modernize their country. And by "fighting professionalism," Mao ended up "fighting modernization." Liu also says that the Maoist use of mass emotion works against institutionalization. He suggests that this mass technique is self-defeating because nation-building depends on the creation of institutions. Finally, Liu says that the political communications in China rely on a combination of mass communications, political penetration of society, and "voluntaristic" participation. An effective Chinese mass media based on journals, books, and the press would require greater urbanization and growth of literacy. Consequently Maoist propaganda is limited in transforming society because it relies on political penetration.[25]

Liu implies that Maoism and ideology are incompatible with modernization and "secularization," that Maoism cannot create the basis for a nation-state by using mass emotion, and that Maoists cannot transform a society by means of political penetration. These implications may serve as a persuasive intuitive basis for Liu's evaluation because they are based on the idea that Maoism is incompatible with its goals or that it is impossible for Maoism to achieve its goals. This idea may be appealing because it suggests that Maoism is inevitably irrational. Indeed, it may seem especially attractive because a counterexample or defense of Maoism as a viable ideology would have to show that Maoism can succeed—a demonstration that by definition is impossible except for true believers.

Lifton's Theory of Propagandistic Limits

In Thought Reform and the Psychology of Totalism, Robert J. Lifton examines the process of "ideological remoulding" (szu-hsiang kai-tsao) in order to determine whether men's beliefs can be changed for a long time.[26] He shows that thought reform can use external force and an appeal to inner enthusiasm to change belief. Since belief and identity affect each other, an emphasis is put on using guilt to induce an individual to empty himself of old ideas, absorb new ones, and eventually find "a new sense of fit" in looking at his environment.

In a later work Lifton, prompted by the Great Proletarian Cultural Revolution, expands his analysis of the psychology of totalism into a psychoanalytic-historical explanation of developments in China.[27] According to Lifton, Mao's strategy for mobilization—"psychicism"— depends on two assumptions: the infinite malleability of the human mind and the all-powerful nature of the will. Mao's "psychistic fallacy" is "the assumption of the interchangeability of psychic state and technology."[28] According to Lifton's "law of diminishing conversions," psychicism was a suitable technique for mobilization in pre-1949 China, but the People's Republic of China has developed a technological society and psychicism interferes with "the internal work" necessary for modernization.[29]

Lifton emphasizes the need for "nonrational" assurance of survival of the self that Maoism satisfies. Maoist revolutionary purity entails transcendentalism that provides a justification for authority. To bolster this authority, Mao's thought, the "Maoist corpus," becomes an "all-consuming prophecy," an "existential absolute."[30] The implication of Lifton's work is that China cannot be transformed and modernized in the Maoist mold.

The problem with Lifton's assessment of Maoist political communication is that he relies on his theorem of impossibility as if it were a valid theorem of logical impossibility concerning modernization. Since this theorem is stated in imprecise terms, it is difficult to test and is relatively invulnerable to criticism. In some disciplines, impossibility proofs have been developed to demonstrate that one cannot logically expect particular outcomes to occur under certain general conditions. For instance, in mathematics, Gödel's incompleteness theorems show that one unified language would not be sufficiently universal for even the purposes of elementary number theory. In contrast, knowledge about the development of political systems is not rigorously deduced from theoretical assumptions. Indeed, analysts have not agreed on the identification of important systemic variables, much less determined the significance of their interaction. Nevertheless, Lifton relies on his theorem as if it were as obvious to a social scientist as Godel's proof might be to a mathematician. However, Lifton does not consider the developmental possibilities that might be generated by taking account of more general conditions. Perhaps this problem would have been obviated if Lifton had compared his analysis with alternative explanations.[31]

Yu's Description of Propagandistic Failure

In Mass Persuasion in Communist China, Frederick T. C. Yu analyzes the techniques that are used to socialize the Chinese population. He concludes that the Chinese Communists have succeeded in integrating a pervasive and penetrating system of communications.

172

This system "is not so successful in the positive aim of producing the particular thoughts and attitudes desired by the Party." It is reasonably effective in screening out all information that will reach the people.[32]

Nevertheless, Yu says the system suffers from serious communications problems. For one thing, although repetition may be a strength in mass persuasion, the "barrage of words" may exhaust the population and impair the potential contributions to the country by the Chinese people. Moreover, the Communist regime politicizes the people while preaching "double-talk." By talking democracy but practicing dictatorship, the regime may have increased its "internal contradictions" and risk being upset by political activists.[33] No matter how shrewdly propaganda is designed, it can only modify thinking, not the conditions themselves.

Although his analysis does not center on the Maoist system of political communications as described above, Yu's ideas are significant because they emphasize the outward contradictory nature of propagandistic "double-talk" and the teleological assumption that human nature tends toward "democracy" even under a Communist system.

Solomon's Model of the Underlying
Dilemma

In contrast with Liu, Lifton, and Yu, Richard H. Solomon does not relate communications to modernization, but considers Maoist "political communication" by postulating a sociological model of Chinese political culture.[34] Specifically, Solomon analyzes the problem of integration in terms of two "contradictions" found in traditional China. One is the contradiction between individual autonomy and group dependence. The other is the contradiction between avoiding aggression and hostility and dealing with luan (chaos) once it explodes into the open.[35]

The traditional solution to this problem was to personalize political action.[36] This solution permitted individual withdrawal, covered over problems, and placed a premium on the suppression of feelings. Both vertically and horizontally, political communications avoided conflict. In contrast, the Maoist solution to the traditional problem is to legitimize conflict and make authority receptive to activism. In order to do this, Mao tried to depersonalize authority, use the mass line to obtain criticism, and shift authority from the Party to the peer group.[37]

Four techniques of political communication were used to implement the Maoist solution. Organization was used to create unified political channels, and ideology was employed to unify the content of everyday life. In this connection, hate and resentment were exploited to create cohesion and to manipulate the isolation of potential anti-Maoists. And criticism was viewed as a dynamic force unifying organizational transactions. That is, criticism was to create unity through mediated conflict and to break up particularistic resistance. Solomon observes that this system of induced nonviolent communication was necessary because of the lack of voluntary habits among Chinese.

The Great Proletarian Cultural Revolution began as an elite-mass problem but became a succession problem involving the future communication of Maoist politics.[38] Specifically, Mao regarded the disagreement of Liu Shao-ch'i and others as factional criticism, not legitimate criticism according to the Maoist model. Consequently, Mao found himself forced to adopt the traditional stance of authority in order to maintain hegemony on the mainland.

Although Solomon's analysis of Mao's problem integrates the developments of the People's Republic of China in an interesting conceptual fashion, one possible implication of his argument is that the combination of anti-Maoist opposition and Red Guard reformism forced conflict out of the nonviolent channels of political change envisioned by Maoism and into the arena of violence, out of the realm of principle.[39] Another possible implication of Solomon's "hypothetical" argument is that Maoism has not made progress in accomplishing the basic attitudinal change that is necessary for carrying out modernization, and has been forced to deviate from its principles of socialization. Thus the Great Proletarian Cultural Revolution can be taken to indicate that Maoism has failed to depersonalize authority or institute mass criticism. However, if one distinguishes between contradictions within the political socialization process and contradictions between the political socialization process and the political process, then the Cultural Revolution can be interpreted more positively as an organic readjustment.

EVALUATING THE EXPLANATIONS

Despite their different theoretical frameworks and approaches, Liu, Lifton, and Yu draw inferences from their analyses that entail some common findings about Maoist political communication and Chinese political behavior:

1. There is a tendency toward "democracy" among the Chinese people.

2. The Maoist system of political communication is irrational.

3. The regime cannot control the preferences of the Chinese population for democracy.

These statements are based on analyses in which the connection between conclusion and explanation is based on intuitive observation.

174

In this type of analysis, one may not infer a causal connection between explanatory factors and conclusion. Consequently, the explanatory power of the analysis is limited by explicit or implicit ad hoc assumptions. In contrast, analyses in which the logical connections between factors and outcomes are postulated as part of a theory allow one to make systematic, theoretical inferences about all similar cases. Solomon's analysis follows this "positive" theoretical approach. The term "positive" is used to indicate that one can draw a "positive" causal inference about the systematic relationship between assumptions and outcomes. Of course, since it is logically possible to deduce confirmed predictions from false assumptions, the validity of "positive" inferences must be regarded as tentative subject to test.[40] Nevertheless, by postulating a model and testing logical predictions against empirical facts, Solomon develops an explanation that is refutable in principle.

In order to highlight the differences between Solomon's analysis and those of Liu, Lifton, and Yu, it is useful to adopt the following threefold typology of models.[41] These models make it possible to examine the relationship of human actors to postulated goals. One type of analysis, the formation of explicative models, focuses on giving meaning to one or more concepts used in explaining the logic behind seemingly paradoxical developments. For example, Scott A. Boorman's wei-ch'i analysis of Maoist revolutionary strategy may be interpreted as a nonmathematical explicative model that explains the logic behind Maoist strategy. (Wei-ch'i is a Chinese board game familiar to Westerners by its Japanese name, go.) For instance, Boorman uses a model to interpret the ostensibly disjointed tactical moves of the Chinese Communists during the civil war as if Communist strategists were following wei-ch'i principles.[42] In other words, this type of analysis is important because it helps us discern patterns in ambiguous phenomena. In this sense, the interpretation of political communication advanced above (see "Propaganda and Decision-Making") explicates the Maoist system of political communication.

Unlike explicative models, representational models do not elaborate the logic of processes. Instead, they record recurrent instances of observed phenomena. For example, Chong-do Hah employs a spatial model of coalition formation to analyze change in coalition alignment during the Great Proletarian Cultural Revolution.[43] In contrast with explicative and representational models, the third type of model—theoretical models—attempts to rigorously deduce predictions about political behavior from systematically related sets of assumptions. This type of model depends on—but logically subsumes—the patterns found in the application of the first two types. By examining the relationship between postulated goals and derived behavior, theoretical models enable one to make "positive" causal inferences about the assumptions of a model.[44]

In the context of this typology, Solomon's explanation is an example of a theoretical model. However, the methodology Solomon uses to test his model is based on an assumption that is testable in principle, but not in practice. Specifically, he makes an untestable assumption about the constancy of the relationship between the preferences of the sample surveyed and the whole Chinese population.[45] Since this assumption is in limbo, Solomon's explanation lacks the experimental basis to serve as a full-fledged positive theory for policy. Nevertheless, his study is different from the analyses of Liu, Lifton, and Yu because it is theoretical. That is, Solomon does not merely rely on a theoretical approach or framework, but systematically links his concepts to derive logical consequences. In contrast, the analyses of Liu, Lifton, and Yu do not provide sufficient theoretical logical connections between their conclusions and tested statements about Chinese politics or politics in general. These nontheoretical studies are valuable because they improve our historical understanding by drawing attention to certain features of the Maoist political communication in practice. But the predictions they yield should be explicitly recognized as speculative, not theoretical, inferences.[46]

The creation of theoretical knowledge about the development of political systems depends on the systematic analysis of the observations of nontheoretical studies. But the development of scientific theory requires that there be no necessary logical connection between the ideological values of analysts and their theories.

For instance, one may predict that the Maoist system is viable without necessarily approving of the system.[47] Some writers have argued that analysts of modernization in China have a bias against the success of Maoist development in China.[48] These critics contend that this bias is explicit and and implicit in studies of modernization in China. Although I have not reviewed the analyses cited by these critics, the evaluation of the work of Liu, Lifton, Yu, and Solomon suggests an explanation for the critics' distress. This evaluation indicated a negative interpretation of the success of mass mobilization techniques in China. Specifically, the fact that these analysts of political communication in China do not explicitly separate their personal values from their theories makes it difficult to distinguish their "scientific" explanations from official or propagandistic explanations. In short, although these explanations purport to be "scientific," they maximize simplicity and minimize information. In order to dispel possible ambiguity about their explanations, analysts need to reorient their studies. In principle, this reorientation may be accomplished by using analytical concepts and techniques that facilitate the elimination of bias.

We may sum up by listing the following points:

1. Scientific and official explanations of the logic of Maoist political communication have different optimal combinations of the variables of simplicity and information. Scientific explanations seek to minimize simplicity and maximize information, while official explanations aim to maximize simplicity and minimize information.

2. Refutability or testability is a distinguishing characteristic of scientific explanation. However, some ostensibly "scientific" explanations of the logic of Maoist political communication are not testable or refutable. Moreover, some of these explanations maximize simplicity and minimize information.

3. In order to clarify the scientific status of their theorizing about Maoist political communication, analysts should adopt theoretical concepts and analytical techniques.

LOGICAL ANALYSIS OF MAO'S PROPAGANDA

Before considering a model for reinterpreting the logic of Maoist political communication, let us examine the implications of applying the "rationalist" and "propagandistic" models of decision-making to the Chinese political system.

One of the implications of Ellul's discussion of propaganda and modernization is that if one cannot use the "rationalist" model of decision-making to evaluate the goals of different societies, then political opinion and political fact may be logically indistinguishable. Accordingly, goals may be seen as ideas that are nonempirical or "metaphysical."[49] They cannot be falsified, because there are no clear standards for determining that they have failed at the level of either education or slogan. Consequently, logical consistency does not obstruct the propagandist. In the Maoist system of political communication, the resiliency of these ideas is reinforced by the technique of creating the slogan but avoiding blame if the propaganda is not verified or is actually falsified by facts vis-à-vis a target audience.

If Ellul's views underline the need for more emphasis on theoretical interpretations of Chinese politics, they raise the problem of how to identify rational behavior if one cannot know the rationality of goals a priori.

Some "neorationalist" analysts of politics have suggested that we turn our attention to consideration of rational alternatives to posited goals, because hypotheses about the achievement of goals are testable.[50] For these neorationalists, the traditional questions about the rationality of goals are transformed into questions about which systems of goals and logic may be postulated to find order in human behavior.[51] This state of affairs has been characterized as a "crisis" by some Western thinkers. Arnold Brecht, for instance, has described the situation as one in which thinkers of a scientific outlook have eliminated traditional goals as irrelevant or unacceptable, but have not been able to deal with the resulting moral vacuum.[52] As Albert Einstein wrote: "If someone approves as a goal the extirpation of the human race from the earth, one cannot refute such a viewpoint on rational grounds."[53]

Einstein's statement dramatizes the difference between traditional rationalism and neorationalism for Western thinkers. For traditional thinkers, the extirpation of the human race was a goal that was unthinkable. For example, the "intellectualism" of Cartesian thought did not defend goals in terms of empirical justifications of the consequences of pursuing them. Instead, traditional rationalists emphasized normative questions about which goals should be pursued. Unlike their predecessors, "neorationalists" emphasize instrumental, not normative, questions about rationality. In other words, neorationalists do not implicitly or explicitly rule out certain goals as unthinkable. Rather, these modern rationalists seek to determine the conditions under which it is reasonable to expect or rule out the achievement of a particular goal or set of goals. This difference in emphasis does not mean that neorationalists are not concerned with normative questions. In fact, the findings of neorationalist analyses can serve as a factual basis for providing normative advice about the achievement of goals.[54]

Propaganda and Maoist Goals

Like neorationalists, Mao Tse-tung attacks traditional rationalism, but he stops short of becoming a neorationalist by deriving the rationality of goals from irrefutable teleological truths. In "On Practice, " for example, Mao describes the perceptual and logical stages of a man's epistemological development. Perceptual knowledge is incomplete, but logical knowledge reaches "the wholeness, the essence and the internal relations of things."[55] For Mao, neither classical rationalism nor empiricism in philosophy recognizes "the historical or dialectic nature of knowledge" and thus cannot provide correct goals.[56] Since the development of human knowledge is open-ended, man must understand the stages of its dialectical development. (Note that Mao and neorationalists both criticize a traditional static view of rationalism.) These stages can be verified historically, but verification may not be fully disclosed because of "scientific or technical limitations or the organic timing of development."[57]

According to Mao, a man's thinking is determined by his social "being."[58] Although Maoists acknowledge that the human experience of struggle involves lessons in success and failure, this does not mean that the regime can fail in upholding the credibility of its propaganda. In fact, Maoism expects people to learn from their mistakes in order to improve their understanding of history and avoid future mistakes. But Maoism does not include falsification as a criterion of truth. If, for example, the official line is self-contradictory or is contradicted by public knowledge, Maoist doctrine is not threatened. Instead, by using ad hoc appeals to "scientific or technical limitations or the organic timing of development," Maoist propaganda can protect the official line from criticism even though the "objective situation" does not support the current line.

By controlling information, the Maoist propaganda apparatus can instill its arational or metaphysical norms in the population, or at least prevent the creation of alternative norms. Nevertheless, Maoism tries to develop a communication system that will use its ability to control information in order to create norms that are not inconsistent with central directives. In this way, Maoism tries to preclude many of the cybernetics problems that Karl Deutsch attributes to the inefficiencies of bureaucratic behavior.[59] Specifically, Maoist leaders depend on a combination of external checks and internalized controls to produce policy that is responsive to feedback about people's needs. This dependence accounts for the emphasis on maintaining direct contact with the masses that is found in Mao's writings on the "mass line." According to this doctrine:

> All correct leadership is necessarily "from the masses;
> to the masses." This means: take the ideas of the
> masses (scattered and unsystematic ideas) and concen-
> trate them (through study turn them into concentrated and
> systematic ideas), then go to the masses and propagate
> and explain these ideas until the masses embrace them
> as their own, hold fast to them and translate them into
> action. Then, once again concentrate ideas from the
> masses and then once again go to the masses so that the
> ideas are persevered in and carried through. And so on,
> over and over again in an endless spiral.[60]

Although the mass line is concerned mainly with the implementation of policy, there is, as James Townsend notes, some informal participation in the formulation of policy by lower levels of the bureaucracy and "the masses."[61] Parris Chang has also pointed out that Maoist bureaucrats would seek the support of lower echelons to overcome the inertia of higher-level conservative bureaucrats.[62]

The system of Maoist political communication tends to reinforce the decentralization of communication by emphasizing vertical communication and preventing the growth of interprovincial lateral communication on a wide scale.[63] This pattern is consistent with the Maoist model for decentralized modernization. As Jack Gray has pointed out, Mao believes that a decentralized strategy is the only way China's peasants can be successfully mobilized for modernization.[64]

The Maoist strategy is based on six tenets.[65] First, peasants must initiate modernization themselves, and not depend on mechanization at an early stage. Second, the peasants must not rely on state investment, because state taxes would drain the surplus value of agricultural produce in order to pay for mechanization. Third, as equipment is introduced, it should be operated by the peasants themselves, in order to maximize the educational multiplier effect of mechanization. Fourth, industries should be decentralized in order to allow the growth of service industries for agriculture. Fifth, profit should not be used as a criterion for the introduction of machinery, because it would tend to concentrate development in richer areas and aggravate the gap between the rich and the poor. Sixth, technicians from outside local areas should not be used exclusively, because their use would sharpen the cleavage between the urban and rural classes.

In order to communicate these tenets to the large target audience of semiliterate Chinese, Maoist propaganda relies on a repetitious, epigrammatic style. In some cases, particularly during the Great Proletarian Cultural Revolution, the small study groups and mass rallies that assimilated Chairman Mao's sayings treated the sayings as a type of incantation. To a foreign observer, this style of communication may seem like a form of "irrational" Pentecostal religion.

But this style of communication is not necessarily irrational. In fact, as long as the repetition of the saying is designed to force individuals to try to relate the truth of the saying to their own lives, this style of communication may serve two important functions. First, it can help individuals define their identity and neutralize the destabilizing influences of anxiety. And second, this communication style may force the individual to consider the results of his actions and become aware of the options that are open to him. In this sense, the individual may be more likely to act rationally.[66] In the context of the Maoist strategy for modernization, these functions may allow China to avoid the destabilizing influences and problems of rapid change that have accompanied modernization in Western countries such as the United States and have threatened the progress of modernization itself. In other words, the Maoist style of political communication may favorably affect the rate of modernization or development in the long run and give China an advantage over Western countries that began to modernize earlier. For example, although the

United States has modernized by producing large amounts of material goods, it is possible that the destabilizing social and political effects of higher stages of economic growth may hinder further production and growth. In such a case, China might avoid this problem because Maoist political communication provided a ritualistic means of re-socializing the individual and creating social stability at an earlier stage of development.

A Neorationalist Approach to Nonelectoral Systems

The above interpretation of Maoist political communication should not be interpreted as a personal evaluation, defense, or endorse-ment of Chinese Communism. Instead, my analysis should be taken as an indication of the divergent implications that may be drawn from a nontheoretical interpretation of Chinese politics. In short, one could argue that the case for an optimistic or pessimistic view of Maoist political communication and modernization is quite equivocal.[67] But if this divergence leads to the conclusion that the neorationalist approach may be worth pursuing, it also suggests doubts about the intellectual payoff of the approach.

Some analysts of Chinese politics have correctly observed that some Western models of politics are inapplicable to the peculiar dynamics of political behavior in China.[68] However, few students of China have attempted to apply models of politics based on general analytical techniques, such as game theory, whose origin is not limited by narrowly defined concepts of rationality. In other words, the uniqueness of historical and cultural events does not preclude the creation of general models that can account for similar patterns of political behavior in different societies. All that is required is that conditions are met in an event that make it logically sufficient for analysts to treat an event as an example of a common type of beha-vior.[69]

COMPETITION IN NONELECTORAL SYSTEMS

Even if we agree that theoretical analysis of Chinese politics is a logical possibility, we may not agree on which hunches might best serve as starting points in the trial-and-error process of devel-oping better models. In order to foster speculation and research on this subject, I offer the following model as an interesting starting point for theorizing about nonelectoral political systems.

These models are inspired by analyses that interpret the com-petition of parties in electoral systems as if the parties were competing for votes distributed along an ideological continuum or policy space. The spatial model considered here is a simple transformation of analytical techniques to fit the constraints placed upon actors in nonelectoral systems. As such, I do not present them as fully elaborated theories, but as an illustration of what simple analytic models may suggest about nonelectoral systems.

Goals and Constrainst for Leaders

In nonelectoral systems, the goals and constraints imposed on actors are quite different from those found in electoral systems. For example, the leader or party in a country like China is concerned with maintaining a position in the policy space that will maximize his popular support and avoid a losing coalition. In an electoral system like that of the United States, units of power may be measured in terms of votes required to obtain a winning coalition in the electoral college system. However, in a nonelectoral system, we may postulate that the support of geopolitical factions or protocoalitions is required to maintain power. Although the identity and constitution of these protocoalitions change, one can postulate that leaders seek their support as if the protocoalitions possessed unequal shares of a finite amount of voting power.[70] In making this postulate, I imply that the decision rules of electoral and nonelectoral systems are simple-majority. Although this implication is not theoretically derived, I suggest that the postulate might be explicated and derived theoretically in further research. In any case, it should be noted that although I postulate similarity of decision-rules, I recognize that the formal definition of actors and division of power in electoral systems may make the competitive situation in nonelectoral systems seem ambiguous by comparison.

On the basis of these postulates, we can represent the leader's problem as adopting a policy orientation that will attract 51 percent of the units of power, given a particular distribution of actor preferences. In the case of China, Figure 2 may be used to interpret the dynamics of Maoist policy behavior as if the actors were rational with respect to the goal of maintaining a winning coalition.

In this model, it is postulated that units of power are unimodal and normally distributed. ("Unimodality" describes the clustering of phenomena under one mode, and "normality" refers to the fact that the phenomena are evenly distributed about the median.) This means that the probability of encountering a unit of power increases as one moves toward the center of policy space. Moreover, in this example the units of power are distributed so that the median position at M marks the unit of power that is the middle point of the population of power units. Given this normal unimodal distribution of power, the optimal strategy for a leader would be to locate himself next to M. Although this strategy would be optimal in the sense that it defeated an opponent competing for votes, the occupancy of the median position would also demonstrate to a potential competitor that the chances of forming a winning coalition are slim.

FIGURE 2

Hypothetical Policy Space

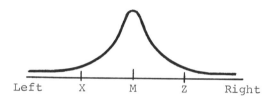

Left   X   M   Z   Right

However, if the government adopts a policy position at X in Figure 2, the prospects for political competitors will improve. For instance, in this case, a "rightist" opponent need capture only half the votes to defeat Maoist policy-makers located at X. The X strategy example logically illustrates the dangers of what Mao calls "adventurism." Conversely, if Maoist policy is located far to the right at Z on Figure 2, then a leftist opponent might find it worthwhile to compete for power. To avoid such a situation, Mao warns against "tailism."

These examples suggest how several points about Mao's conception of the distribution of preferences in China may be interpreted. First, he acts <u>as if</u> he believes that the distribution of preferences is unimodal and is gradually moving to the left. Second, he seems to assume that opponents on the right and left possess an insignificant amount of power. In his words, they are literally a "handful" of "capitalist roaders" or other opponents. Third, since information on the actual distribution of preferences is imperfect, the "mass line" serves as a feedback mechanism for indicating the distribution of preferences. Fourth, if Maoist administrators deviate significantly from a dominant position in policy space, the Maoist leadership has two options. First, it can adopt various degrees of mass mobilization to persuade holders of power to reorder their preferences and support Maoist policy. In effect, this first option involves an attempt to redistribute preferences along policy space.[71] For example, in the type of "adventuristic" situation depicted above, the Maoist leadership might try to identify the tendency toward "opportunism" with disloyalty, in order to reverse or preclude a shift in preferences.

The second option open to Maoist leaders is to change the distribution of preferences by introducing new elements into the competition for power. For instance, during the Great Proletarian Cultural Revolution, Mao found that his policies were in an adventuristic position in policy space vis-à-vis the emerging hostile coalition of bureaucratic forces. His response was to expand the population of power by mobilizing social elements such as the Red Guard and splitting traditional holders of power into Maoist and anti-Maoist groups. This strategy allowed Mao to create uncertainty in order to neutralize the power of his enemies and eventually mobilize a coalition to dominate his opponents.

CONCLUSION

This study has presented a case for reorienting the study of political communication in China toward the development of theoretical explanations of political behavior. I have demonstrated that such explanations are required to distinguish science from propaganda. I have also introduced a simple spatial model to explicate political competition from the viewpoint of leadership in nonelectoral systems. This model is not fully elaborated, but is designed to spur interest in the development of a theoretical understanding of Chinese politics.

NOTES

1. This approach is explained and illustrated in William H. Riker and Peter C. Ordeshook, An Introduction to Positive Political Theory (Englewood Cliffs, N.J.: Prentice-Hall, 1972); and Steven J. Brams, "Positive Coalition Theory: The Relationship Between Postulated Goals and Derived Behavior," in C. P. Cotter, ed., Political Science Annual: Conflict, Competition, and Coalitions, 4 (Indianapolis: Bobbs-Merrill, 1973), pp. 3-40.

2. Cf. Anthony Downs, An Economic Theory of Democracy (New York: Harper and Row, 1957); and Richard G. Niemi and Herbert F. Weisberg, eds., Probability Models of Collective Decision Making (Columbus, Ohio: Charles E. Merrill, 1972), Pt. 4. It should be noted that uncertainty does not necessarily lead to the problems for voters found in Downs's original analysis. This point is developed in Kenneth A. Shepsle, "Parties, Voters, and the Risk Environment: A Mathematical Treatment of Electoral Competition Under Uncertainty," in Niemi and Weisberg, op. cit., pp. 273-97.

3. Jacques Ellul, The Political Illusion, translated by Konrad Kellen (New York: Alfred A. Knopf, 1967); Propaganda, translated by Konrad Kellen and Jean Lerner (New York: Alfred A. Knopf, 1965); and The Technological Society, translated by Konrad Kellen (New York: Alfred A. Knopf, 1964).

4. Ellul, Propaganda, p. 61.

5. Ibid., p. 21.

6. Ibid., p. 26.

7. Ibid., pp. 26 ff.

8. Ibid., p. 34.

9. Ibid., p. 35.

10. Ibid., p. 305.

11. This technique is mentioned in F. T. C. Yu, Mass Persuasion in Communist China (New York: Praeger Publishers, 1964), pp. 3-33. However, Yu's interpretation of its significance is more negative than Ellul's assessment. According to some sources, Mao used this technique to launch the Great Proletarian Cultural Revolution by having Yao Wen-yuan initiate the call for revolution. See W. A. C. Adie, "China's 'Second Liberation' in Perspective," in Dick Wilson, ed., China After the Cultural Revolution (New York: Vintage Books, 1970), pp. 52 ff.

12. Ellul, Propaganda, p. 79.

13. Ibid.

14. Ibid., p. 155.

15. The importance of refutation in testing a theory is emphasized in Karl R. Popper, The Logic of Scientific Discovery (London: Hutchinson, 1959), passim.

16. Ibid., pp. 44-46.

17. Ibid.

18. Among other views that might be considered is A. Doak Barnett's China After Mao (Princeton: Princeton University Press, 1967). Although Barnett holds that Maoism is incompatible with modernization, he tends to assert his position without elaborating a rationale for it. For example, he says that Maoism is "in many ways obsolete as a guide to action for China as it moves along the road to modernization and increasingly plays the role of a great power" (p. 66). This conclusion seems trivial, since all ideologies or systems of ideas eventually need to be revised. Moreover, Barnett disparages Mao's prescriptions as "romantic ' (p. 67) without considering their potential value in the process of modernization. If Maoism is characterized as a thought system, then it is "romantic" by definition because it depends on abstractions and/or imaginary ideas. By emphasizing the "Yenan complex" and other sources of inspiration for Maoist thought, Barnett implies that Maoism is "romantic" in a perjorative sense that entails irrationality as well

as irrelevance. However, as I will argue, Maoist thought can be interpreted in a more positive manner.

19. For a critical review of these approaches, see James A. Bill and Robert L. Hargrave, Jr., Comparative Politics: The Quest for Theory (Columbus; Ohio: Charles E. Merrill, 1973), Chs. II and III.

20. This analysis is based on Alan P. L. Liu, "Mass Media in the Cultural Revolution: Problems of Mass Mobilization in Communist China," Current Scene 8, no. 8 (Apr. 20, 1967); and Communications and National Integration in Communist China (Berkeley: University of California Press, 1972), passim.

21. Cf. Foreign Broadcast Information Service (FBIS) Daily Report, July 7, 1969.

22. For a further description of this practice, see New York Times, Nov. 21, 1970, p. 62.

23. The example is drawn from an FBIS daily file report of Mar. 17, 1969.

24. Although Red Guard publications helped fill the communications void, the full extent of their impact is not known. Examples can be found in translations published by U.S. Department of Commerce, Joint Publications Research Service, "Samples of Red Guard Publications," vol. I Aug. 1 1967) and vol. II (Aug. 8, 1967). Many of these publications are described in "US FBIS Special Memorandum: Annotated List of Red Guard Publications (Washington, D. C.: Foreign Broadcast Information Service, May 1, 1968).

25. Cf. Liu, "Mass Media," passim.

26. Robert J. Lifton, Thought Reform and the Psychology of Totalism: A Study of Brainwashing in China (New York: Norton, 1961.

27. Robert J. Lifton, Revolutionary Immortality: Mao Tse-tung and the Chinese Communist Revolution (New York: Vintage, 1968).

28. Ibid., p. 105.

29. Ibid., p. 134.

30. Ibid., p. 136.

31. For a discussion of Gödel's theorems and the use of impossibility proofs in general, cf. Karl R. Popper, Conjectures and Refutations (London: Routledge and Kegan Paul, 1963).

32. Yu, Mass Persuasion, p. 155.

33. Ibid., p. 158.

34. Richard H. Solomon, "Mao's Effort to Reintegrate the Chinese Polity: Problems of Authority and Conflict in the Chinese Socialization Process, " in A. Doak Barnett, ed., Chinese Politics in Action (Seattle: University of Washington Press, 1969), pp. 271-304; and Mao's Revolution and the Chinese Political Culture (Berkeley: University of California Press, 1972).

35. Solomon, "Mao's Effort to Reintegrate the Chinese Polity," p. 310.

36. Ibid., p. 303.

37. Ibid., pp. 310 ff.

38. Ibid., pp. 342 ff.

39. Ibid.

40. Cf. Riker and Ordeshook, op. cit., Ch. I; Brams, op. cit.; and Popper, The Logic of Scientific Discovery.

41. This typology is discussed in Joseph Berger, Bernard P. Cohen, J. Laurie Snell, and Morris Zelditch, Jr., Types of Formalization in Small Group Research (Boston: Houghton Mifflin Company, 1962).

42. Cf. Scott A. Boorman, The Protracted Game: A Wei-Ch'i Interpretation of Maoist Revolutionary Strategy (New York: Oxford University Press, 1970), pp. 3-5; and Arnold B. Urken, "Coalitions in the Chinese Civil War" (unpublished Ph.D. dissertation, New York University, 1973), pp. 39-43.

43. Chong-do Hah, "The Dynamics of the Chinese Cultural Revolution: An Interpretation Based on an Analytical Framework," World Politics 24, no. 2 (Jan. 1972).

44. Cf. Urken, op. cit.; and Brams, op. cit.

45. Cf. Solomon, "Mao's Effort to Reintegrate the Chinese Polity," and the appendixes in Mao's Revolution and the Chinese Political Culture.

46. A good example of the need for making this distinction may be found in Lucian W. Pye's "Mass Participation in China," in John M. Lindbeck, ed., China: Management of a Revolutionary Society (Seattle: University of Washington Press, 1971), pp. 3-33. Pye argues that Western "theories of political development" such as "group theory," "mass politics," and "interest group theory" do not explain the pattern of politics in China. Similarly, Pye maintains that the viability of Maoist techniques of mobilization is "questionable" and that the Maoist policies may "paradoxically" lead to the development of "capitalism." In analyzing Western and Maoist political theory, Pye ostensibly believes that predictions "logically follow" from certain explanatory factors. However, in neither case does Pye systematically deduce his inferences to show that his predictions carry any more force than Maoist prognoses as logical predictions. Cf. op. cit., pp. 22-29.

47. For a discussion of logical possibilities and valid argument, see J. G. Kemeny, J. L. Snell, and G. L. Thompson, Introduction to Finite Mathematics (Englewood Cliffs, N.J.: Prentice-Hall, 1957), pp. 32-49.

48. Cf. Mark Selden, "People's War and the Transformation of the Peasant Society," in Edward Friedman and Mark Selden, eds.,

America's Asia: Dissenting Essays on Asian-American Relations (New York: Vintage, 1971), pp. 357-92. For example, Selden maintains that the "creativity" or "the dedication" of the resistance "lies behind" the success of revolutionary nationalist movements (p. 359). Since "lies behind" implies an unarticulated concept of explanation, Selden's analysis is hardly more theoretical than the "abuses" of modernization theory he criticizes. In other words, Selden does not demonstrate that there is any necessary or inevitable compatibility between the strategy of the people's war and modernization. The need for deductive theories of politics and mathematical reasoning in the creation of scientific cures for the "ills of humanity" is discussed in Robert T. Holt and John E. Turner, 'Competing Paradigms in Comparative Politics," in R. T. Holt and J. E. Turner, eds., The Methodology of Comparative Research (New York: The Free Press, 1970), pp. 21-72.

49. For example, in early Western science, Parmenides and Democritus disagreed about metaphysical ideas. Parmenides argued that there is not space between matter and that there is no change in the world. Democritus argued that things do change in the world and that there is space between matter. Although Democritus' theory of change and structure of the world is closer to the view accepted today, it is just as metaphysical as Parmenides' theory. For a fuller discussion of this debate, see "Back to the Presocratics," in Popper, Conjectures and Refutations. For a brief discussion of metaphysics and politics, see J. W. N. Watkins, "Is Political Philosophy Dead?" Encounter (June 1954). More detailed exposition of these ideas can be found in two other works by Watkins: a paper in Proceedings of the Aristotelian Society Supp. 37 (1963); and "Confirmable and Influential Metaphysics," Mind (July 1958): 344-66.

50. Cf. Riker and Ordeshook, op. cit.

51. Marion J. Levy, Jr., Modernization and the Structure of Societies (Princeton: Princeton University Press, 1966). Levy treats these metaphysical ideas as types of "arational knowledge" useful in understanding "the ideas, the attitudes, and the action of the membership of all societies including the most highly modernized ones" (p. 663). For example, Levy suggests that there is no contradiction between the goals derived from "arational knowledge" and "rational" or scientific knowledge about the achievement of goals (p. 717).

52. Arnold Brecht, Political Theory: The Foundations of Twentieth Century Political Thought (Princeton: Princeton University Press, 1969), pp. 17 ff.

53. Quoted in ibid., p. 9.

54. Cf. Brams, op. cit.

55. Mao Tse-tung, "On Practice," in Anne Fremantle, ed., Mao Tsetung: An Anthology of His Writings (New York: Mentor, 1962), p. 203.

56. Ibid., p. 208.

57. Ibid., p. 209.

58. Mao Tse-tung, Where Do Correct Ideas Come From? (Peking: Foreign Languages Press, 1966).

59. Karl Deutsch, The Nerves of Government (New York: The Free Press, 1966).

60. Mao Tse-tung, Selected Works of Mao Tse-tung, III (Peking: Foreign Languages Press, 1966), p. 119.

61. James R. Townsend, Political Participation in Communist China (Berkeley and Los Angeles: University of California Press, 1967), p. 74.

62. Parris Hsu-cheng Chang, "Patterns and Processes of Policy-Making in Communist China, 1955-1962: Three Case Studies" (unpublished Ph.D. dissertation, Columbia University, 1969), passim.

63. One notable exception to this pattern is the interprovincial broadcasts that were encouraged as a preliminary step in the creation of a new military region between Inner Mongolia and Heilungkiang Province. Also cf. Richard H. Solomon, "Communications Patterns and the Chinese Revolution," China Quarterly no. 32 (Oct.-Dec. 1967), pp. 88-110.

64. Jack Gray, "The Economics of Maoism," in Dick Wilson, ed., China After the Cultural Revolution, pp. 130-131.

65. Ibid., pp. 128-130.

66. Mao Tse-tung's epigrams can be thought of as metaphysical truths. That is, they are not refutable and therefore, strictly speaking, not verifiable; but they are nevertheless influential in inspiring individuals to rationalize their thought and action. The use of epigrams in problem-solving helps to internalize control in bureaucracies. Cf. Anthony Downs, Inside Bureaucracy (Boston: Little, Brown, 1967), pp. 215 ff.

67. The informational richness and logical limitations of functionalist analyses are outlined in George J. Graham, Methodological Foundations for Political Analysis (Waltham, Mass.: Xerox Publishing Company, 1971), pp. 79-82.

68. Cf. Richard W. Wilson, "Chinese Studies in Crisis," World Politics 1 (Nov. 1970).

69. Cf. Riker and Ordeshook, op. cit., Ch. I. Rare examples of studies of China based on analytic models are listed in notes 42 and 43.

70. This type of postulate is justified in Urken, op. cit., Ch. V.

71. The advantages of a "despot" in determining the ranking of preferences among a population is analyzed in Gordon Tullock, "A Model of Social Interaction," in James F. Herndon and Joseph L. Bernd, eds., Mathematical Applications in Political Science, V (Charlottesville: University Press of Virginia, 1971).

8

THE SUBSTITUTION OF "PEOPLE" FOR "INDIVIDUAL" IN THE ETHOS OF THE MAOIST POLITY

James Chieh Hsiung

I shall attempt to define the logic of actors in the Maoist political system by offering a set of interpretations deduced from a basic postulate: that the willful imposition of social rationality over private self-interests (in a nonmarket ambience) has significantly modified the game of politics. Underlying the imposed sociability norm is Mao's conviction about the corrigibility of man in an edifying social environment and about what collective "voluntarist" action can do to alter the external world. Besides the seeming tautology in this perceived man-milieu relationship, there is an element of self-fulfilling prophecy: While the collective meliorist assumption gives rise to the enforced sociability norm, once the latter's primacy is established, the individuals in the morally pressured society, as it were, are disposed or conditioned to respect the larger public well-being over their private preferences.

The enforceability of the collective norm results from, and perpetuates, the peculiar power distribution between government and citizenry reflecting the integration of the economic and political systems. So long as the pressurized social environment exists, the Maoist polity can expect to be freed of the obstacles to achieving "optimal" social states that Anthony Downs imputes to the Western capitalistic democracy posited on the self-interest axiom.[1] Much of the rest of this paper will be devoted to discussing the problem of optimality within the general context of the contrasting "givens" and assumptions about man and social environment between the Maoist socialistic model and Downs's market-economy model of electoral democracy.

---

*The author wishes to acknowledge with gratitude many valuable comments made by Professors Steven Brams, a colleague at New York University, Arnold B. Urken, and Martin K. Whyte.

By "optimality" we mean either a Paretian state of socioeconomic well-being in which everyone is made better off without sacrificing anyone (except in a noncumulative way, such as during a transition), or the achievement of such goals as the equitable distribution of the costs and benefits of "collective goods." A "collective good" is defined by Mancur Olson, Jr., as "any good such that, if any person X_i in a group $X_1, \cdots, X_i, \cdots, X_n$ consumes it, it cannot feasibly be withheld from the others in that group."[2] In other words, those who do not pay the cost cannot be excluded from sharing in the consumption of the good because it is indivisible, such as police protection, national defense, law and order, and similar services provided by the government. We generally follow this definition but extend it to what are sometimes categorized as "externalities," or spill-over benefits accruing to other groups, at no extra cost, from activities financed by a specific civic group, such as the "clean air" movement in the United States today. In a collective economy, such fine distinctions made on the basis of public or private cost-bearing can hardly be maintained. In our frame of reference, collective goods include not only such socialist benefits as job security, free insurance, and public housing— what Robert J. Osborn calls "social wage"[3]—but also such vital societal changes as increase in distributive justice and leveling down of alienation in social and production relations. Pursuits of these collective goods or of the Paretian state are defined in this study as pursuits of optimality.

Our purpose is to propose a single hypothesis to explain the political relationships between government and citizenry in the People's Republic of China and to suggest what behavior can be expected if the actors act "rationally," or in accordance with goals found in the system's prevailing norms. "Rationality" is often defined in terms of the goals that individuals seek for themselves (guided by their own "self-interests") in electoral systems. For reasons that will become obvious, we define rationality not by reference to individual preferences so much as to the collective goals postulated in the system's prevailing norms, as defined by the Maoist leadership. Furthermore, in order to understand the significance of the system's goals, we have found it necessary to examine the basic premise about human motives (human nature) on which these goals are based. Both the goals and the premise on which they are postulated would be totally unrealistic if they were out of touch with the limiting conditions ("givens") in reality. Thus, we shall look into the system's "givens" as well.

In this study, we aim at bringing together and relating systematically certain vital observable phenomena in an explainable relationship that is deducible from the basic postulate laid out at the very outset. We hope to show that the Maoist system can be understood as if there is a logic to its scheme of things, which cannot be summarily discounted simply because of our own preconceptions. My own understanding has gained enormously from an intellectual exercise contrasting the Maoist logic with that inherent in the Downs model of Western democracy. I shall therefore use the Downs model as a basis for some close comparisons as well as a counterpoint for theorizing. Downs proposes an "economic theory of democracy," and argues that economics and politics must be merged in a unified theory of social action. We need a similar approach in assessing the axioms of the Maoist system, because of its full integration of the economic, political, and social subsystems.

My discussion of the Downs model is based on my understanding of the model, which may or may not be the same as Downs has conceived it, just as Downs's model may or may not be identical with the reality he is attempting to represent. Moreover, the Maoist model I am presenting may or may not be true of the reality of which it is a model, any more than Downs's model may or may not be true of its empirical referent. Models are judged not by their truth or falsity, but by their theoretical utility. Strictly speaking, models are analogues or isomorphs of reality and, as such, are in purely abstract form, with no empirical referents. They are not theories per se, which, while more or less abstract, are explanatory devices (and sometimes more) for observable phenomena. In an explanation, isolated observable phenomena, loosely defined, are brought together and related systematically. The use of cognitive models involves a process of learning that relates the new or unfamiliar patterns to those already established in our heads, and it is capable of telescoping complex phenomena into an isomorphic structure of symbols that is intellectually more manageable. The ultimate aim is to identify a set of axioms or generalizations that are universal in form and inferentially fertile, and can suggest relationships that need further exploration or areas in which new generalizations may appear. The modeling endeavor is thus an essential step toward theory-building, through a process known as "retroduction" (testing and refining the model by relating it to the empirical referents).[4] Our attempt at comparing the two models, therefore, has this epistemological value in view.

DOWNS'S CAPITALIST-DEMOCRATIC MODEL

To make the comparisons meaningful, it will be necessary to discuss briefly the essential and relevant portions of Downs's theory, so that the stage will be set for our later discussions of the Maoist model. For convenience' sake, and without doing the author undue injustice, we shall first restate certain essential assumptions in Downs's theory, including its accepted premise about human nature and the perceived "givens" of its empirical referent, the Western capitalistic democracy. We shall then summarize his analysis of the characteristics of democratic government and the consequences that logically follow.

Premise and "Givens"

The most crucial starting point in the Downs model is the premise that human nature can be understood as if it is nonaltruistic and, indeed, "selfish," so much so that self-interest defines an individual's "rational" behavior. This self-interest view recognizes the conflict of what is "individually rational" with what is "socially rational," though the specific boundaries are sometimes hard to define. But the same view assumes that, despite rhetoric to the contrary, the former often predominates over the latter in political behavior. All economic theory from Adam Smith on down (with the exception of the Marxists) is based on this premise; and to Downs, the same applies to politics as well.[5]

Closely associated with this premise are two essential "givens" of society in Downs's analysis of the democratic model: free market and party politics (or election politics). From these two "givens," Downs infers at a relatively high level of abstraction two competitive but not always compatible distribution systems: the unequal reward system, determined by the invisible hand of the market, and the equal distribution of votes (as conventionally known in the "one man, one vote" watchword)—except where modified by antiquated institutions such as the Electoral College—as found in the electoral competition between political parties.[6] The disparities between the two distribution systems are particularly significant in a comparison with the Maoist polity, as will become clear later.

Characteristics of Democratic Government

"Democratic government" is defined in Downs's model as a "vote-maximizing government," since the motivation of political parties is to be "in office" and the government must therefore maximize its support in terms of the number of votes it can muster. Vote-maximizing, according to Downs, is not only distinct, in its motivation, from working for the people's optimal well-being, but could actually run counter to welfare-maximizing.[7]

Because each adult citizen has one vote, his welfare preferences are weighted in the eyes of the government, which is interested <u>only in his vote</u>, <u>not his welfare</u>.[8]

Agreeing with Joseph Schumpeter, Downs sees a motivation in politics similar to that in economic activity. No economic man produces out of a moral conviction that production is essential for mankind and that he is fulfilling his social function (division of labor) for its own sake. Just as productivity is the motive force of economic activity, so the competitive struggle for power and office, not promotion of social welfare, motivates political activity. In this analogy, the common link is the self-interest axiom; social functions are not ruled out but are seen as merely a by-product, rather than the cause, of human action.[9]

Consequences of the System as Defined

The word "system" is used here to encompass the "rational" man, the society, and the democratic government as defined by Downs above. Because of the combined effects of voters' self-interest rationality and the vote-maximizing nature of party government, the system has a built-in bias against attaining a "Paretian optimum." Although Downs does not define the concept, which is borrowed from economic theory and named after the economist Vilfredo Pareto, he uses "Paretian optimum" broadly to denote an imagined perfect equilibrium in which nobody can be made better off without hurting somebody else. For all its market-economy implications, this usage has a great deal in common with the way we use "optimality." An operational difference, however, lies in Downs's derivation of social ends from individual ends, whereas optimality in reference to the Maoist polity denotes a reversal of the relative importance of the two sets of ends, in which the happy state of maximal welfare is either attained at the societal level (subsuming the individual interests) or not at all.

Following the self-interest axiom, every citizen in Downs's model attempts to maximize his utility income (what he can get from government actions such as police protection or highways) but evades paying the cost for it unless coerced to do so, as in taxation. The reason is that the utility income consists mainly of collective (indivisible) goods, which can be enjoyed by every man, no matter who pays for them.[10] Theoretically, the private sector may automatically reach a Paretian optimum when there is "perfect competition," under conditions of certainty, as the general equilibrium economists claim. But certainty in the market economy is the exception rather than the rule. Left to itself, the private sector is not likely to reach a Paretian optimum even if there are no collective goods or other similar complications.[11] Furthermore, Downs adds, acquisition of political information necessary for influencing policy-making, as distinct from acquiring it in order to vote, is costly. Not every voter in the market economy—with its unequal income distribution—can equally afford the cost. Thus, despite equality in franchise, corporate units and the wealthy are more likely to become influencers than are the less financially endowed individual voters.[12]

Government action, in Downs's view, is essential for reaching an optimal social state. However, since the government depends for its survival on its ability to marshal the votes, such action may not be forthcoming where there is a temporal gap between the present and the future time point when the optimal utility incomes are received. The government may not survive the next election, owing to the costs or temporary sacrifices that its long-term optimal program calls for. Without denying that governments are vitally concerned with the effects of their actions upon the voters' future utility returns, Downs emphasizes that a government in the electoral system cannot trade present votes for future votes the way a voter can trade present income for future income.[13] He notes other reasons why government is unable, in his model, to achieve optimality or may even consciously block it.

First, in a market economy, the government cannot infallibly judge every individual's income-earning potential; measure his benefits and costs cheaply, directly, and without error; and pass individually discriminatory laws to equalize the utility returns for everyone.[14]

Second, the interparty competition in election politics does not always cause the government to move society to a Paretian optimum, if the preferences of individual citizens are sufficiently diverse. The government's choice is foreclosed when there is a conflict between different optimal states, or between an optimal position (reflecting social rationality) and a dominant preoccupation of a majority of the voters (following individual self-interests). With the diversified interests of the voters, Downs notes, every optimum is dominated by a suboptimal position. Assume, for example, that there are three citizens in society—P, Q, and R—and three suboptimal positions—X, Y, and Z—each of which is dominated by a corresponding optimum—X', Y', and Z'. Every citizen prefers each optimum to its corresponding suboptimal position, but they do not rank the optima in the same way. Their preferences are as follows:

Ranking	Citizen		
	P	Q	R
First	X'	Y'	Z'
Second	X	Y	Z
Third	Y'	Z'	X'
Fourth	Y	Z	X
Fifth	Z'	X'	Y'
Sixth	Z	X	Y

It is plain that in this case every optimum is dominated by a suboptimal position: X' by Z, Z' by Y, and Y' by X. Thus, concludes Downs:

> Even in a world of perfect certainty, with no technical obstacles to achieving a Paretian optimum, a two-party democracy would not necessarily arrive at one. No matter what stand the incumbents took, the opposition could defeat them by taking a suboptimal stand, because a majority would prefer the latter to the former.[15]

Under the circumstances, whether society arrives at a Paretian optimum is largely "a matter of chance," and in a two-party system "society will not attain a Paretian optimum."[16]

Third, the attainment of a Paretian optimum is impossible in uncertain circumstances. No party in uncertainty knows which social states are optimal or in what way various states "dominate" each other in voters' preferences. From the citizens' point of view, on the other hand, uncertainty may cause them to oppose giving government the powers necessary to achieve optimal states for fear that, once granted, such powers might be employed against them, either collectively or individually, in the future.[17] Although the actual effects of uncertainty may not necessarily produce the same problems for voters as Downs infers, it is important to note that in a larger sense uncertainty perpetuates the two disparate distribution systems alluded to earlier: money and votes. On the one hand, the vote-maximizing goal of the government causes it to act in favor of the most numerous income groups, the middle-class voters (Downs calls them the "low-income receivers").[18] But, for fear of mortgaging their political freedom to the high-income groups, the lower-income voters will jealously guard their votes and prohibit any trading of votes (even if the law can be changed to make it legal) for monetary gains.[19] On the other hand, though the financially better-off groups may attempt to influence policy-making by offering political bribes, they invariably find it more profitable (or less costly) to injure some affected citizens than to bribe all of them. A majority of citizens, realizing this, have legitimate reasons to band together to outlaw bribery, because uncertainty makes each fear that he may be in the injured minority.[20]

For like reason, therefore, the beneficiaries in both distribution systems (money and vote) want to perpetuate the status quo with its disparities, and refrain from using their advantage in one system to alter the other in their own favor. The end result, from society's point of view, is that while government interference with the normal operation of the economy is an index of the political effectiveness of democracy, uncertainty not only reduces government intervention to a suboptimal level but, more important, prevents the achievement of optimal positions in the Paretian sense.

THE MAOIST ANTITHESIS

Our discussion of the Maoist logic will follow the same procedure as above, beginning with the underlying assumptions and the modus operandi of the system, especially from the post-Cultural Revolution vantage point. Following that, we shall examine the characteristics of the government and the logical ramifications attendant thereto, in close comparison with the Downs model.

Premise and "Givens": A Crucial Difference

In the Downs model, the self-interest premise is accepted without having to question how the principals themselves feel about it, since politics in this model parallels the market economy and in neither is there societal challenge to the dictum of private ends. The "givens" in the Chinese system stand in stark contrast, however. Parallel to its planned economy, the system politically operates under the overall orchestration and stewardship of the Communist Party. Politics begins not with the citizen-qua-voter (counterpart to the consumer in the market economy) but with the Party, from which flows civic virtue, or collective will, to which all individual (partial) wills must bend. In these circumstances, how the Party—or its Chairman—feels about the question of human nature and rationality has a decisive bearing on the system's modus operandi.

In the command economy, profitability has been willfully replaced by the glorified social function of the worker-producer; and within the command structures typical of the socialist system the self-interest axiom has lost much, if not all, of its economic and political implications. What matters in political behavior is not so much the conflict of private interests as the enforcement of the social rationality promoted by the Party. Politics in this case does not ignore human nature, but follows quite different assumptions. In the Maoist view, human nature is tied to "class nature. "Classes," to Mao, are not only structurally defined—by reference to one's relationship to the mode of production—but also ideologically defined, in the sense that a proletarian may "think bourgeois" and thus betray his own class, or vice versa. Behind this view of ideological convertibility is the basic assumption that human nature is not immutably predisposed to good or evil, sociability or selfishness, but subject to the conditioning, or reconditioning, effects of one's class background or the surrounding sociopolitical conditions.

What shapes human nature, in this view, is not only the "corrupting" influence of the external material conditions but, equally, how the individual relates himself to them. Society has an edifying function and must see that all "corrupting" influences are expurgated. It follows, therefore, that in the "correct" society, individual selfishness is contained and social rationality asserted. This voluntarist assumption about human nature (that it can be helped) thus complements, rather than replaces, its "mechanistic" counterpart (that human nature is conditioned by external environment). It finds expression in the Party's enforcement of the collective rationality, which sets in motion a political process significantly different from what results solely from the self-interest axiom.[21]

Characteristics of the Maoist Polity

The term "polity" is used here to accommodate the complex structure under study. In the first place, there is the structure of the "dual government," the Party and the state bureaucracy. Second, there is a special division of labor in which a "monocratic" group of professional cadres staffs both the Party and the state structures.[22] Third, members of this monocratic group are chosen not only because of their ideological commitment and their organizational skills, but also because they purportedly have close ties with the various strata of society they hail from. (Although individual private motivations are not to be ruled out, the conditions just described are generally representative of the Party's recruitment practices.) The Party can be said to constitute an extensive web of human and organizational ties with the entire society that cannot be portrayed by the term "government" as we normally use it.

"Polity" therefore conveys an all-enveloping process in which "formal" government and "informal" governance blend into one closely knit fabric. In contrast with its vote-maximizing counterpart in the Downs model, government in the Maoist model does not depend upon the franchise for its coming to power. But it has staked its legitimacy on a commitment to realize optimal welfare for society, as promised by its Communist ideology; and its continued legitimacy depends on translating this commitment into action. The government's desire to maximize its legitimacy causes it to maximize public welfare and, in doing so, to make the entire society share more or less evenly the benefits as well as the costs of the pursuit of optimality.[23] The welfare-maximizing tendency offers a contrast with the vote-maximizing tendency in the Downs model, for reasons already explained.

Ramifications of the Maoist Premise

We shall concentrate on the more distinct ramifications ensuing from the Maoist premise about human nature and the imposition of social rationality on human behavior. Some of these have been touched upon before but will be elaborated upon for their significance.

(a) Neither the motivation of government action nor political behavior in general can be explained solely by the self-interest axiom, because the government is not vote-maximizing and the individual citizens are under restraints placed on them by the collective norm. Competition for power is not absent but exists in different forms, almost exclusively within the Party, among leaders representing varying views and policy preferences. The competition is often ideologically tainted, in that the principals wrangle over the most efficacious ways of achieving the promised optimal goals (and also over what are the intermediate goals that constitute a means for other goals). The Cultural Revolution, for example, climaxed a long-smoldering conflict in this fashion.[24] Competition among Party leaders represents an inverted manifestation of the conflict of the articulated interests of citizens in the Western democratic system. The inversion is a logical consequence of the fact that the political process in the socialist system starts from the Party's stewardship, rather than from the electoral process. To the extent that they exist, elections in this system are more like referenda than are their counterparts in the party-politics systems in the West.

Since encroachments upon individual (private) interests are not to be presumed under the Party-enforced collective norm, the protection of these interests is not left to the self-help of the citizens themselves. Moreover, since the enforced norm defines "rationality" as being concerned with interests larger than—sometimes in spite of—one's own selfish ends, the reward system also reflects this bias. Those who accept the norm are better rewarded in the end than those who do not. By the rules of the game, therefore, it is a "rational" individual who bows to and works for the collective well-being on his own accord. To do otherwise, in the circumstances, would be contrary to his own self-interests. Though coercion is necessary to enforce the sociability code where persuasion fails, once the norm is firmly established and internalized, the individuals acting "rationally" will, without coercion, be disposed to minimize their own utility returns and contribute their shares to the cost of the collective goods. By contrast, government coercion is applied in the Downs model to make individuals pay the cost of collective goods, but no coercion is used specifically to change the self-interest axiom itself.

(b) In the command economy the vast disparities between (economically defined) classes have been leveled down, leaving no intervening classes between the Party and the masses. While the planned economy frees itself of the unequal distribution that besets a market economy, the dominance of the Party leaders creates a disparity of a different sort, in the distribution of political power. Yet there is complementarity between the two distribution systems: the economic system (which is equal) and the political (which is unequal). Both the Party and the masses have a common stake in the elimination of the erstwhile pouvoirs intermédiaires and the prevention of any new ones from arising, so as to control the allocation of resources. The Party relies on economic egalitarianism as both a means for blocking the ascendancy of any intermediate power blocs and as a way to rally the support of the masses on its side. The masses, on their part, support the Party's political dominance because it alone guarantees the economic egalitarianism they cherish.

To the extent that recruitment to the Party-predominant political system is still open (the Party is not a hereditary aristocracy), it offers a reasonable hope of self-elevation for the more enterprising individuals. Egalitarianism in the economic system has, to be sure, made the political system the only arena where there is room for sufficiently attractive social mobility.[25] If we grant that in the real world it is not always the surety, but the possibility of success, that motivates human endeavors, then this prospect of self-elevation, however limited in reality, is additional cause for the masses' support for the system. In this case, private motivation runs with, but not against, the system's modus operandi.

(c) Because of the two disparate distributions culminating in economic equality but political inequality, and because social rationality has to be enforced, the relative strength of private and public motivations differs in two types of politics, in direct proportion to society's capability of enforcement. In the narrower realm of politics found exclusively within the Party, such as in the pure power struggles among the top leadership, private motives play a greater role, since the masses cannot enforce the collective norm on the Party leadership as effectively as the Party can on them. Political behavior during the Cultural Revolution, so far as the intra-Party power-struggle aspect (as distinct from the ideological aspect) is concerned, is a lot more explainable when compared with coalition behavior in Western electoral systems, in which rationality is defined mainly in terms of the actors' self-interests. Mao acted as if he followed the three principles that William Riker has deduced from general coalition behaviors. He put together a coalition large enough to win but not too large to overburden the sharing of the "spoils" (the "minimal winning coalition," or size principle). To keep the coalition on his side, he had to make concessions or dole out payoffs to its members, allowing them even to inflict unnecessary harsh violence on the "power-holders," from whom power was being wrested (the side-payment principle). Toward the later stages of the game, Mao had to drop some of the partners, to ease the overwhelming burden of side-payments and/or to maximize the gains (the strategic principle).[26] The final group of coalition partners to be dumped was the Lin Piao faction, which demanded too high a price that Mao could not pay without jeopardizing his own position.[27]

In the larger polity involving the Party-mass relationships, on the other hand, the nature of the pursuit of optimality (as distinct from pure power) causes the Party to promote a grand (not minimal-winning) coalition. In order to distribute evenly the costs and benefits of the collective goods, it is imperative that every citizen accept and live out the sociability dictum. So long as the Party is able to enforce the dictum, private motivations defer to larger social ends. It is as "rational" for the Party to maintain the grand coalition and enforce the collective norm (because the entire system, including the Party's predominance, depends on it) as it is for the masses to accept the symbiosis of the two discrete types of politics at work, as just described. In this sense, individual rationality and social rationality converge.

(d) The integration of economic functions into the socialist polity has created qualitative changes in government-citizenry relationships. Whereas in the market economy the tasks of planning and spurring productivity, managerial supervision and control, generating a work ethic, and shaping consumer habits are in the hands of business and industry, these functions are transferred to the government's domain of responsibilities in the planned economy. So are the tasks of surveillance and regimentation that exist in the private productive sector of the capitalist economy, such as the punching of the time card and various other means of monitoring worker performance. As manager of production, the government spurs economic productivity by recourse to political power. (This is known by the Maoist watchword "Politics in Command," which means that macrodevelopment must take precedence over microdevelopment, or that economic planning is not merely an economic decision but must consider the overall welfare of society.) While the abolishment of private ownership and the consequent elimination of <u>pouvoirs intermédiaires</u> have obviated many interclass disputes (such as those between management and labor, landlords and tenants, creditors and debtors), the masses are bound to the government in a direct economic relationship in which the profitability motive is subsumed under higher goals of productivity and distributive justice.

Given its political predominance, the government in this model has the resources to equalize the utility incomes for every citizen. The obstacles that prevent the government from moving society to optimality in the Downs model are not duplicated here. In the first place, the planned economy removes the difficulty of arriving at a clear definition of optimal states, and the uncertainty about judging the individual's income-earning potential and measuring his benefits and costs is either mitigated or unknown under the system. The a priori dominance of the Communist Party rules out the kind of inter-party competition for votes that blocks the attainment of Paretian optimality in many instances in a two-party system, as encapsuled in the Downs model. Free from the vote-maximizing preoccupation, the government transcends any possible conflicts of interest among the different groups of the citizenry, while the enforcement of the collective norm transforms or mitigates the dimensions of these conflicts.

The transcendence gives the government the freedom it needs to determine, or arbitrate, what is an optimal position to pursue or, in the event of competing alternative optimal states, which one is to be chosen at a given time. However, certainty is only relative in the real world, even in a socialist system; and to the extent that the Party's legitimacy depends on its optimality-pursuing capability, the government cannot completely ignore the possible conflicting preferences of the citizen groups where more than one option is open. We have noted in the Downs model that where citizen preferences are diverse, every optimal position is dominated by a suboptimal one. Granting that the imposition of social rationality reduces the diversity in citizen preferences, and granting that the government has the freedom to choose among alternative optimuma, the determination of the ultimate optimal position among competing choices still requires perfect knowledge on the part of the decision-makers. Lack of perfect knowledge makes the government's transcendental freedom meaningless, or else it leads to abuse of that freedom, with drastic consequences.

The desire to avoid these consequences and their future recurrence compels the government, as under the Maoists during the Cultural Revolution and beyond, to engage in constant dialogues with the masses, so as to generate the necessary information for the state planners in decisions and choices regarding optimal policies, on the one hand, and to ensure citizen acceptance of the policies, on the other.[28] Unlike the government in the Downs model, the competition between different optimal states and between citizens' preferences does not foreclose the government's choice or action in the Maoist system. In the event of conflicting preferences between citizen groups P, Q, and R, the government can, after sufficient dialogues with all three groups and possibly others concerned, make sure that one of the competing optimums, X', Y', and Z', is chosen, and prevent any of the suboptimal positions, X, Y, and Z, from dominating the chosen optimal position.

In doing so, the Maoist government could duplicate the errors and excesses of Stalinism, with its heavy reliance on complete centralized planning and ubiquitous external control, which smothered mass initiative and creative participation. But Mao is not Stalin. His major difference lies in his deep-seated belief in the voluntarism of the masses when they are given the "correct" social environment. This belief, more than the attempt to avoid the Stalinist mistakes, accounts for his "mass line," under which the masses are involved in finalizing, not just implementing, the economic plans and also in decisions affecting the allocation of resources and fruits of their labor. Similarly, the overriding concern to effect optimal returns for the system explains why Mao turns against the Party operatives when the latter's excessive power stands in the way of the masses' productive zeal or of achieving optimality.

For very similar reasons, Mao has taken steps to contain the overspecializing effects of industrialization, which could thwart or upset the egalitarian distribution principle. On both the state-mass balanced planning and the "three eliminations" questions, Mao is undoubtedly reacting to the antisocialist degenerations ("revisionism") he finds in the Soviet Union, as well as to the evils that Marxists attribute to the capitalist system. (The "three eliminations" are Mao's program to eliminate the disparities and contradictions between agriculture and industry, between rural and urban development, and between manual and mental work.) Central to these Maoist policies is the removal, by the citizenry's voluntarist action under the Party's stewardship, of all obstacles to achieving a state of optimality for society. The enforcement of this collective voluntarist strain is a guarantee against natural tendencies (including private selfishness and widening gulfs between classes due to increasing professional specialization) that militate against the attainment of optimality for the system.

CONCLUSION

We have attempted to demonstrate how the introduction of the Maoist collective voluntarist strain has changed or modified the modus operandi and behavior of actors in the Maoist polity and that there is

203

a logic to be understood in its own terms. There is also a self-ful-filling prophecy, to the extent that the voluntarist assumption (about the corrigibility of man through an edifying society) and the enforced primacy of social rationality tend to reinforce each other. The en-forceability of the collective norm is assured under the socialist system, in which the Party's role parallels that of the planner in the command economy, and the Party's a priori predominance is the starting point of the political process (as contrasted with suffrage in the Downs model).

In reality, private motivations or self-interests still play a residual role in political behavior, so long as they are consistent with the collective frame of reference. Private motives explain why the masses support the Party's predominance (because it guarantees their economic equality) and why the government is committed to welfare-maximizing (this is the government's way of maximizing the legitimacy of its uncontested power). In the power struggles among the top Party leaders, as during the Cultural Revolution, self-interests are more explanatory of the actors' behavior than they are in the larger polity. The sociability norm, nonetheless, poses a challenge to any definition of "rationality" that is presented in terms of individual self-interests alone. So long as it remains operative, the Maoist emphasis on collec-tive voluntarism will mark the Chinese polity apart from other sys-tems, including even the Soviet Union under its present operative code.

The mobilization of the community's collective voluntarist spirit, in other words, is the sourse of the Maoist polity's potential for at-taining optimality. "Potential" because our discussion has focused on the logic of the voluntarist code of the Maoist polity as a develop-mental system, not on its actual accomplishments. The latter, while bountiful, are beyond the pale of this discussion. It is nevertheless true that, just as the enforcement of the sociability norm is a dis-tinguishing quality, the actual realization of optimal returns for the entire citizenry is a test of the system's success. (Throughout this discussion I have used "citizenry" in a manner that excludes the officially ostracized persons or classes [until rehabilitated]. I have also preferred "citizenry" to "citizens," to suggest the collectivity rather than individuals.)

It may be added at this point that comparative studies of social organization have shown that where supply of collective goods is in-volved, there is a tendency for nonmarket groups or organizations to seek the largest possible membership, so that the costs of the goods will be lower for all members. Whereas firms in a market lament an increase in the number of competitive firms (because of splits in profits), nonmarket associations that supply collective goods invariably drive for an enlargement of their ranks and sometimes even attempt to make membership compulsory.[29] The Maoist socialist entity may be likened to such a large nonmarket association, which seeks an even distribution of the costs (and benefits) in order to insure a steady supply of maximal collective goods. The compulsory enforcement of the Maoist communal voluntarism and the extent to which it has been practiced are, therefore, but indicators of the size of the Chinese population and the magnitude of tha task of enlisting all of them as active participants in the pursuit of optimality.

Both Downs and Kenneth Arrow have argued that if most choice situations involve two or more alternatives, and if voter preferences are sufficiently diverse, the government in an electoral system cannot move society to a Paretian optimum unless some part of society dictates to the rest.[30] The Communist Party in the Maoist system performs exactly this function, being that part of society that has both the power and transcendent discretion to move the rest. The potentials for achieving optimality, as noted, lie in the facts that (a) the social utility function is (unlike the Downs model) not overridden by the vote function of government, (b) the elusive "majority" (whose specific components shift from issue to issue) is replaced by the conceptually more definitive "community," and (c) government policy is no longer a compromise of conflicting voter preferences and of tensions resulting from optimal and suboptimal choices.

The obvious question here is, if the Party is the guardian of community interests and the executor of the transitive general welfare function, who is the guardian of the Party? The answer again goes back to the Maoist assumption about an edifying social environment. Society, in possession of socialist conscience and ethics, is the counterweight to the Party during times when the latter has gone astray, just as the Party is the catalyst of social action during normal times. The Cultural Revolution has clearly demonstrated that the Maoist polity is no perfect system, yet society enlightened by an accepted socialist civic virtue (with all its conflicting interpretations at times) can be such a corrective mechanism. Like normative political-theory questions regarding where sovereignty lies between the ruler and the ruled, the question regarding the validity of the Maoist assumption about man and society can be pushed only so far and has to stop at some point. The crucial fact is that the Maoist polity, as an institution and a community of human beings, does proceed from the very premise that has given the system its vitality as well as raison d'être.

For two reasons, I have eschewed ethical questions, such as whether the seeming loss of individual "freedom" by the people and the denial of "pluralism" in the Maoist society are justifiable costs for its purported optimal potentials. First, questions of this sort cannot be answered unless and until it can be established that terms such as "freedom" and "pluralism" have universal meanings for all societies, no matter what their systems and stages of development. Furthermore, if one accepts "pluralism" to be an ideological justification for, and product of, the conflict of private self-interests typical of a market economy, and if one accepts "freedom" to be a prerequisite for the fighting out of those interests, then they make little sense in a planned-economy ambience. In the latter, as noted, private interests are not to be left to the self-help of the individuals themselves, one pitted against another, because their encroachment is not to be presumed under the enforced rules of the collective game. Second, though important of and in themselves, ethical questions do not directly shed any significant light on political behavior. What governs the workings of politics in the system under study, as elsewhere, is not so much whether the individual citizen is convinced of the intrinsic value of the prevailing norms, but whether under the given structure of expectations he views it as "rational" for him to follow the norms and actually does so.

By the same token, I have not speculated on such questions as whether the government in the Maoist polity may abandon its pronounced commitment to fulfilling optimal social ends. I have taken this commitment as a "given." We are concerned with "rational" or expectable behavior vis-à-vis the existing conditions of the system at the present time. An abandonment by the Party of its professed goal-values would result in a systemic transformation, or disappearance of the very system we have defined to be the object of our scrutiny. In that eventuality, a totally new analysis would be called for. Our analysis here, needless to say, is valid to the extent that the "givens" are validly perceived and postulated within the present temporal framework.

Like those of Downs, our efforts are not merely explicative by intent but also seek to provide some inferential value. Much of what we have stated in regard to the Maoist model—such as the enforcement and enforceability of social rationality—is not only testable, but offers something from which future political behavior of the system's actors can be deduced. Of course, its predictive capability is subject to the willful changes that the Party may make in the future. No "scientific" theory in the social sciences is expected to predict every single event, decision, or action, simply because of the nature of the human world. But it should be able to establish correlations between conditions and events, anticipate trends, and offer a fairly reliable prevision of the environment in which decisions will be made or of what actors will do if they act in accordance with the rules of the game.[31] A test of possible bias in the model developed herein is for other scholars to create alternative sets of assumptions that will explain better than mine. As stated in the beginning, modeling is an essential step toward theory-building; and I hope that what I have done—comparing two distinct models at close range—has some epistemological value to offer.

I cannot, in closing, resist making an obiter dictum that it could be unproductive and even dangerous to try to blindly borrow concepts and apply social-science methodology derived from essentially market-dominated polities. The question of Pareto optimality in the West is often studied from assumptions rooted in the symbiosis of the market system and the voting system as two coequal but separate avenues of social choice. Implicit in this perspective is the concept of "voter sovereignty," very much parallel to that of "consumer sovereignty." Since social ends are derived from private ends, Pareto optimality is therefore defined, implicitly or explicitly, as the highest coincidence or convergence of individual preferences. Little or no attention is given to the normative considerations of social choice in nonmarket systems. With whatever precious little is said about the "centralized procedures" for arriving at an optimal social choice in the socialist systems, it is frequently alleged that decisions are "centralized" and made by "a single decision authority with accurate knowledge of individuals' preferences."[32]

This "centralized decision" view is troubling, if not disturbing, on a number of grounds. First, it still shows a preoccupation with "accurate knowledge of individuals' preferences," totally ignoring the complicated process we have discussed in reference to the Maoist polity, where the purported optimal social choice is determined by the state planner, whose function it is to make decisions with the community's overall interests in view, though in close consultation with the masses. While involving two-way communication with the masses, this decision-making mode could transcend or even go against specific individual preferences, for the achievement of community interests may entail temporary individual sacrifices or self-denials. Second, the "decision authority," at least in the Maoist polity (as contrasted with other socialist systems), is by no means as singular and centralized as is assumed. There are standard divisions in the making of social choice between the center and the local levels. Even decisions made at the center are to be, at least since the Great Leap, "fleshed out" or "made realistic" (lo shih) at the various levels, all the way down to the rice-roots. This collective or communal approach to social choice makes meaningless the Western-centered notion of Pareto optimality derived from individual preferences.

Another troubling element in the "centralized decision" view, which is more serious, is the implicit assumption that outside the convergence of individual preferences, there is no Paretian optimum to speak of. It is an unfair and unwarranted definitional game. I admit that the communal-derived definition of optimal choice presents a totally different problem of testing, for there is no way of proving that a policy so decided is an optimal choice unless (tautologically) one goes back to its source, the community decision-makers (dominated by the Communist Party). Furthermore, since the purported optimal policy decided through the communal process may require temporary individual self-denials, dissent or even opposition from those individuals or groups called upon to make the sacrifices ceases to be a meaningful indicator of the falsity or nonsuccess of the policy itself.

In my discussion above, I did not deal with the questions just raised, because I was not dealing with analytical measures for appraising the validity or success of optimal choices, as already explained. In any continuation of the study beyond what I have done, I believe the question of identifying the measures for making the appraisal must be solved. Offhand, I have only a few suggestions to make on how the question could be approached. First, I believe that the policy in question can be evaluated against the goals and standards set by the norms prevailing in the Maoist system. Second, as a more "independent" measure, the actual benefits accruing to the community must be weighed against the costs. Also, the distribution of the benefits must be weighed against the distribution of the costs within the community. Moreover, in weighing the distribution scales, comparisons should be made with a balance sheet likewise established for another society, preferably a market system, provided the goals pursued are comparable.

In any event, I believe that comparisons between a nonelectoral polity such as the Maoist system and a market-economy electoral system can be made, if we apply caution and make judicious adjustments, working from the postulated assumptions for each system and then building up therefrom, but not before this elemental hurdle is cleared. Returning to the principal concerns of this book, what I hope to have done in my study is to demonstrate the absolute necessity to grasp the basic assumptions on which "Maoism" and the Chinese system under its aegis are predicated, if we are to know anything about the subject matter in the epistemological sense.

NOTES

1. Anthony Downs, An Economic Theory of Democracy (New York: Harper and Row, 1957), esp. pp. 18, 172, 177 ff., 184, 283.

2. Mancur Olson, Jr., The Logic of Collective Action (New York: Shocken, 1965), p. 14.

3. Robert J. Osborn, Soviet Social Policies: Welfare, Equality and Community (Homewood, Ill.: Dorsey Press 1970), p. 31 ff.

4. Abraham Kaplan, The Conduct of Inquiry (Scranton, Pa.: Chandler, 1964), pp. 258-93, 349; also Kul B. Rai and John C. Blydenburgh, Political Science Statistics (Boston: Holbrook Press, 1974), pp. 4 ff.

5. Downs, op. cit., pp. 27, 283.

6. Ibid., pp. 184 ff.

7. Ibid., pp. 23, 27, 184.

8. Ibid., p. 18. Emphasis added.

9. Ibid., pp. 27-29.

10. Ibid., pp. 16, 170.

11. Ibid., p. 182.

12. Ibid., p. 254.

13. Ibid., p. 175.

14. Ibid., p. 178.

15. Ibid., pp. 180-81.

16. Ibid., p. 181.

17. Ibid., p. 183. For a comment that uncertainty does not necessarily lead to the problems for voters found in Downs's analysis, see Kenneth A. Shepsle, "Parties, Voters, and the Risk Environment: A Mathematical Treatment of Electoral Competition Under Uncertainty," in Richard G. Niemi and Herbert F. Weisberg, eds., Probability Models of Collective Decision Making (Columbus, Ohio: Charles E. Merrill, 1972), pp. 273-97.

18. Downs' op. cit., p. 202.

19. Ibid., p. 191.

20. Ibid., p. 193.

21. For this section, see generally James C. Hsiung, Ideology and Practice: The Evolution of Chinese Communism (New York: Praeger, 1970), esp. pp. 106-65; Benjamin I. Schwartz, Communism and China: Ideology in Flux (Cambridge, Mass.: Harvard University Press, 1968), pp. 162-85; Donald J. Munro, "The Malleability of Man in Chinese Communism," China Quarterly no. 48 (Oct.-Dec. 1971): 609-40; John G. Gurley, "Capitalist and Maoist Economic Development," in Edward Friedman and Mark Selden, eds., America's Asia (New York: Vintage, 1971), pp. 324-56; E. L. Wheelwright and Bruce McFarlane, The Chinese Road to Socialism (New York: Monthly Review Press, 1970).

22. I have borrowed the concept of "monocratic" elite from Frederick Fleron, Jr., "Toward a Reconceptualization of Political Change in the Soviet Union: The Political Leadership System," Comparative Politics 1, no. 2 (Jan. 1969); 236. As used here, the term suggests a group of careerist political leaders who, originally recruited from society, constitute an independent center of power not rivaled by any other group, and whose eminent position is due to an assumed delegation of authority by the people at large in recognition

of their political vision, empathy, organizational ability, and special endowment necessary for the governance of public affairs. The existence of a "monocratic" elite presupposes a peculiar division of labor that recognizes its special place and functions.

23. See Hsiung, op. cit., pp. 85-105.

24. Ibid., pp. 169 ff.

25. Franklin Houn, A Short History of Chinese Communism (rev. ed.; Englewood Cliffs, N.J.: Prentice-Hall, 1973), pp. 112-28; James P. Harrison, The Long March to Power (New York: Praeger, 1972), pp. 432-511.

26. For three principles (size, side-payment, and strategic), see William Riker, The Theory of Political Coalitions (New Haven: Yale University Press, 1962).

27. For the downfall of Lin Piao and his ilk, see the various Chung-fa (Center-issued) documents, disseminated by the Central Committee of the Chinese Communist Party, esp. nos. 56 (1970) and 4, 12, and 24 (all 1972), copies of which are available in the United States at the Chinese Document Center, School of International Affairs Library, Columbia University. On the Cultural Revolution, see also Hsiung, op. cit., pp. 217-90; William Dorrill, Power, Policy, and Ideology in the Making of China's Cultural Revolution, Memorandum RM-5731-PR, (Santa Monica, Calif.: RAND, Aug. 1968).

28. On this question, see Franz Schurmann, Ideology and Organization in Communist China (new and enl. ed.; Berkeley: University of California Press, 1968), pp. 175 ff; and Audrey Donnithorne, China's Economic System (New York: Praeger, 1967), pp. 460 ff. See also generally Gurley, op. cit., and Wheelwright and McFarland, op. cit., n. 21 above.

29. Cf. Olson, op. cit., p. 37 and passim.

30. Kenneth J. Arrow, Social Choice and Individual Values (New York: John Wiley & Sons, 1951); Downs, op. cit., p. 18 and Ch. 4.

31. See generally Kaplan, op. cit., also Louis D. Hayes and Ronald D. Hedlund, eds., The Conduct of Political Inquiry (Englewood Cliffs, N.J.: Prentice-Hall, 1970); Eugene J. Meehan, The Foundations of Political Analysis: Empirical and Normative (Homewood, Ill.: Dorsey Press, 1971); James N. Rosenau, The Drama of Politics: An Introduction to the Joys of Inquiry (Boston: Little, Brown, 1973).

32. Richard Zeckhauser, "Voting Systems, Honest Preferences and Pareto Optimality," American Political Science Review 67, no. 3 (Sep. 1973): 934-46. For a somewhat different discussion of the question of Pareto optimality, see William H. Riker and Steven J. Brams, "The Paradox of Vote Trading," ibid. no. 4 (Dec. 1973): 1235-47.

SELECTED BIBLIOGRAPHY

Soviet and Russian-Language Sources

"Antileninskaya sushchnost maoistskikh vzglyadov na gosudarstvo i demokratiyu" (Anti-Leninist essence of Maoist views on state and democracy), Sovetskoe gosudarstvo i pravo no. 2 (1972): 54-63.

Antimarksistskaya sushchnost vzglyadov i politiki Mao Tse-duna, sbornik statei (Anti-Marxist essence of the views and policy of Mao Tse-tung, collection of articles). Moscow: Izd. Politicheskoi Literatury, 1969.

Apalin, G. "Antinarodnyi rezhim maoistov" (Anti-popular regime of the Maoists), Sovety deputatov trudyashchikhsya no. 1 (1972): 104-07.

Burlatsky, F. Maoizm ili Marksizm? (Maoism or Marxism?). Moscow: Izd. Politicheskoi Literatury, 1967.

_____. Maoizm—ugroza sotsializmu v Kitae (Maoism—threat to socialism in China). Moscow: Izd. Politicheskoi Literatury, 1968.

_____. "China at the Cross-Roads," Chinese Law and Government (White Plains, N.Y.) Translated from Mirovaya ekonomika i mezhdunarodnye otnosheniya, 1968 no. 6.

_____. The True Face of Maoism. Moscow: Novosti Press Agency Publishing House, n.d.

A Destructive Policy. Moscow, Novosti Press Agency Publishing House, 1972.

Gavrilov, I. "Orudie despoticheskoi vlasti Maoistov" (Weapon of despotic authority of the Maoists), Sovety deputatov trudyashchikhsya, 1969, no. 6, pp. 108-10. '

Gelbras, V. Mao's Pseudo-Socialism. Moscow: Novosti Press Agency Publishing House, n.d.

Gudoshnikov, L. "Political Mechanism of Present-Day China," New Times no. 37 (1972): 24-25.

Gudoshnikov, L. M., and Topornin, B. N. "Krizis politiko-pravovogo razvitiya v Kitae" (Crisis of political and legal development in China), Sovetskoe gosudarstvo i pravo, 1969, no. 5, pp. 11-20.

Kalinychev, F. "Narushenie demokratii i zakonosti v KNR" (Violation of democracy and legality in the PRC) Sotsialisticheskaya zakonnost, 1968, no. 2, pp. 32-34.

Kitaiskaya Narodnaya Respublika, ekonomika, gosudarstvo i pravo, kultura (The People's Republic of China, economy, state and law, culture). Moscow: Nauka, 1970.

Kritika teoreticheskikh kontseptsii Mao Tse-duna (Critique of the theoretical conceptions of Mao Tse-tung). Moscow: Mysl, 1970.

Kyuzadzhyan, L. S. Proletarskii internatsionalizm i melkoburzhuaznyi natsionalizm (Proletarian internationalism and petite bourgeois nationalism). Moscow: Izd. Politicheskoi Literatury, 1968.

_____ The Chinese Crisis: Causes and Character. Moscow: Novosti Press Agency Publishing House, n.d.

Lenin i problemy sovremennogo Kitaya, sbornik statei. (Lenin and the problems of contemporary China, collection of articles). Moscow, Izd. Politicheskoi Literatury, 1971.

"Lzherevolyutsionery bez maski" (Pseudo-revolutionaries unmasked) (editorial), Pravda, May 18, 1970, pp. 6-7. English translation, Pseudo-Revolutionaries Unmasked. Moscow: Novosti Press Agency Publishing House, 1970.

Opasnyi kurs (Dangerous course). 3 vols. Moscow: Izd. Politicheskoi Literatury, 1969-72.

Ostroumov, G. S. "Politiko-pravovaya ideologiya i krizis politicheskoi vlasti v Kitae" (Political and legal ideology and the crisis of political authority in China), Sovetskoe gosudarstvo i pravo, 1967, no. 6, pp. 59-66. English translation in Chinese Law and Government (White Plains, N.Y.) no. 3 (Fall 1968): 4-22.

Perlov, I. D. "Otkhod ot demokraticheskikh printsipov pravosudiya v KNR" (Departure from the democratic principles of justice in the PRC), Sovetskoe gosudarstvo i pravo, 1968, no. 1, pp. 75-82. English translation in Chinese Law and Government no. 1 (Fall 1968): 23-36.

Rakhimov, T. "Velikoderzhavnaya politika Mao Tse-duna i ego gruppy v natsionalnom voprose" (Great Power policy of Mao Tse-tung and his group in the national question), Kommunist, 1967, no. 7, pp. 114-19.

_____. Natsionalizm i shovinizm—osnova politiki gruppy Mao Tse-duna. (Nationalism and chauvinism—basis of the policy of the Mao Tse-tung group). Moscow: Mysl, 1968.

_____ and Bodoslovskii, V. "Velikoderzhavnyi shovinizm Mao Tse-duna" (Great Power Chauvinism of Mao Tse-tung), Aziya i Afrika segodnya, no. 7, 1969.

_____ and Taldomskii, V. "Velikokhanskii shovinizm" (Great Han chauvinism), Novoe vremya, 1972, no. 5.

Shirendyb, B. "Velikoderzhavnyi shovinizm gruppy Mao Tse-duna" (Great Power chauvinism of the group of Mao Tse-tung), in V.A. Krivtsova, ed., Maoizm glazami Kommunistov, Mirovaya kommunisticheskaya i rabochaya pechat o politike gruppy Mao Tse-duna (Maoism through the eyes of Communists. The world Communist and workers' press concerning the policy of the group of Mao Tse-tung), pp. 79-92. Moscow: Progress, 1969.

Sidikhmenov, V. Klassy i klassovaya borba v krivom zerkale. (Classes and class struggle in a flawed mirror). Moscow: Mysl, 1969.

Titov, M. "Velikoderzhavnyi shovinizm—osnova politiki maoizma" (Great Power chauvinism—basis of the policy of Maoism), Partiinaya zhizn, 1970, no. 3.

Za chistotu marksizma-leninizma. (For the purity of Marxism-Leninism). Moscow: Mysl, 1964.

Zanegin, B.; Mironov, A.; Mikhailov, Ya. K sobytiyam v Kitae (Concerning events in China). Moscow: Izd. Politicheskoi Literatury, 1967. English translation, Developments in China. Moscow: Progress Publishers, 1968.

Other Books and Published Materials

Barnett, A. Doak. China After Mao. Princeton: Princeton University Press, 1967.

_____, ed. Chinese Communist Politics in Action. Seattle: University of Washington Press, 1969.

Berger, Joseph; Cohen, Bernard P.; Snell, J. Laurie; and Zelditch, Morris, Jr. Types of Formalization in Small Group Research. Boston: Houghton Mifflin, 1962.

Bill, A. James, and Hargrave, Robert L., Jr. Comparative Politics: The Quest for Theory. Columbus, Ohio: Charles E. Merrill, 1973.

Blum, Robert. The United States and China in World Affairs. Edited by A. Doak Barnett. New York: McGraw-Hill, 1966.

Boorman, Scott A. The Protracted Game. A Wei-chi Interpretation of Maoist Revolutionary Strategy. New York: Oxford University Press, 1969.

Boyd, R. G. Communist China's Foreign Policy. New York: Praeger, 1962.

Bridgham P.; Cohen, A.; and Jaffe, L. "Mao's Road and Sino-Soviet Relations: A View from Washington, 1953." China Quarterly no. 52 (Oct./Dec. 1972) 670-698.

Ch'en, Jerome. Mao and the Chinese Revolution. New York: Oxford University Press, 1965.

Chen, Pi-chao. "In Search of Chinese National Character via Child-Training," World Politics 25, no. 4 (July 1973) 608-635.

Cohen, Jerome ed., Contemporary Chinese Law: Research Problems and Perspectives. Cambridge, Mass.: Harvard University Press, 1970.

Cotter, C. P., ed., Political Science Annual: Conflict, Competition, and Coalitions. Vol. 4. Indianapolis: Bobbs-Merrill, 1973.

Deutsch, Karl. The Nerves of Government. New York: The Free Press, 1966.

Diamant, Alfred. "The Bureaucratic Model: Max Weber Rejected, Rediscovered, Reformed," in Ferrel Heady and Sybil L. Stokes, eds., Paper in Comparative Public Administration. Ann Arbor: Institute of Public Administration, University of Michigan, 1962.

Dimitrov, Georgi. The United Front, the Struggle Against Fascism and War. London: Lawrance and Wishart, 1938.

Donnithorne, Audrey. China's Economic System. New York: Praeger, 1967.

Downs, Anthony. An Economic Theory of Democracy. New York: Harper and Row, 1957.

Ellul, Jacques. The Technological Society. Translated by Konrad Kellen. New York: Alfred A. Knopf, 1964.

_____. Propaganda. Translated by Konrad Kellen and Jean Lerner. New York: Alfred A. Knopf, 1965.

_____. The Political Illusion. Translated by Konrad Kellen. New York: Alfred A. Knopf, 1967.

Fleron, Fredrick, Jr. "Toward a Reconceptualization of Political Leadership System," Comparative Politics 1, no. 2 (Jan. 1969) 228-244.

Friedman, Edward, and Seldon, Mark, eds. American's Asian-American Relations. New York: Vintage, 1971.

Funnel, Victor C. "Bureaucracy and the Chinese Communist Party," Current Scene 9, no. 5 (May 7, 1971) 1 ff.

Gelbras, V. Mao's Pseudo-Socialism. Moscow: Novosti Press Agency Publishing House.

Graham, George J. Methodological Foundation for Political Analysis. Waltham, Mass.: Xerox Publishing Company, 1971.

Greene, Fred. U. S. and Security of Asia. New York: McGraw-Hill, 1968.

Halper, A. M. Policies Toward China: View from Six Continents. New York: McGraw-Hill, 1965.

Harrison, James P. The Long March to Power. New York: Praeger, 1972.

Herndon, James F., and Berna, Joseph L., eds. Mathematical Applications in Political Science. Charlottesville: University Press of Virginia, 1971.

Hinton, Harold C. China's Turbulent Quest; an Analysis of China's Foreign Relations Since 1949. Bloomington: Indiana University Press, 1972.

_____. An Introduction to Chinese Politics. New York: Praeger, 1973.

Hodges, Donald C., and AbunShanab, Robert Elias, eds. National Liberation Fronts, 1960-1970. New York: William Morrow, 1972.

Holubnychy, Vsevolod. "Mao Tse-tung's Materialist Dialectics," China Quarterly no. 19 (July-Sept. 1964).

Houn, Franklin. A Short History of Chinese Communisum. Rev. ed. Englewood Cliffs, N.J.: Prentince-Hall, 1973.

Hsiung, James Chieh. Ideology and Practice. New York: Praeger, 1970.

_____. Law and Policy in China's Foreign Relations. New York: Columbia University Press, 1972.

Huck, Arthur. The Security of China. New York: Columbia University Press, 1970.

Hudson, G. F.; Lowenthal, Richard, and MacFarquhar, Roderick. The Sino-Soviet Dispute. New York, Praeger, 1962.

Johnson, Chalmers. Ideology and Politics in Contemporary China. Seattle: University of Washington Press, 1973.

Kao Ying-mao. Bureaucracy and Political Development in Communist China. Stanford: Stanford University Press, 1974.

Kemey, J. G.; Snell, J. L.; and Thompson, G. L. Introduction to Finite Mathematics. Englewood Cliffs, N.J.: Prentice-Hall, 1957.

Kuomintang, Central Reform Committee. Fei-tang te tsu-chih yü ts'e-lüeh lu-hsien (The organization and tactical lines of the Chinese Communist Party). Taipei, Taiwan: Chung-yang wen-wu kung-yin she, 1952.

Lall, Arthur. How Communist China Negotiates. New York: Columbia University Press, 1968.

Lenin, Nikolai. Lieh-ning ch'uan-chi (Collected Works of Lenin). Peking: Jen-min ch'u-pan she, 1953.

Levy, Marion J., Jr. Modernization and the Structure of Societies. Princeton: Princeton University Press, 1966.

Lifton, Robert J. Thought Reform and the Psychology of Totalism. New York: Norton, 1961.

_____. Revolutionary Immortality: Mao Tse-tung and the Chinese Communist Revolution. New York: Vintage, 1968.

Lindbeck, John M., ed. China: Management of a Revolutionary Society. Seattle: University of Washington Press, 1971.

Liu, Alan P. Communications and National Integration in Communist China. Berkeley: University of California Press, 1972.

Liu Shao-ch'i. "Self-Cultivation in Organization and Discipline," in Chinese Law and Government (White Plains, N.Y.) 5, no. 1 (Spring 1972).

Mao Tse-tung. Lun hsien chieh-tuan (On new stage). Chungking: Hsin-hua jih-pao kuan, 1939.

_____. Lun jen-min min-chu chuan-cheng (On people's democratic dictatorship). Dairen: Hsin-hua shu-tien, 1949.

_____. Hsuan-chi (Selected works). 4 vols. Peking: Jen-min ch'u-pan she, 1960.

_____. Where Do Correct Ideas Come From? Peking: Foreign Languages Press, 1966.

_____. "Chairman Mao Discusses Twenty Manifestations of Bureaucracy." Translation in U.S. Department of Commerce, Joint Publications Research Service. Translations on Communist China no. 90 (Feb. 12, 1970).

_____. "Sixty Articles on Work Methods (Draft)," Chinese Law and Government 5, no. 1 (Spring 1973).

Maxwell, Neville. India's China War. New York: Doubleday, 1972.

Mayo, Henry B. Democracy and Marxism. New York: Oxford University Press, 1955.

Michels, Robert. Political Parties. New York: The Free Press, 1962.

Munro, Donald J. "The Malleability of Man in Chinese Communism," China Quarterly no. 48 (Oct.-Dec. 1971) 609-640.

Niemi, Richard, and Weisberg, Herbert F., eds. Probability Models of Collective Decision-Making. Columbus, Ohio: Charles E. Merrill, 1972.

North, Robert C. The Foreign Relations of China. Belmont, Calif.: Dickenson, 1969.

Oksenberg, Michel, ed. China's Developmental Experiences. New York: Praeger, 1973.

Patterson, George N. Peking Versus Delhi. New York: Praeger, 1963.

Pentony, Devere E., ed. China, the Emerging Red Giant. San Francisco: Chandler, 1962.

_____. ed. Soviet Behavior in World Affairs. San Francisco: Chandler, 1962.

Popper, Karl R. The Logic of Scientific Discovery. London: Hutchinson, 1959.

_____. Conjectures and Refutations. London: Routledge and Kegan Paul, 1963.

Riker, William H. The Theory of Political Coalitions. New Haven: Yale University Press, 1962.

Riker, William H., and Ordeshook, Peter C. An Introduction to Positive Political Theory. Englewood Cliffs, N.J.: Prentice-Hall, 1972.

Scalapino, Robert A., ed. The Communist Revolution in Asia: Tactics, Goals, and Achievements. Englewood Cliffs, N.J.: Prentice-Hall, 1969.

Schram, Stuart R. Mao Tse-tung. Baltimore: Penguin, 1966.

_____. The Political Thought of Mao Tse-tung. New York: Praeger, 1970.

Schwartz, Benjamin. "China and the West in the 'Thought of Mao Tse-tung,'" in Ping-ti Ho and Tang Tsou, eds., China in Crisis. vol. 1, book 1. Chicago: University of Chicago Press, 1968.

_____. Communism and China: Ideology in Flux. Cambridge, Mass.: Harvard University Press, 1968.

Schwartz, Harry. Tsars, Mandarins and Commissars: A History of Chinese-Russian Relations. New York: Doubleday, 1973.

Selden, Mark. The Yenan Way in Revolutionary China. Cambridge, Mass.: Harvard University Press, 1971.

Selznick, Philip. The Organizational Weapon: A Study of Bolshevik Strategy and Tactics. New York: McGraw-Hill, 1952.

Snow, Edgar. Red Star over China. New York: Random House, 1938 and 1944.

_____. Red China Today. New York: Vintage Books, 1970.

Solomon, Richard H. Mao's Revolution and the Chinese Political Culture. Berkeley: University of California Press, 1972.

Stalin, Joseph. Foundation of Leninism. London: Lawrance and Wishart, 1942.

Tang, Peter S., and Maloney, J. M. Communist China: The Domestic Scene, 1949-1967. South Orange, N.J.: Seton Hall University Press, 1967.

Thomson, James. While China Faced the West. Cambridge, Mass.: Harvard University Press, 1969.

Thornton, Ricard C. The Comintern and the Chinese Communists, 1928-1931. Seattle: University of Washington Press, 1969.

Townsend, James R. Political Participation in Communist China. Berkeley: University of California Press, 1967.

Tsou, Tang. "The Cultural Revolution and the Chinese Political System," China Quarterly no. 38 (Apr.-June 1969) 63-91.

U.S. Congress, Joint Economic Committee. People's Republic of China: An Economic Assessment. Washington, D.C.: U.S. Government Printing Office, 1972.

Van Slyke, Lyman P. Enemies and Friends: The United Front in Chinese Communist History. Stanford: Stanford University Press, 1967.

Vogel, Ezra F. "From Revolutionaries to Semi-Bureaucrats: The 'Regularization' of Cadres," China Quarterly no. 29 (Jan.-Mar. 1967).

Wakeman, Frederic. History and Will. Berkeley: University of California Press, 1973.

Weber, Max. The Religion of China. Glencoe, Ill.: The Free Press, 1951.

_____. Economy and Society. New York: Bedminster Press, 1968.

Whiting, Allen S. China Crossess the Yalu: The Decision to Enter the Korean War. New York: Macmillan, 1960.

Whitson, William. The Chinese High Command: A History of Communist Military Politics, 1927-1971. New York: Praeger, 1972.

Whyte, Martin King. "Bureaucracy and Modernization in China: The Maoist Critique," American Sociological Review 38, no. 2 (Apr. 1973) 149-165.

Wilbur, C. Martin. "The Ashes of Defeat," China Quarterly no. 18 (Apr.-June 1964).

Wilson, Richard W. "Chinese Studies in Crisis," World Politics no. 1 (Nov. 1970).

Wint, Guy. Communist China's Crusade. New York: Praeger, 1965.

Wo-men cheng-tsai ch'ien-chin (We are forging ahead). Peking: People's Publishing House, 1972.

Young, Kenneth T. Negotiating with the Chinese Communists. New York: McGraw-Hill, 1968.

Yu, Frederick T. C. Mass Persuasion in Communist China. New York: Praeger, 1964.

Yu, George T. China and Tanzania: A Study of Cooperative Interaction. Berkeley: University of California Press, 1970.

Zagoria, Donald. The Sino-Soviet Conflict, 1956-1961. Princeton: Princeton University Press, 1962.

Long March, 62, 76
Luan, 173
Luxemburg, Rosa, 55

Malik, Adam, 130
Manchuria, 142, 145
Mao Tse-tung, 90, 91, 105-107, 108
  108, 110-111, 114-115, 163, 167,
  168, 170; on bureaucracy, 44;
  coalition patterns of, 200-201;
  on contradictions, 56; cult of, 63;
  on human nature, 49, 197f.; and
  Leninist legacy, 55; meliorist
  view of, xvii, 190; organizational
  ideal of, 45; power position, 74
  (see also "Maoism"; Maoists)
"Maoism," new approach to, vii-
  viii; logic of, 191-192; Marxist-
  anthropologist strain in, xvii
Maoist government and polity,
  202-203
Maoist polity, optimality in, 190f.
  or Ch. 8
Maoists, 115-120, 122-123, 126-
  127, 128, 130
Marx, Karl, 8-11, 13, 15, 24, 107,
  108
Marxism-Leninism, 23-26, 112,
  115-116
Mass line, 51, 179, 203
Masses, relations with Party, 200f.
May 7 cadre schools, 51-52
Mechanical materialism, 15, 21
Mediterranean Sea, 120-121
Meisner, Maurice, 23
Mencius, 8
Metaphysics, 177
Michels, Robert, 38; on oligarchy,
  48-51
Middle East, 121
Militarization, 144, 146-147
Military-control committees, 147,
  155
Models, 164-166, 175-176, 181-183
Modeling, defined in relation to

theory, 192-193
"Modern revisionism," 115
Modernization, 163-164, 171-172,
  180
Mojsov, Lazar, 96
Moleiro, Moises, 91
Mongols, 141-142
Moscow, 108, 128-129
Moscow Conference of the Com-
  munist Parties, 115
"Mountaintop stronghold men-
  tality," 51
Mozambique, 91; Liberation Front
  for, 89;

National assimilation, 143
National minorities, 138-143, 161
National People's Congress, 143,
  146-147, 149
National united front, 107-108
Nationalist government, 106-107,
  113
Nehru, 99
Neorationalism, 177-178, 181-184
New Three-Anti Campaign, 52
New Zealand, 117, 120
Newton, Isaac, 26
Ningtu Conference, 62f., 64, 66,
  67-75
Ninth Party Congress, 120
North Korea, 117
North Vietnam, 117

Oceania, 93, 94
"Official" explanations, 168
Oligarchy, 48; American trade
  unions, 54; Chinese campaigns
  against, 51; in China, 51;
  democracy, 48-49, 54f.; "iron
  law" of, 48; and the Leninist
  legacy, 55; origins, 49; and
  socialism, 48-50
Olson, Mancur, Jr., 191
Open-door rectification, 52
Optimality, in capitalist-democratic

VINCENT CHEN is Professor of Political Science at the Graduate School, St. John's University. He received his M.A. from the University of Chicago and his Ph.D. from Yale. A student of international relations and Chinese Communist affairs, Dr. Chen is the author of Sino-Russian Relations in the Seventeenth Century and scholarly articles. He is completing a book entitled People's Republic of China's Behavior in World Politics.

WILLIAM F. DORRILL is Associate Professor of Political Science and Asian Studies at the University of Pittsburgh, where he is also Director of the East Asian Center and Chairman of the Department of East Asian Languages and Literatures. After graduate study at Virginia, the Australian National University, and Harvard, where he received the Ph.D., he served successively in the U.S. Government, RAND Corporation, and the Research Analysis Corporation. His publications include works on contemporary Chinese politics and foreign policy as well as the history of the Chinese Communist movement.

GEORGE GINSBURGS is Professor of Law at the School of Law, Rutgers University (Camden, N.J.). He received his M.A. and Ph.D. in political science from the University of California at Los Angeles, and taught at the University of Iowa and the Graduate Faculty of the New School of Social Research. He is a recipient of research grants from the Ford Foundation, the Social Science Research Council, and the National Endowment of Humanities. Among his publications are Soviet Citizenship Law (1968) and Communist China and Tibet (co-author, 1964). He also wrote "Constitutional Foundations of Socialist Commonwealth" for the Yearbook of World Affairs, 1972. He is a contributor to China's Practice of International Law, Jerome A. Cohen, ed. (1972).

JAMES CHIEH HSIUNG is Associate Professor of Politics at New York University, where he is also Director of Graduate Studies, Department of Politics. He is the author of Ideology and Practice: The Evolution of Chinese Communism (1970) and Law and Policy in China's Foreign Relations (1972), and is a contributor to Law in Chinese Foreign Policy (1972) and China's Practice of International Law (1972). He received his Ph.D. in political science from Columbia University, where he also taught, and is affiliated with its East Asian

Institute as a Research Associate. His current research interests are in the cross-fertilization of social science and East Asian studies.

ARNOLD B. URKEN is currently teaching at Stevens Institute of Technology. He received his M.A. at Rutgers and his Ph.D., in political science, at New York University. Professor Urken has also studied Chinese language and politics at Columbia University and did research in the philosophy of science and politics at the London School of Economics and Political Science. Formerly an analyst of Chinese Communist propaganda in the U.S. Army, Professor Urken's research interests are in formal modeling and its use in explicating Chinese political phenomena.

MARTIN KING WHYTE is Assistant Professor of Sociology and Associate of the Center for Chinese Studies, University of Michigan. He received his M.A. in Russian area studies and his Ph.D. in sociology at Harvard. During 1973-74 he served as Director of the Universities Service Center in Hong Kong. Dr. Whytes Research on small study-groups and mutual criticism sessions in China will be published in Small Groups and Political Rituals in China (1974). His current research focuses on contemporary family patterns and kin ties in rural areas of Kwangtung Province.

BRANTLY WOMACK is a doctoral candidate in political science at the University of Chicago. A Fulbright Scholar in philosophy at the University of Munich in 1969-70, he holds a B.A. from the University of Dallas and an M.A. from the University of Chicago.

GEORGE T. YU is Professor of Political Science at the University of Illinois (Urbana). He is author of Party Politics in Republican China: The Kuomintang 1912-1924 and China and Tanzania: A Study in Cooperative Interaction, and is coauthor of The Chinese Anarchist Movement. Professor Yu is a contributor to The Dynamics of China's Foreign Relations and The Year Book of World Affairs 1970. He has written articles and reviews for Asian Survey, Journal of Asian Studies, Journal of Politics, Problems of Communism, Race, and other journals. He received his doctorate in political science from the University of California (Berkeley).

CHINA AND THE GREAT POWERS: Relations
with the U.S., the USSR, and Japan
edited by Francis O. Wilcox

CHINA AND SOUTHEAST ASIA: Peking's
Relations with Revolutionary Movements
John J. Taylor

LAND REFORM IN THE PEOPLE'S REPUBLIC
OF CHINA: Institutional Transformation in
Agriculture
John Wong

THE MAOIST EDUCATIONAL REVOLUTION
Theodore Hsi-en Chen

THE MILITARY AND POLITICAL POWER IN
CHINA IN THE 1970s
edited by William W. Whitson

THE NET COST OF CHINA'S FOREIGN AID: A
Quantitative Analysis of an International Grants
Economy
Janos Horvath

SINO-AMERICAN DÉTENTE AND ITS POLICY
IMPLICATIONS*
edited by Gene T. Hsiao

*Also available in paperback as a PSS Student Edition.